# Disfarmer: Man Behind the Camera

# Map of Counties, Towns & Railroads in Arkansas circa 1910

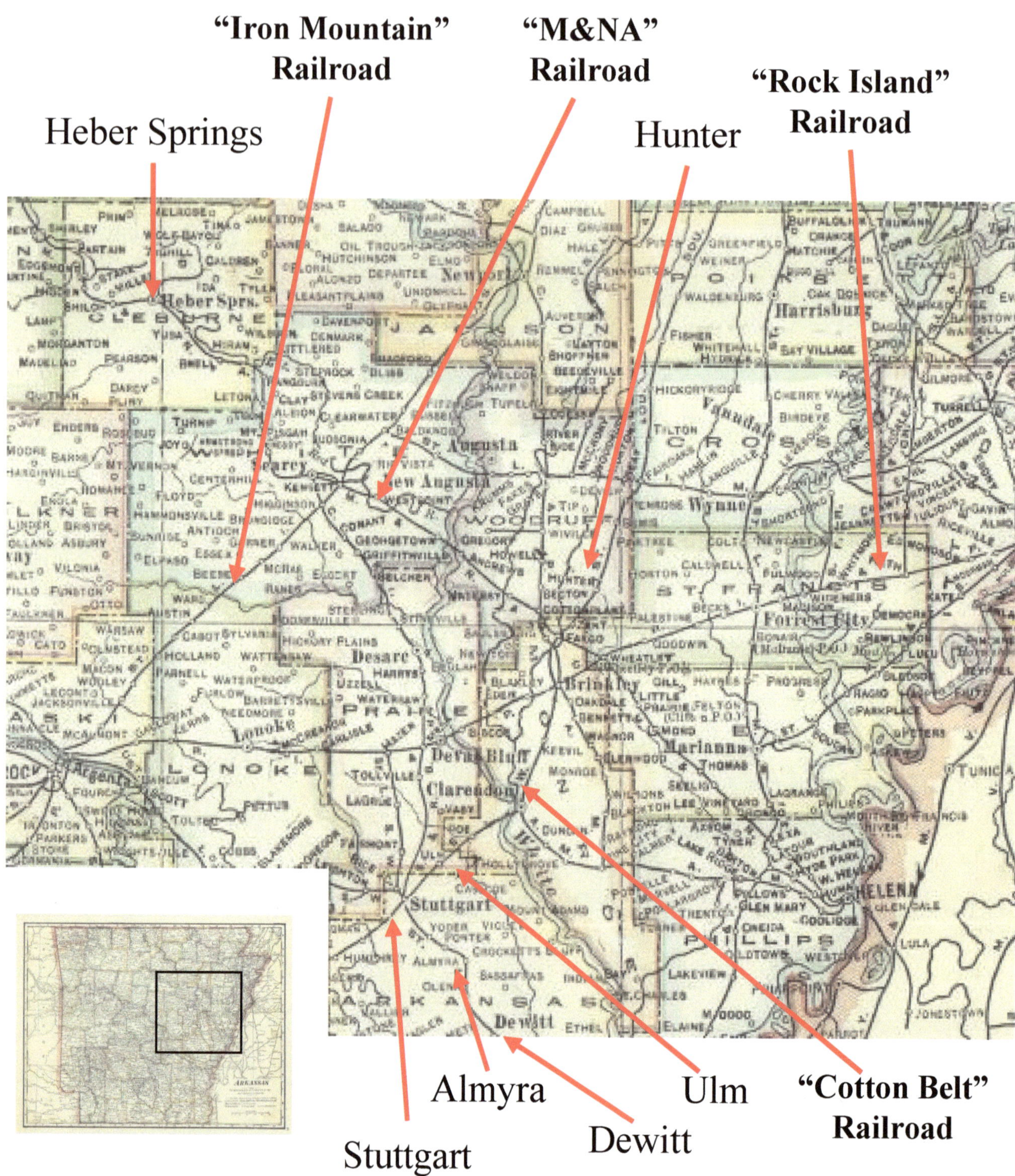


Source: "Select Counties, Arkansas," map, Historical Maps of Arkansas, George F. Cram, 1913 <http://alabamamaps.ua.edu>.

# Map of Counties, Towns & Railroads in Arkansas circa 1910

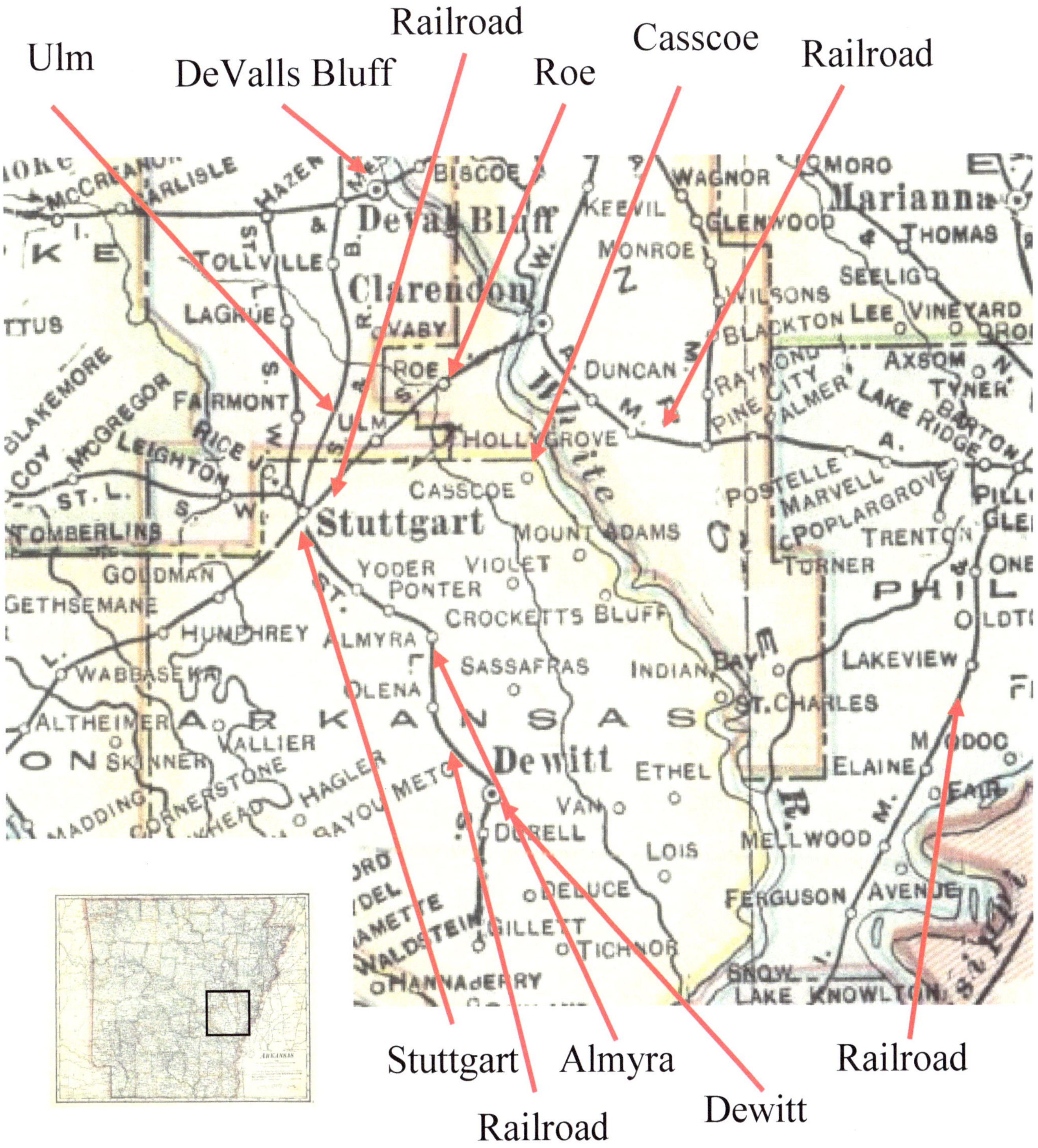


Source: "Select Counties, Arkansas," map, Historical Maps of Arkansas, George F. Cram, 1913 <http://alabamamaps.ua.edu>.

# Disfarmer: Man Behind the Camera

**Kim O. Davis**

Book Designed and Edited by Kim O. Davis

Self-published
*Sherwood, Arkansas*

First Edition

Printed in the United States of America.

FIRST EDITION

First Printing, February 2014

Library of Congress Cataloging-in-Publication Data has been applied for:

ISBN-10: 0991394321
ISBN-13: 978-0-9913943-2-6

**Cover Photo:** Photo of Disfarmer holding his Kodak No. 3-A Folding Camera standing behind his home on Sugar Loaf Street circa 1920. This photo was provided by the James Calvin Minor, Sr. Family.

# Dedication

This book is dedicated to the loving memory of my mother, Robbie Dean Davis (1934-2012), who would have been proud of me had she lived to see this book completed. She defined the meaning of the word love everyday in the lives of her husband, children and extended family.

I would also like to dedicate this book to my father, A. Odean Davis, who was born in rural Arkansas in 1933 at the beginning of the Great Depression. His childhood stories and his demonstrated work ethic were invaluable to me during the long hours of effort required to produce this biography.

I would like to mention my inspirational grandparents, Jim V. and Arizona Davis and Isaac C. and Oletta Trammell, who raised families during the Great Depression and World War II. Their true-life stories of their struggles to raise families during extremely difficult times in Arkansas helped me to empathize with the subjects of Disfarmer's thought-provoking photographs. It gave me an emotional connection to Disfarmer's time and place.

Last but certainly not least, I would like to thank my wife, Judy, and my daughter, Sydney, for their patience and understanding during the long hours of my absence from family activities and slacking on household chores during the two year span of time required for me to research and write this biography.

*- Kim O. Davis*

# *Table of Contents*

**Dedication** ..... **vii**

**Table of Photos & Illustrations** ..... **x**

**Preface** ..... **xv**

**Acknowledgements** ..... **xvi**

**Chapter I. Introduction: Mike Disfarmer** ..... **18**

**Chapter II. The Formative Years: Birth to Age 26** ..... **22**

**Chapter III. The Photographer's Apprenticeship - 1900 to 1914** ..... **26**

Supposition 1: A Photography Venture Enters the Viewfinder ..... 31

**Chapter IV. Heber Springs: A Brief Introduction** ..... **34**

**Chapter V. Penrose & Meyer Photographers: 1914 to 1920** ..... **40**

Supposition 2: Penrose & Meyer Focus on Heber Springs ..... 42

Vignette: William Orestus Penrose ..... 44

Vignette: Palmer School of Chiropractic ..... 45

**Chapter VI. The Meyer Photography Studio: 1921 to 1938** ..... **48**

Vignette: Heber Springs' Early Twentieth Century Tornados ..... 52

Vignette: The Skylight Photography Studio ..... 52

Vignette: Ford Model T ..... 55

**Chapter VII. The Classical Period: Disfarmer Photography Studio / 1939 to 1945** ..... **56**

Supposition 3: A Unique Combination of Ingredients ..... 58

Vignette: Origin of the Name Disfarmer ..... 60

Vignette: The Great Depression's Impact on Cleburne County ..... 60

**Chapter VIII. Decline and Death: 1946 to 1959** ..... **61**

**Chapter IX. Man Behind the Camera: A Psychological Profile** ..... **65**

**Chapter X. Cameras, Equipment, Supplies and Technique.............................71**

Supposition 4a: Possible Cameras........................................................................................72

Supposition 4b: Reliance on Glass Plates............................................................................73

Supposition 4c: Possible Dark-Room Equipment..................................................................75

Vignette: Rochester Camera and Lens Companies.................................................................77

Vignette: Eastman Kodak Company.......................................................................................77

Vignette: Real Photo Postcards.............................................................................................79

**Chapter XI. The Disfarmer Family Album.......................................................81**

**Appendix 1: Disfarmer Family History as Told by Relatives to Louise Fricker ...............................................................................................................94**

The Meyer Family History as Told by Harry Neukam...............................................................95

What I Can Remember About Uncle Mike.................................................................................96

Written to Me [Louise Fricker] by Marie Fricker Fillman July 1, 1986........................................96

Ione Goodrich Riedell-neice [sic] of Mike Meyer Who Lived in Santa Cruz, California Wrote:........96

Roy's [Fricker] Memories of his Uncle Mike:...........................................................................96

Mike Meyer / Disfarmer Biographical Sketch by Louise Fricker...............................................98

**Appendix 2: Meyer Family Timelines...........................................................101**

**Appendix 3: Heber Springs Times and the Headlight Article on Name Change ...............................................................................................................106**

**Appendix 4: James Calvin Minor, Sr., Country Music Star and Great Nephew of Mike Disfarmer.............................................................................................107**

**Appendix 5: Disfarmer Exhibit - Cleburne County Historical Society, Heber Springs, Arkansas...........................................................................................110**

**Links to Disfarmer Photos...........................................................................113**

**About the Author.........................................................................................114**

# Table of Photos & Illustrations


| Chapter / Appendix | Number | Subject | Photographer (if known) | Source |
|---|---|---|---|---|
| I | 1 | Disfarmer | Bessie Utley | Cleburne County Historical Society |
| I | 2 | Disfarmer | | Author's Private Collection |
| I | 3 | Disfarmer | Disfarmer Self-portrait | James Calvin Minor, Sr. Family Collection |
| | | | | |
| II | 1 | Ursula & Christopher Meyer | | Louise Fricker Family Collection |
| II | 2 | Margaretha & Martin Meyer | | Louise Fricker Family Collection |
| II | 3 | Disfarmer | | Louise Fricker Family Collection |
| II | 4 | Meyer Home, Almyra, Arkansas | Disfarmer | Author's Private Collection |
| II | 5 | Barbara Krodel & Michael Griiner | | Louise Fricker Family Collection |
| II | 6 | Meyer Home, Stuttgart, Arkansas | | Louise Fricker Family Collection |
| II | 7 | Auto Parade, Stuttgart, Arkansas | | Author's Private Collection |
| II | 8 | Main St., Stuttgart, Arkansas | | Author's Private Collection |
| II | 9 | Rice Harvesting, Grand Prairie, Arkansas | | Author's Private Collection |
| II | 10 | Cotton Belt Depot, Stuttgart, Arkansas | | Author's Private Collection |
| | | | | |
| III | 1 | Mike & Charley Meyer | Dayton Bowers | Author's Private Collection |
| III | 2 | Dayton Bowers Studio | Dayton Bowers | The Butler Center, Anna Grace Bowers Collection |
| III | 3 | Dayton Bowers Home | Dayton Bowers | Steven & Ray Hanley |
| III | 4 | Dayton Bowers | | The Butler Center, Anna Grace Bowers Collection |
| III | 5 | Unidentified Man, Crawfordsville, Indiana | Lawson | The Butler Center, Anna Grace Bowers Collection |
| III | 6 | Payer Sisters | E.K. Blush | William G. Coleman Family Collection |
| III | 7 | Gettle Children | E.K. Blush | William G. Coleman Family Collection |
| III | 8 | Reverend Edward Kornbaum | James Ball | William G. Coleman Family Collection |
| III | 9 | Eda Clawitter | Charles Buerkle | William G. Coleman Family Collection |
| III | 10 | Gettle Children | Charles Buerkle | William G. Coleman Family Collection |
| III | 11 | Immigration Train | E.K. Blush | The Encyclopedia of Arkansas History & Culture |
| III | 12 | Ida Payer | E.K. Blush | William G. Coleman Family Collection |
| III | 13 | Rev. Edward Kornbaum, Jr. | | William G. Coleman Family Collection |
| III | 14 | Ulm, Arkansas Depot | E.K. Blush | William G. Coleman Family Collection |
| | | | | |

# Table of Photos & Illustrations (continued)


| Chapter / Appendix | Number | Subject | Photographer (if known) | Source |
|---|---|---|---|---|
| IV | 1 | Sugar Loaf Mountain | | www.CityofHeberSprings.com |
| IV | 2 | Little Red River / Sugar Loaf Mountain | | Author's Private Collection |
| IV | 3 | Max Frauenthal | | The Encyclopedia of Arkansas History & Culture |
| IV | 4 | Black Sulphur Spring | E.G. Spellman | Author's Private Collection |
| IV | 5 | Spring Park Entrance, Heber Springs, Arkansas | | www.CityofHeberSprings.com |
| IV | 6 | M&NA Railroad Map | | Author's Private Collection |
| IV | 7 | 3rd Street, Heber Springs, Arkansas | | The Encyclopedia of Arkansas History & Culture |
| IV | 8 | 1912 Cover: Oak Leaves Magazine | | Author's Private Collection |
| IV | 9 | 3rd Street, Heber Springs, Arkansas | | The Encyclopedia of Arkansas History & Culture |
| IV | 10 | Main St. Heber Springs, Arkansas | | www.CityofHeberSprings.com |
| IV | 11 | Black Sulphur Springs | | Author's Private Collection |
| IV | 12 | Red Sulphur Springs | | Author's Private Collection |
| IV | 13 | White Sulphur Springs | | Author's Private Collection |
| IV | 14 | Red Sulphur & Eye Springs | | Author's Private Collection |
| | | | | |
| V | 1 | Penrose & Meyer Studio | | Cleburne County Historical Society |
| V | 2 | Penrose Wedding Announcement | | The Rutherford B. Hayes Presidential Center |
| V | 3 | Main Street, Heber Springs, Arkansas | | The Encyclopedia of Arkansas History & Culture |
| V | 4 | George A. Penrose | | The Palmer School of Chiropractic Archives |
| V | 5 | Edith Penrose | | The Palmer School of Chiropractic Archives |
| V | 6 | 1914 Cover: Oak Leaves Magazine | | Boone County Historical Society |
| V | 7 | Ad: The Palmer School of Chiropractic | | |
| V | 8 | Socialist Party Presidential Campaign Button | | |
| V | 9 | The Palmer School of Chiropractic | | |
| V | 10 | Penrose & Meyer Studio | | Cleburne County Historical Society |
| | | | | |
| VI | 1 | Meyer Home, Heber Springs, Arkansas | Disfarmer | Author's Private Collection |
| VI | 2 | Margaretha Meyer feeding chickens | Disfarmer | James Calvin Minor, Sr. Family Collection |
| VI | 3 | Meyer Home after Tornado, Heber Springs | Disfarmer | Author's Private Collection |
| VI | 4 | Interior of Meyer Home after | Disfarmer | Louise Fricker Family Collection |
| VI | 5 | Disfarmer Studio | Disfarmer | James Calvin Minor, Sr. Family Collection |

# Table of Photos & Illustrations (continued)


| Chapter / Appendix | Number | Subject | Photographer (if known) | Source |
|---|---|---|---|---|
| VI | 6 | Heber Springs after Tornado | Disfarmer | www.TheSunTimes.com |
| VI | 7 | Margaretha Meyer in front of Disfarmer Studio | Disfarmer | James Calvin Minor, Sr. Family Collection |
| VI | 8 | Margaretha Meyer in bed after fall | Disfarmer | Louise Fricker Family Collection |
| VI | 9 | Mike Meyer playing violin | | Louise Fricker Family Collection |
| VI | 10 | Model T Ford | Disfarmer | James Calvin Minor, Sr. Family Collection |
| | | | | |
| VII | 1 | Newspaper Article on Name Change | | Arkansas History Commission |
| VII | 2 | Meyer Petition to Court | | Cleburne County Clerk |
| VII | 3 | Margaretha Meyer RPPC | Disfarmer | Author's Private Collection |
| VII | 4 | Disfarmer | | Author's Private Collection |
| VII | 5 | Disfarmer of Men Holding Catfish | Disfarmer | Author's Private Collection |
| VII | 6 | Disfarmer Draft Card | | Ancestry.com |
| | | | | |
| | | | | |
| VIII | 1 | Maggie Minor | Disfarmer | Author's Private Collection |
| VIII | 2 | Martha Price / Eanes | | Ruth Kirkemeier Family Collection |
| VIII | 3 | Disfarmer | Roy Fricker | Louise Fricker Family Collection |
| VIII | 4 | Maggie Minor Klinger 2nd Home, De Valls Bluff, Arkansas | Author | Author's Private Collection |
| VIII | 5 | Disfarmer Grave Marker | | Author's Private Collection |
| | | | | |
| IX | 1 | Little Man Syndrome Illustration | | Psychology Today |
| IX | 2 | Margaretha Meyer & Unidentified Friend | Disfarmer | Louise Fricker Family Collection |
| IX | 3 | Margaretha Meyer on Back Porch | Disfarmer | Author's Private Collection |
| IX | 4 | Narcissus Painting | Caravaggio | Public Domain |
| | | | | |
| X | 1 | Kodak Ad | | |
| X | 2 | Kodak 3-A Folding Camera | Author | Cleburne County Historical Society |
| X | 3 | Kodak Print Ads | | "Kodakery" magazine |
| X | 4 | "Kodakery" cover and print ad | | "Kodakery" magazine |
| X | 5 | RPPC Back | Disfarmer | Author's Private Collection |
| X | 6 | George Eastman | | |
| X | 7 | George Eastman | | |
| X | 8 | Disfarmer & Pearl Fricker | Disfarmer | Louise Fricker Family Collection |
| | | | | |
| XI | 1 | Charley Meyer Draft Card | | Ancestry.com |
| XI | 2 | Margaretha Meyer after fall in chair | Disfarmer | James Calvin Minor, Sr. Family Collection |
| XI | 3 | Margaretha Meyer | Disfarmer | Louise Fricker Family Collection |
| | | | | |

# Table of Photos & Illustrations (continued)


| Chapter / Appendix | Number | Subject | Photographer (if known) | Source |
|---|---|---|---|---|
| XI | 4 | Margaretha Meyer | Disfarmer | Louise Fricker Family Collection |
| XI | 5 | Margaretha Meyer | Disfarmer | Louise Fricker Family Collection |
| XI | 6 | RPPC Back | Disfarmer | Louise Fricker Family Collection |
| XI | 7 | Andrew Meyer's children | Charles Buerkle | Louise Fricker Family Collection |
| XI | 8 | Andrew Meyer | | Louise Fricker Family Collection |
| XI | 9 | Evelyn Meyer | Charles Buerkle | Louise Fricker Family Collection |
| XI | 10 | George Meyer | | Louise Fricker Family Collection |
| XI | 11 | Evelyn Meyer | | Louise Fricker Family Collection |
| XI | 12 | Pearl Marie Fricker | Disfarmer | Louise Fricker Family Collection |
| XI | 13 | George Meyer | Disfarmer | Louise Fricker Family Collection |
| XI | 14 | Grace Meyer | | Louise Fricker Family Collection |
| XI | 15 | Barbara Neukam | | Louise Fricker Family Collection |
| XI | 16 | Katy Meyer | | Louise Fricker Family Collection |
| XI | 17 | Disfarmer & Barbara Neukam | | Author's Private Collection |
| XI | 18 | John Joseph Fricker | | Louise Fricker Family Collection |
| XI | 19 | Mary Ursula Fricker | Disfarmer | Louise Fricker Family Collection |
| XI | 20 | John J. Fricker Family | Disfarmer | Louise Fricker Family Collection |
| XI | 21 | John Joseph Fricker | | Louise Fricker Family Collection |
| XI | 22 | Pearl Fricker, Disfarmer, Anna Meyer | Disfarmer | James Calvin Minor, Sr. Family Collection |
| XI | 23 | Anna Meyer | Disfarmer | Louise Fricker Family Collection |
| XI | 24 | Anna Meyer, Disfarmer, Pearl Fricker | Disfarmer | James Calvin Minor, Sr. Family Collection |
| XI | 25 | Ione Goodrich | | Ruth Kirkemeier Family Collection |
| XI | 26 | Maggie Meyer | Disfarmer | Louise Fricker Family Collection |
| XI | 27 | Children of Maggie & Theodore H. Minor | Disfarmer | Louise Fricker Family Collection |
| XI | 28 | Maggie, Theodore H. Minor & Family | Disfarmer | Ruth Kirkemeier Family Collection |
| XI | 29 | William Minor | Disfarmer | Ruth Kirkemeier Family Collection |
| XI | 30 | Mike & Velma Minor | Disfarmer | Author's Private Collection |
| XI | 31 | Marion & Clara Minor | Disfarmer | Author's Private Collection |
| XI | 32 | Maggie Minor | Disfarmer | Ruth Kirkemeier Family Collection |
| XI | 33 | Geppert Studio Stamp | | Ruth Kirkemeier Family Collection |
| XI | 34 | Theodore Hursley Minor | Disfarmer | Ruth Kirkemeier Family Collection |
| XI | 35 | Maggie & Theodore H. Minor | Disfarmer | Author's Private Collection |
| XI | 36 | Maggie & Theodore H. Minor | Disfarmer | Author's Private Collection |
| XI | 37 | Maggie & Theodore H. Minor | Disfarmer | James Calvin Minor, Sr. Family Collection |
| XI | 38 | Charley & Mike Meyer | Disfarmer | Louise Fricker Family Collection |
| XI | 39 | Charley & Mike Meyer | Disfarmer | James Calvin Minor, Sr. Family Collection |
| XI | 40 | Charley & Mike Meyer | Dayton Bowers | Author's Private Collection |
| XI | 41 | Charley Meyer & George Penrose | Disfarmer | James Calvin Minor, Sr. Family Collection |
| XI | 42 | Charley Meyer, wife and children | | Author's Private Collection |

# Table of Photos & Illustrations (continued)


| Chapter / Appendix | Number | Subject | Photographer (if known) | Source |
|---|---|---|---|---|
| XI | 43 | Joe Neukam & Minor Girls | Disfarmer | Author's Private Collection |
| XI | 44 | Joe Neukam | Disfarmer | Louise Fricker Family Collection |
| XI | 45 | Maggie Minor and Daughters | Disfarmer | Author's Private Collection |
| XI | 46 | Minor Girls | Disfarmer | Ruth Kirkemeier Family Collection |
| XI | 47 | Young Maggie Minor on Farm | Disfarmer | Author's Private Collection |
| XI | 48 | Margaret, Frank Kirkemeier, Calvin Minor & daughter Ruth | | Author's Private Collection |
| XI | 49 | Lucy Kirkemeier and son, Lester | | Ruth Kirkemeier Family Collection |
| XI | 50 | Stephen & Alvina Kirkemeier | Disfarmer | Author's Private Collection |
| | | | | |
| A4 | 1 | James Calvin Minor, Sr. | | James Calvin Minor, Sr. Family Collection |
| A4 | 2 | Jimmy Minor & the Diamond K Ranch-hands | | James Calvin Minor, Sr. Family Collection |
| A4 | 3 | Jim Minor on the Grand Ol' Opry | | James Calvin Minor, Sr. Family Collection |
| A4 | 4 | Jim Minor | | James Calvin Minor, Sr. Family Collection |
| A4 | 5 | James C. Minor, Sr. | | James Calvin Minor, Sr. Family Collection |
| A4 | 6 | Jimmy Minor & Mickey Minor | | Ruth Kirkemeier Family Collection |
| A4 | 7 | Disfarmer's Violin & Case | Author | James Calvin Minor, Sr. Family Collection |
| | | | | |
| A5 | Various | Disfarmer Exhibit | Author | Cleburne County Historical Society Museum, Heber Springs, Arkansas |
| | | | | |

# Preface

Why is there such international interest in a small-town photographer's portraits of ordinary, rural people from Heber Springs, Arkansas taken in the 1930's and 1940's? The answer: his body of work reflects an artistic genius that captured the soul of rural, agrarian people as they endured tremendous hardship brought on by the Great Depression and World War II. His timeless photos can now be found in photography museums, exhibitions and private collections in the United States, Canada and Europe. Quite a change in status for these photographs from such humble beginnings.

Much has been published about Disfarmer's photography and little about his life. He is the subject of a documentary film, a puppet play and the inspiration for music. Despite this volume of work, many significant questions have remained unanswered about Disfarmer. This biography will attempt to answer these lingering questions and to shed new light on Disfarmer's life, his psyche and technique and how the confluence of these yielded near photographic perfection. This book is not focused on his work – several great compendiums of his photographs have been published. However, many of Disfarmer's photographs and those of other photographers are presented herein to illustrate his life and times – many of which have never been seen by the public.

Disfarmer died in relative obscurity in 1959 at the age of 75 in a small town in Arkansas by the name of Heber Springs. After his photographic genius was discovered in the early 1970's, he had been dead some thirteen years. He did not leave a journal. He never married and had no children. He did not have any close friends. Some Heber Springs citizens knew him through limited interactions in the course of small town life. Many others knew him only through brief encounters while having their portraits made. Disfarmer was separated by distance from most relatives for much of his life. As a result, what we know about his life to date has been pieced together largely through hearsay with those that knew him superficially.

Due to this lack of first-person narrative, some have attempted to piece together a picture of Disfarmer's life. However, many aspects have remained out of focus. Based largely on hearsay and few surviving primary source documents, his odd, bohemian lifestyle has been superficially reconstructed. My intent is to fill in voids in Disfarmer's life through extensive research. I will also attempt to debunk or confirm some of the Disfarmer myths.

The eccentricities and idiosyncrasies of the quirky photographer created a fertile environment for the Disfarmer legend to take root and flourish. The legend revolves around a Van Gogh-like persona -- a town-loner who changed his name because of a bizarre story about his childhood. Was the Disfarmer myth watered and fed by those that would benefit by the embellishment of his eccentricities? From a promotional perspective, it certainly helps create and perpetuate "buzz" if the man behind the camera was an eccentric that local townsfolk shunned.

The Disfarmer myth created an interesting dichotomy that has baffled fans and family for almost 40 years. How could a hermit-like, anti-social, outsider take such thought-provoking and insightful portraits of ordinary people – his lens like a window into their souls? Was he anti-social? Did he truly not like to be around people other than to briefly take their photographs? Was Disfarmer close to his family even though he chose to live away from them? Was he empathetic with his photographic subjects having grown up in a family of farmers that endured hardships in post-reconstruction Arkansas?

My research includes discussions with surviving relatives, gathering and examining family photos -- many of which were made by Disfarmer or were of Disfarmer, genealogy research, study of numerous publications and visits to regional museums and libraries. Close study of primary source documents such as family photos and artifacts has yielded clues that were in turn pursued yielding additional leads and discoveries. From this body of research, I will draw conclusions or suppositions that will fill in gaps and answer some of the lingering questions about his life and photography. When offering conjecture, I will identify it as "supposition."

I hope to dispel some of the myths about the man and to confirm others. The myth-busting does not detract but enhances Disfarmer's photographic genius by casting it in a different light. Much like how Disfarmer's use of the camera illuminated the soul of his subjects, the legend of Disfarmer is enhanced by a closer examination of his life through the lens of truth rather than viewing him through the distorted filters of hearsay and innuendo. I present *Disfarmer: Man Behind the Camera.*

*- Kim O. Davis*

# Acknowledgements

L. Frank Baum quotes, Goodreads.com, © 2014, <http://www.goodreads.com/author/quotes/3242.L_Frank_Baum>.

I would like to acknowledge the following for their permission to reproduce photos and other documents that were instrumental in bringing this biography of Mike Disfarmer to the printed page:

- David Fricker, Disfarmer's Great-Nephew, and his wife, Verma Fricker, De Valls Bluff, Arkansas
- The Louise Fricker Family Photograph & Genealogy Collection, De Valls Bluff, Arkansas
- Lester Kirkemier, Disfarmer's Great-Nephew, Sherwood, Arkansas
- The James Calvin Minor, Sr. Family Photograph Collection, De Valls Bluff, Arkansas
- Ruth (Kirkemier) Newkirk, Disfarmer's Great-Niece, De Valls Bluff, Arkansas
- The William G. Coleman Family Photographs, San Francisco, California
- The Cleburne County Historical Society, Heber Springs, Arkansas
- Special Collections and Archives, Palmer College of Chiropractic, Davenport, Iowa
- The Butler Center for Arkansas Studies, Little Rock, Arkansas, Anna Grace Bowers Brown Collection, 1881-1944
- Ancestry.com®
- Mr. Greer Lile, photographer and photography collector, Little Rock, Arkansas
- Mr. Hubert Smith, photographer and photography collector, Maumelle, Arkansas

I would also like to recognize the following people and organizations for their assistance with this publication:

- Mr. Tom Prince, Esq. of North Little Rock, Arkansas, a former Mayor of Little Rock, a Civil War historian and reenactor who proofread the draft and made other content suggestions
- Dr. Michael "Mickey" Barnett, Disfarmer Historian, Cleburne County Historical Society, Heber Springs, Arkansas
- Mr. Brian Robertson, Butler Center for Arkansas Studies, Little Rock, Arkansas
- Mr. Daniel Smith and Ms. Rosemary Riess, Special Collections and Archives, David D. Palmer Health Sciences Library, Palmer College of Chiropractic, Davenport, Iowa
- James Calvin Minor, Jr., Disfarmer's 2nd Great-Nephew, De Valls Bluff, Arkansas

I would like especially to recognize the assistance of the following individuals who spent considerable time and energy in helping me with this biography. These individuals are passionate about preserving their respective family histories:

- Mr. Todd W. Minor, Disfarmer's 2nd Great-Nephew, De Valls Bluff, Arkansas: Todd provided considerable assistance throughout the researching and writing of this biography. His insights and knowledge of the Meyer Family history were instrumental in helping me "connect the dots" on Disfarmer's life story.
- Mr. William G. Coleman, San Francisco, California: William is a descendant of the Clawitter-Gettle-Payer families who resided in and around Ulm, Arkansas. William's extensive collection of family photographs from the late 1800's and early 1900's – many of which were made by early photographers in the Stuttgart, Arkansas, area. – provided valuable insights into possible connections among these photographers, Disfarmer and Disfarmer's early partner, George A. Penrose.

# Chapter I. Introduction: Mike Disfarmer

*"...and the next moment all of them were filled with wonder. For they saw, standing in just the spot the screen had hidden, a little old man, with a bald head and a wrinkled face, who seemed to be as much surprised as they were."*

- L. Frank Baum, The Wonderful Wizard of Oz

Mike Disfarmer died alone on newspapers strewn on his studio floor at age 75 in 1959, never imagining that the penny portraits he made of working class people in the hills of Arkansas would one day sell for several thousand dollars each and would hang in museums, private collections and photography galleries in New York, San Francisco, Canada and Europe. The hard-working, blue-collar residents of Cleburne County, Arkansas, who scraped together their nickels, dimes and quarters during the Great Depression and World War II to have their keepsake portraits made would have been equally shocked and disbelieving. But for the apparent generosity of the town mortician who paid for a modest headstone, his grave might remain unmarked today.

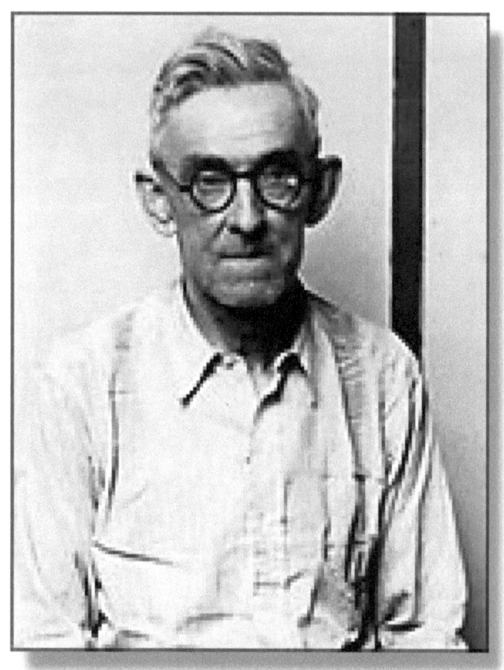

**1. Mike Disfarmer photo taken circa 1946, about age 63, by his assistant, Bessie Utley. The distinctive vertical stripe of Disfarmer's reversible backdrop is clearly visible.**

Disfarmer earned a modest living as a photographer in Heber Springs, Arkansas, a small town in the Ozark foothills, from 1914 until his death in 1959. For a few years during the Roaring Twenties, his photography income was sizable by small town standards. He was an eccentric, small town character – odd, reclusive and sometimes downright rude to people. For most of those years, he made small portraits of ordinary people using glass plate negatives and contact printing from a unique skylight-studio situated on the corner of Main and North First Streets. By a bit of luck and pluck, the photographic negatives which hold up well over a number of years, were discovered by accident after his death and eventually brought to the attention of an influential editor of a photography magazine in New York. The editor was enraptured by the striking photographs which were haunting in the way they captured the soul of ordinary people living under extraordinary conditions from the end of the Great Depression through the end of World War II – a unique time in American History when such photos are rare.

Disfarmer was born Mike Meyer but on March 29, 1939 at the age of 54, he petitioned the Cleburne County Circuit Court to have his name legally changed. The bizarre but imaginative story he provided to the court as the reason for his name change contained elements that strangely foreshadowed a more famous imaginative story that would appear on the silver screen later that same year. Disfarmer alleged to the court that he was not truly a Meyer but as a mere infant, he was blown by a tornado to the Indiana doorsteps of his mother and father, Margaretha and Martin Meyer, who raised him as a Meyer. He went on to claim that on many an occasion, he was an embarrassment to the Meyer clan and that his relatives frequently commented that they wished to disown him. The judge granted his request.

In August of 1939, the classic film, *The Wizard of Oz*[1], was released to a nationwide audience. In the now well-known story based on a 1900 novel by L. Frank Baum, an adolescent Dorothy and her dog Toto are blown by a tornado from Kansas to the Emerald City where they encounter a wizard – or at least a man posing as a wizard. Unlike Dorothy and Toto who were eventually reunited with family and friends in Kansas, Mike Meyer became Mike Disfarmer and chose to sever all ties with his past and his family.

1939 marked the beginning of what I call the classical phase for Disfarmer. He appears to have become more reclusive and concentrated his photography almost exclusively on in-studio work. Between 1939 and 1946, Disfarmer produced photos that are the most sought after by collectors.

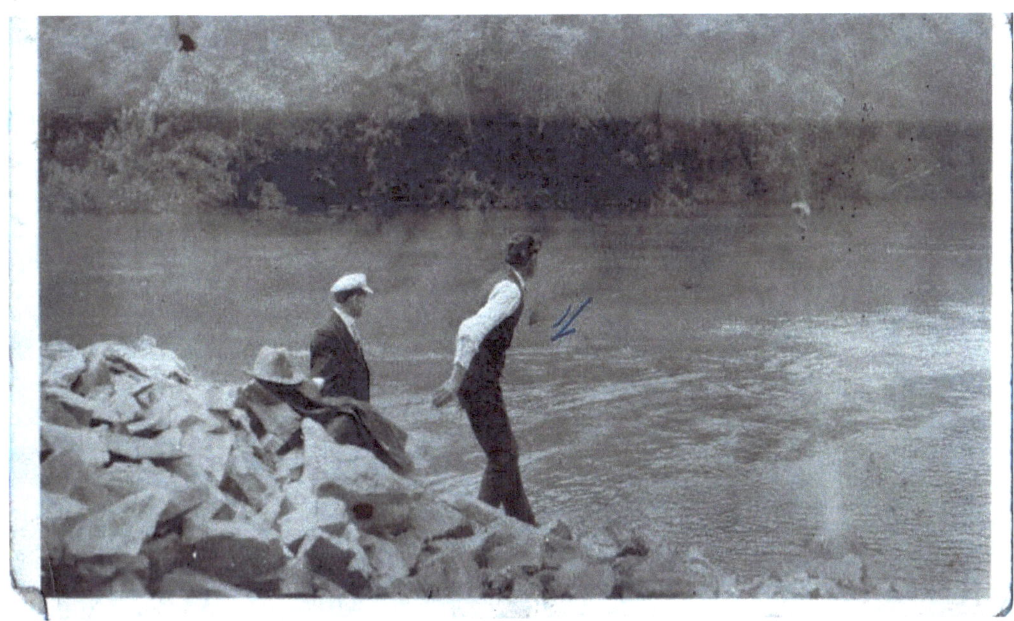

**2. Mike Disfarmer skipping rocks at the river. The river is believed to be the Little Red River near Heber Springs, Arkansas. The gentleman seated on the rocks may have been his early partner, George A. Penrose. The date of the real photo postcard (RPPC) is circa 1918. Below is the correspondence side of the RPPC stamped "PENROSE & MEYER / PHOTOGRAPHERS / HEBER SPRINGS, ARK." The AZO stamp block with the 4 corner triangles pointing up dates the paper between 1904 and 1918.**

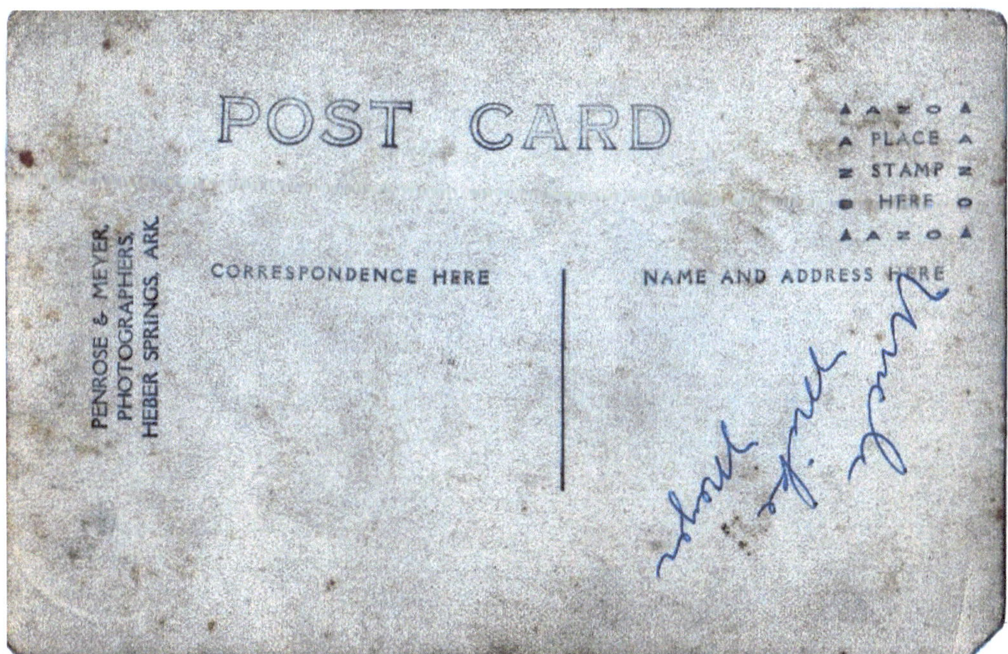


After World War II, Disfarmer's photography business fell into decline. He began to drink more and eat less, which inevitably took its toll on his health. In 1959, after a couple of townsfolk become alarmed that they had not seen Disfarmer on the streets for a few days, they went to his studio and found him dead on the floor where he appeared to have lain for several days. And that's where the story should have ended but fate intervened.

Shortly after Disfarmer's death, Joe Albright, a former Heber Springs mayor, a real-estate agent and photography buff, purchased the contents of Disfarmer's decaying studio at an estate sale for five dollars from a local bank acting as the administrator of the estate.[2] Albright hoped to find some interesting photo equipment to add to his collection. While digging through the contents of the studio, Albright found a stack of about 4,000 glass plate negatives in the studio. While rifling through the glass plates, Albright allegedly found $8,000 in U.S. Savings Bonds and several hundred dollars in cash stored in between the plates which helped Albright recoup his original investment plus a tidy profit.[3*] Albright, not thinking that the glass plate negatives had any intrinsic value, stored the negatives away at his home. And yet fate intervened again to prevent the Disfarmer saga from an ignoble ending.

In the late 1960's, the local Heber Spring newspaper editor, Peter Miller, who had moved to the rural community from New York, ran a photo contest to spark community interest in the small town paper. The photo contest was cleverly called "Some Day Your Prints Will Come" and ran for several weeks seeking entries from the community. Albright contacted Miller informing the editor that he was in possession of some glass plate negatives that might be of interest to the photo contest. Miller examined the glass plate negatives and decided to publish some of the photos. After seeing the local community's reaction to the reprints of the Disfarmer negatives that had lain dormant for some 20 to 30 years, Miller acquired the glass negatives from Allbright for five dollars in 1973.[4] Miller eventually salvaged about 3,000 of the 4,000 glass plate negatives using a cleaning solution supplied to him by Kodak® to remove mold and dirt from the aging plates. Afterwards, Miller produced some prints from the restored negatives.

Miller then contacted an old acquaintance in New York, Julia Scully, the then editor of Modern Photography magazine. On seeing the prints, Scully's discerning eye observed unique qualities in the glass plate negatives and grew keenly interested in learning more about the little known photographer, Mike Disfarmer. In 1976, Miller and Scully collaborated in publishing the first of two books displaying high-quality reprints of some of the more interesting negatives taken by Disfarmer. The publishing of this first book occurred contemporaneously with an exhibition at the International Center of Photography in New York. These events catapulted Disfarmer's photography to international prominence.[5] Since the publishing of that first book, several other books have been published showcasing Disfarmer's work.

Then in the early 2000's, a couple that had lived in Heber Springs but had moved to Chicago, approached Michael Mattis, a well known photography collector and showed him some original Disfarmer prints. Previously, it was erroneously believed that no actual Disfarmer prints had survived and that the Albright-Miller glass plate negatives were the only surviving artifacts from Disfarmer's lengthy career. Around 2005, Mattis commissioned the Disfarmer Project, a small team lead by art researcher, Hava Gurevich, to move to Heber Springs to buy Disfarmer prints from Cleburne Coun-

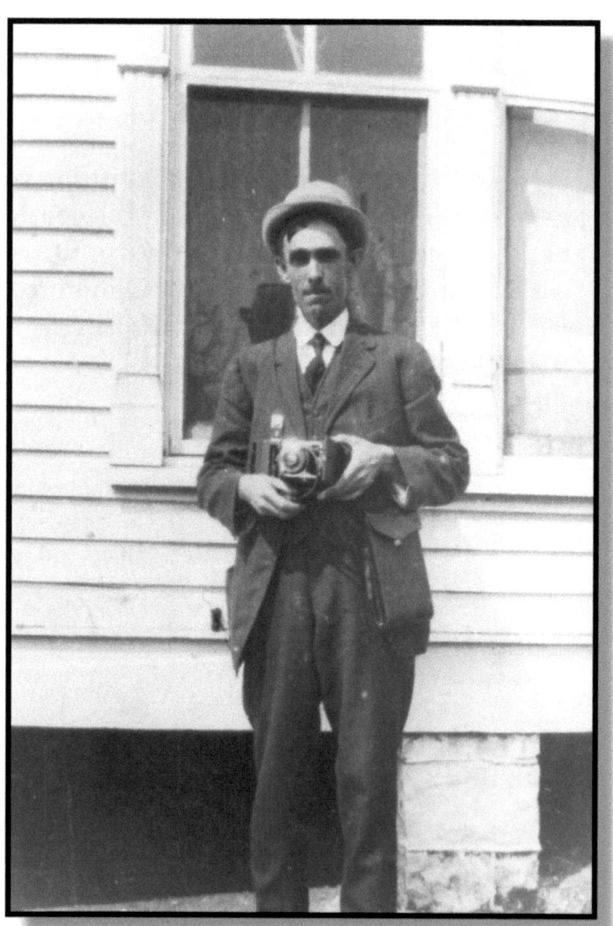

**3. Mike Meyer / Disfarmer in photo taken circa 1920, at approximately 36 years of age. Meyer is holding his Kodak No. 3-A Folding Brownie camera and is standing behind his Heber Springs, Sugar Loaf Street home where his studio was located on the back porch from about 1920 to 1926.**

* According to family oral history shared by Todd and Jim Minor, Jr., Disfarmer did not trust banks after living through the Great Depression.

ty residents. Mattis appears to have spent about $3 million of his own money acquiring original Disfarmer prints. Those prints in turn made their way into his personal collection, into the hands of various galleries and dealers and eventually into certain photography museums. Some of those original Disfarmer prints are reported to have sold for between $10,000 and $30,000 each.

So who was this almost-forgotten, small-town photographer who took these "frozen in time" portraits that provide a window into the souls of ordinary Americans struggling to survive and raise families during a time of great hardship in this country's history – the Great Depression and World War II? Was he a wizard or simply an ordinary photographer who by a sheer twist of fate found himself in the right place at the right time? Or perhaps he was an above-average photographer who had mastered his craft and continued to rely on tried and true tools of his trade, unwilling to embrace or invest in the latest technology. How significant was the eccentric, off-putting personality of the town's odd-ball photographer in generating a certain stilted reaction in the studio from his photographic subjects? Or perhaps it was the nature of the subjects themselves to "be who they were" and not put on a facade which led to a stark realism in the photos. Perhaps all these ingredients came together at a place in time to create the perfect soufflé. The purpose of this biography is to allow the reader to draw his/her own conclusions about Disfarmer, the man behind the camera.

**NOTES**

[1] The Wizard of Oz, dir. Victor Fleming, Metro-Goldwyn-Mayer, premiered in Hollywood on August 15, 1939, released nationally on August 25, 1939, based on the novel The Wonderful Wizard of Oz by L. Frank Baum, 1900.

[2] "HEBER SPRINGS COMMERCIAL HISTORIC DISTRICT, HEBER SPRINGS, CLEBURNE COUNTY," Arkansas Historic Preservation Program, <http://www.arkansaspreservation.com/historic-properties/_search_nomination_popup.aspx?id=2459>.

[3] Richard Woodward, Disfarmer: A Biography, <http://disfarmer.org/Disfarmer%20Bio.htm>.

[4] HEBER SPRINGS COMMERCIAL HISTORIC DISTRICT.

[5] Richard Woodward.

# Chapter II. The Formative Years: Birth to Age 26

*"To 'know Thyself' is considered quite an accomplishment."*

— L. Frank Baum, The Marvelous Land of Oz

Michael "Mike" Meyer was a second generation American and was descended from German immigrants. He was born April 12, 1884 in Portersville, Indiana to Martin Meyer and Margaretha (Weidenhammer) Meyer and was the sixth child of eight children. He was the second son of three sons born to the couple. The children of Martin Meyer and Margaretha Weidenhammer in birth order were:

1. Andrew (1869-1951)
2. Barbara (1871-1952)
3. Anna Kathrina (1874-1881)
4. Mary Ursula (1877-1926)
5. Anna (1881-1972)
6. Michael "Mike" (1884-1959)
7. Margaretha "Maggie" (1887-1975)
8. Charles H. "Charley" Wolfgang (1889-1976)

Mike's father, Martin, was the only son of Christopher Meyer and Ursula (maiden name may have been Maier) Meyer. Christopher (b. April 21, 1809) and Ursula (b. 1814) were both born in Germany. Christopher came to the United States in 1841, landing at Baltimore, Maryland. After landing, he moved first to Dubois County, Indiana, and later, moved to Crawford County, Indiana. Christopher and Ursula were married in Dubois County in March, 1843. Martin was born June 2, 1846 in Indiana.

On August 24, 1864, Martin Meyer joined the Union Army, Company A, 49th Indiana Veteran Voluntary Infantry in which he served for over a year. He was discharged on September 18, 1865, and lived for a period of time in Crawford and Dubois Counties, Indiana. Martin received a military pension for a disability incurred from an illness he suffered in Kentucky in 1865. He was married to Margaretha Weidenhammer on May 26, 1868, in Haysville, Indiana by Reverend Vernhart Sheifterling, a Lutheran Minister. Martin apparently was known as a carpenter, a harness-maker, a farmer, and a musician. Martin's musical talent would be passed down to his son, Mike, his daughter Maggie and at least one of Maggie's grandchildren, James Calvin Minor, Sr. (see Appendix 4). A December 27, 1881, land transaction shows that Martin Meyer was a trustee of the Emmanuel Lutheran Hill Church in Dubois County, Indiana.

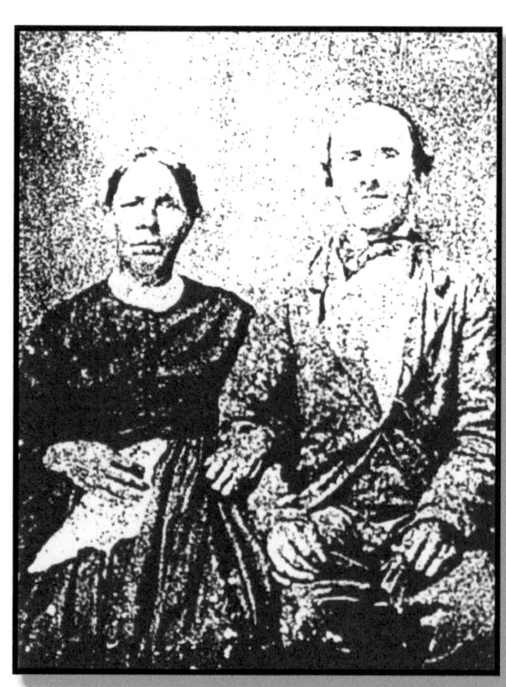

**1. Ursula and Christopher Meyer, Mike Meyer/Disfarmer's paternal grandparents were both born in Germany.**

Mike's mother, Margaretha Weidenhammer, was born near Haysville, Indiana, on March 25, 1849. She was baptized in infancy and confirmed at age 13 in the Lutheran Church at Haysville, Indiana. Margaretha was the third of four children born to Johann Weidenhammer and Barbara (Krodel) Weidenhammer. Johann was born October 3, 1812 at Mistelback, District Bayreuth, Bavaria, Germany. Barbara was born August 21, 1821 in Germany. Johann Weidenhammer and Barbara Krodel were married on February 5, 1841, at St. Paul's Lutheran Church in Jasper, Indiana. Johann died in Indiana before 1860 making Margaretha less than 10 years old at the time of his death. Barbara died at the age of 85 on September 16, 1906 and is buried at Emmanuel Lutheran Hill Cemetery, Dubois County, Indiana.

When Mike was about eight years of age, his father moved his family to Almyra, Arkansas County, Arkansas, in 1892, to the Delta region where they settled and took up farming southeast of town in Keaton Township. Keaton Township is a long, narrow township that runs north and south in Arkansas County. Mike's paternal grandfather, Christopher, died on January 13, 1895 at Patoka Township, Crawford County, Indiana. It appears that sometime after the death of his grandfather, Disfarmer's paternal grandmother, Ursula Meyer, relocated to Almyra, Arkansas, and moved in with her only son, Martin, and his young family.

It is not known why Martin Meyer decided to uproot his young family and move them south of the Mason-Dixon line to take up farming in Arkansas. We do not know if he left Indiana due to a hardship there or if he was drawn to Arkansas County as was the case with many other families of Germanic descent. Almyra lies about 25 miles south of Stuttgart, Arkansas, and was connected to Stuttgart by the St. Louis Southwestern Railway, more commonly known as the "Cotton Belt." Stuttgart, Arkansas, was founded by the Reverend Adam Buerkle, a Lutheran minister in 1883. Reverend Buerkle actively recruited Germanic families from the Midwest with an effective promotional campaign that offered cheap land and attractive farming opportunities. Many German-Americans residing in the Midwest relocated south to the natural prairie area of Arkansas to raise grain crops which they were very adept at growing. Around the time that Martin Meyer relocated his large family to Arkansas County near Stuttgart, rice farming was introduced to the area. Stuttgart promotes itself today as the rice capital of the United States.

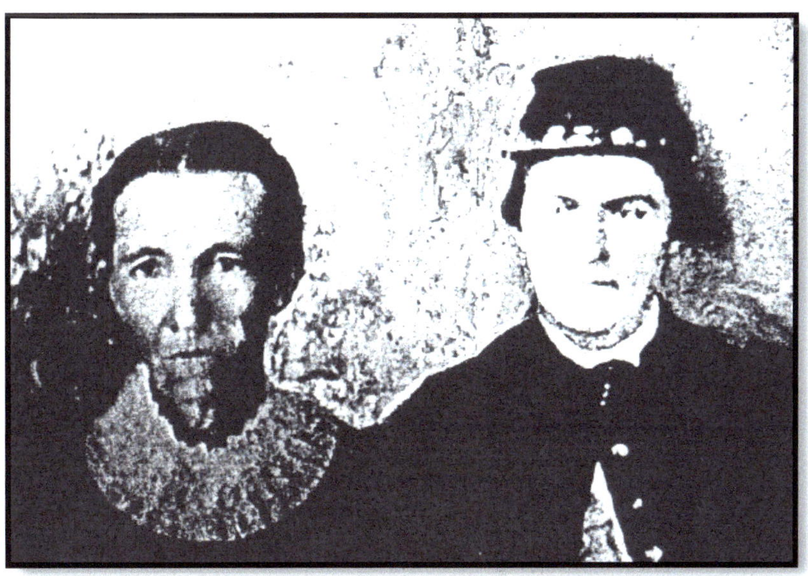

**2. Mike Meyer/Disfarmer's mother, Margaretha (Weidenhammer) Meyer and his father, Martin Meyer. Martin fought for the Union Army during the Civil War.**

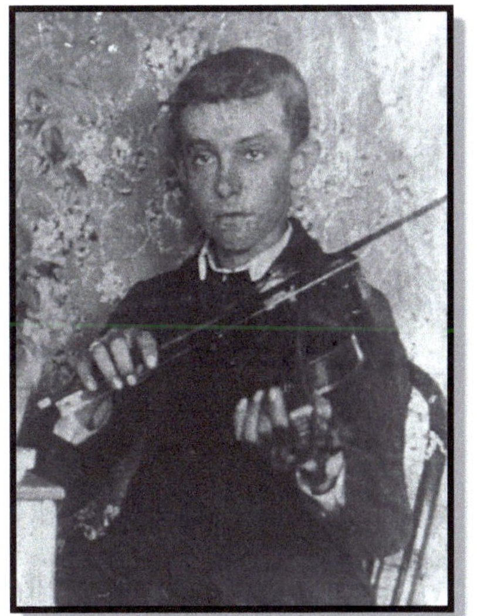

**3. Mike Meyer about 8 years old playing his violin.**

In 1898, a mere six years after moving his family to Almyra, Mike's father, Martin, died at the age of 52. His young family was left without the primary breadwinner -- a financially devastating event for a family trying to eke out its livelihood from tilling the soil. Mike Meyer was only 14 when his father died.

The 1900 U.S. Census shows that Mike's mother, Margaretha (Weidenhammer) Meyer, was the head-of-household and young Mike was the oldest son still living at home. Living with

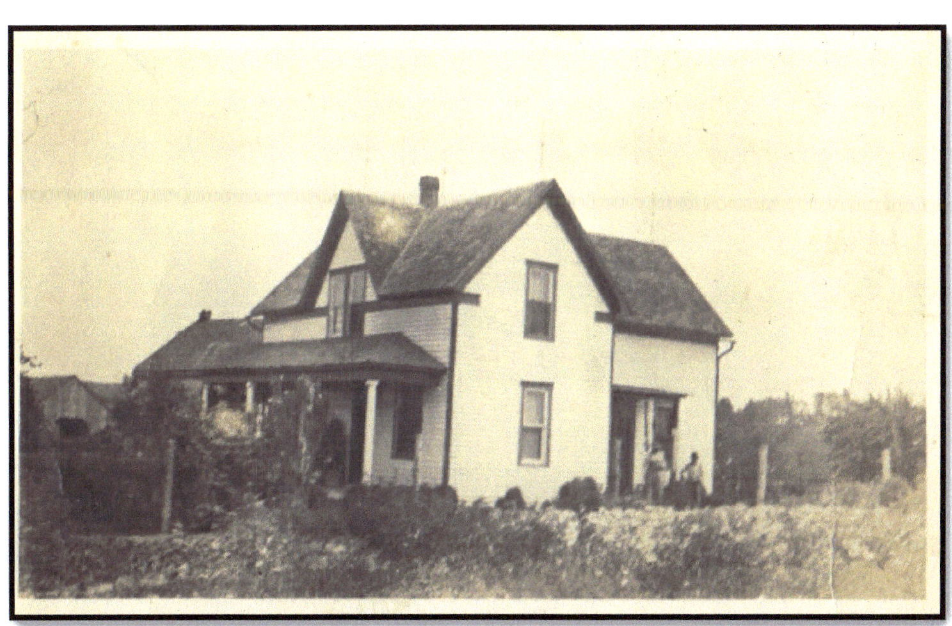

**4. The Meyer Family home in Keaton Township near Almyra, Arkansas (not confirmed). This photo was likely taken by a young Disfarmer circa 1900. Two people can be seen at the back of the house.**

Mike and his mother, Margaretha, were:

- his oldest sister, Barbara - 28, and her husband, William Neukam - 34;
- the Neukam children, John - 8, Sophia - 7, Harry - 4 and Clara - 1;
- his older sister, Anna - 19;
- his younger sister, Maggie - 13;
- and his youngest brother, Charley - 10.

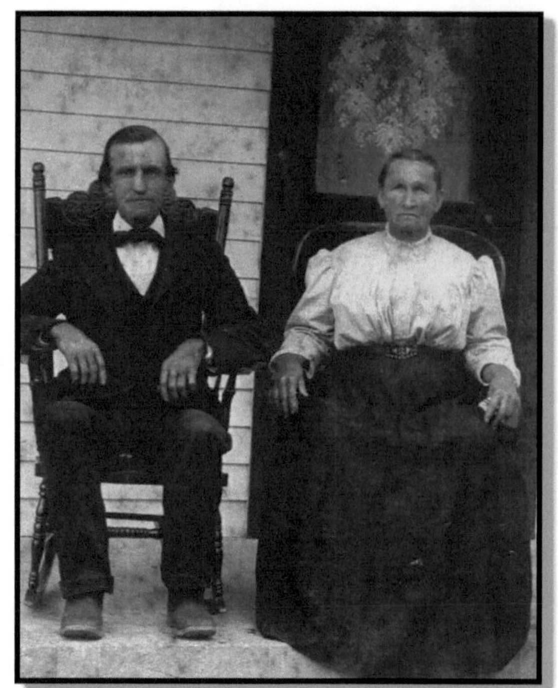

**5. Barbara Krodel, mother of Margaretha Weidenhammer, with her second husband, Michael Griiner or Greener.**

Mike Meyer's remaining siblings that were not living in the household in 1900 were Andrew Meyer, 31, Mary Ursula, 23, and Anna Katherina, who died at the age of 7. Andrew married Lillian Uleah Lewis in 1896 and had moved out on his own to start his new family. Mary Ursula married John Joseph Fricker on Christmas Eve, 1895 and had also moved out of the household before 1900. In 1902, Disfarmer's youngest sister, Maggie, at the age of 15 married Theodore Hursley Minor, and moved out of the Meyer household. More detail about Mike's next older sister, Anna, his younger brother, Charley, both with whom he was very close, as well as extensive family photographs can be found in Chapter 11.

By the time of the 1910 U.S. Census, Mike Meyer, now 26, was the only one of Margaretha Meyer's living children still unmarried and still living at home with his widowed mother who was now 61. The two of them were then living on Cleveland Street in the city of Stuttgart, Gum Pond Township, Arkansas County, Arkansas. The census record shows that Mike's mother had her "own income" which appears to have been a military pension drawn on her deceased husband, Martin, a Union Army veteran. The 1910 census shows that at the age of 26, Mike was a "laborer" performing "odd jobs." Mike Meyer did not yet consider himself a professional photographer at the age of 26. However, he was likely learning his future profession and may have been an amateur photographer for some time.

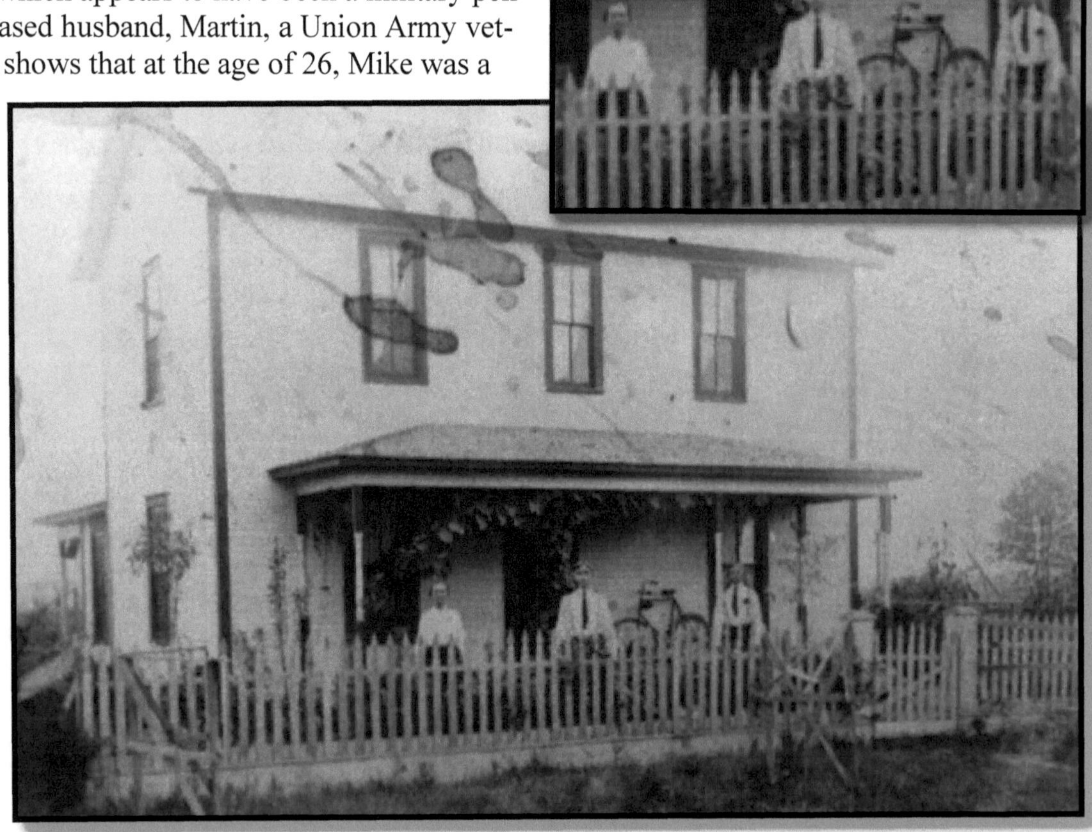

**6. Mike Meyer's home in Stuttgart, Arkansas circa 1910. In front of the house are Meyer's mother, Margaretha (left), Mike (middle) and his brother, Charley (right). See the inset above for an enlarged view.**

# Early Scenes of Stuttgart, Arkansas

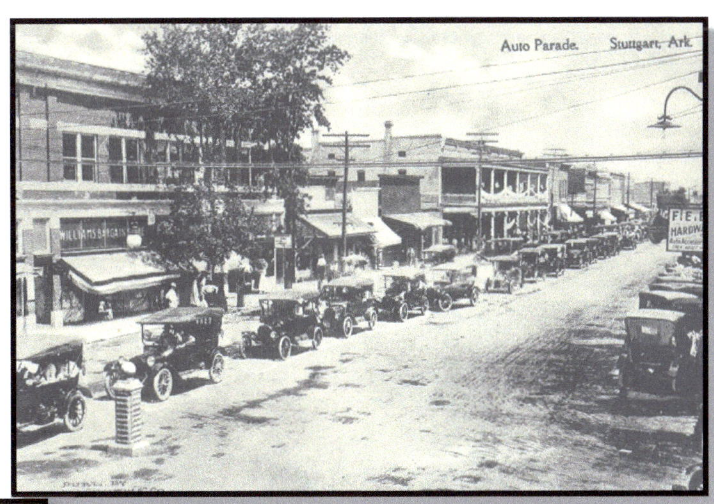


7. View of "Auto Parade," Stuttgart, Arkansas, circa 1914.

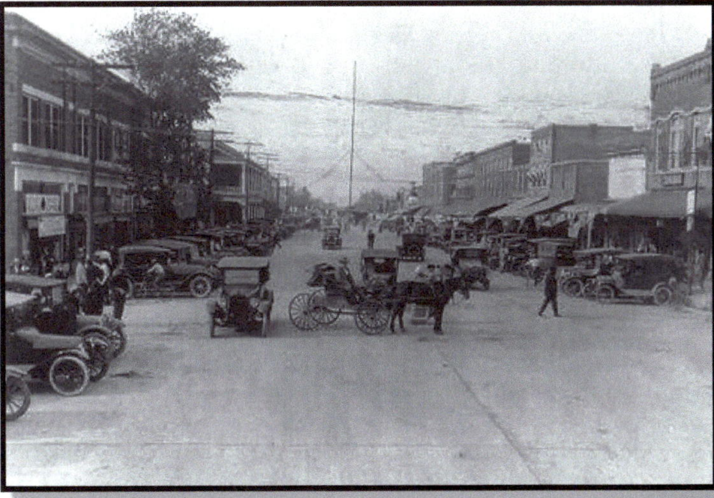

8. Main Street, Stuttgart, Arkansas, 1914.

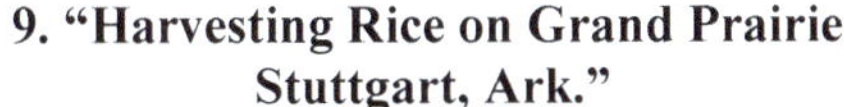

9. "Harvesting Rice on Grand Prairie, Stuttgart, Ark."

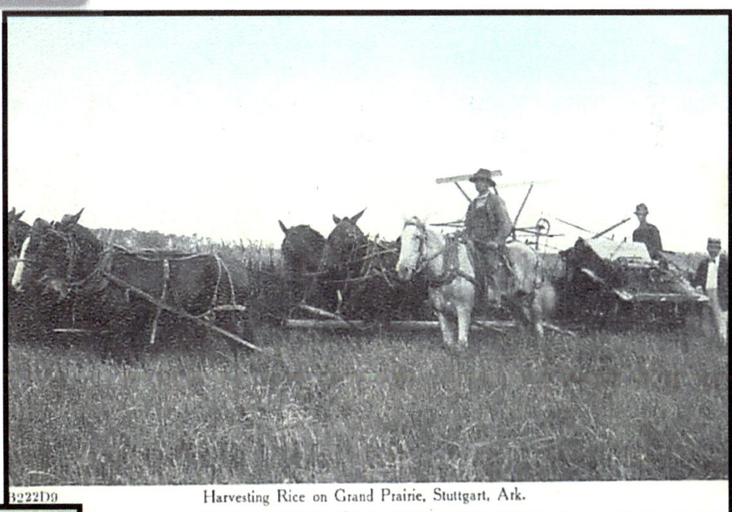


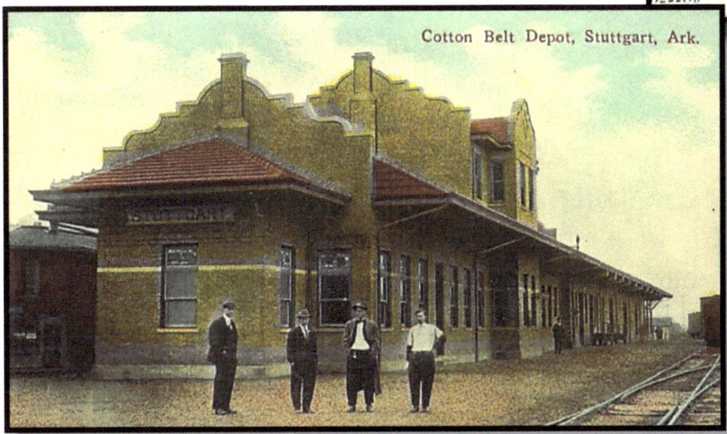


10. "Cotton Belt Depot, Stuttgart, Ark."

# Chapter III. The Photographer's Apprenticeship - 1900 to 1914

*"That proves you are unusual," returned the Scarecrow; "and I am convinced that the only people worthy of consideration in this world are the unusual ones. For the common folks are like the leaves of a tree, and live and die unnoticed."*

— L. Frank Baum, The Land Of Oz

One of the biggest unanswered questions about Disfarmer is where did he learn his craft? I believe I can answer that question based on compelling, circumstantial evidence uncovered. Other researchers have noted that several early photographers operated in the Stuttgart, Arkansas area and that Disfarmer may have learned his trade from one of these photographers. The same source noted that Disfarmer once stated that he been to Elmyra (New York), implying that maybe Disfarmer traveled a great distance from his Arkansas home to learn the profession that would eventually make him a post-mortem, iconic photographer. As noted in Chapter 2, Disfarmer lived in Almyra, Arkansas, and his reference was to Almyra, not Elmyra, New York. I concur with the supposition that Disfarmer learned his craft in Arkansas County, Arkansas, sometime between 1900 and 1914. According to the 1910 census, Disfarmer listed his occupation as a laborer. My supposition however, is that he was learning the photography trade between 1900 and 1914, in Arkansas County possibly from at least two photographers, Dayton Bowers and Edward K. Blush. In January, 1914, Disfarmer moved from Stuttgart, Arkansas County, to Heber Springs, Cleburne County, Arkansas, along with his elderly mother.

According to research performed by D.L. Ewbank* who compiled a list of early Arkansas photographers using several sources such as city directories at the Arkansas History Commission, there were four (4) professional photographers working in Arkansas County in the late 1800's to the early 1900's:

- Dayton Bowers, DeWitt, Arkansas County, Arkansas, 1884 - 1913
- Edward K. Blush, Stuttgart, Arkansas County, Arkansas, 1898 - 1900
- Charles W. Buerkle, Stuttgart, 1906 - 1907
- Chester W. Vandusen, Stuttgart, 1912 - 1913

These dates represent known dates of operation but are not absolute dates of operation. The photographers may have operated for more years than listed here. Based on corroborating evidence, I know that two of these four made photographs earlier than the dates listed in the Ewbank research. Dayton Bowers opened his photography studio in 1881 which is three years before the 1884 date listed by Ewbank. And Edward K. Blush made a professional photograph in 1894 which is four years before the 1898 date noted by Ewbank.

**Dayton Bowers**

The first link in the chain of evidence is a studio photograph obtained from Disfarmer's great niece, Ruth (Kirkemier) Newkirk that was taken by Dayton Bowers, an early Arkansas County photographer. The subjects in the photograph are two youthful boys wearing hats and smoking cigars. Ms. Newkirk was unable to identify the young boys in the photo. However, after carefully studying the photograph and comparing it with other early photos of Disfarmer and his brother, Charley, I believe the subjects are Mike Meyer, age 14 to 16, and his youngest brother, Charley, age 9 to 11, which dates the photo to around 1898 to 1900. The age difference between Disfarmer and his younger brother

* Ms. Ewbank is an award winning author whose articles and columns have appeared in Writer's Digest, Family Tree Magazine, ScreenTalk-the International Voice of Screenwriting and MovieScope. She has a B.A. in Political Science from the University of Arkansas, and an M.A. in Media Psychology & Social Change from Fielding Graduate University.

Charley was five years and the two boys in the photograph appear about five years apart in age. This appears to be one of the earliest surviving photographs of Disfarmer and his youngest brother, Charley. Mike and Charley were photographed together at numerous times in their lives (see Chapter 11). The brothers were usually stylishly dressed in the fashion of the day. The Dayton Bowers photograph taken around 1900, would be the first known picture of the teen-aged Disfarmer and his younger brother, Charley.

So why is this Dayton Bowers photo of Disfarmer and Charley significant? Dayton Bowers was a very early photographer in Arkansas, apparently the earliest professional photographer in Arkansas County. He opened a photography studio in DeWitt, Arkansas County, Arkansas, in 1881, shortly after the arrival of the dry plate photographic process. R.L. Maddox invented the dry plate photographic process in 1871 which was a major technology breakthrough. In 1879, George Eastman invented a machine that quickly and efficiently produced dry plates – marking his first major success in the field of photography. In 1880, Eastman began commercial production of dry plates and in 1881, he and Henry Strong formed the Eastman Dry Plate Company. Dayton Bowers apparently embraced the new technology, opening his photography studio in 1881.

Bowers was a prolific photographer – taking photos in his studio and around the small farming town of DeWitt. He operated his photography business until about 1913 and took photos of residents and of many buildings and other landmarks in the DeWitt area during its early years. Besides his photography business, Dayton Bowers was also a real estate speculator. He sold farms and farmland to new settlers that were relocating to the area around DeWitt. As a result of his photography and real estate business, Bowers was apparently a successful entrepreneur. Many of his pho-

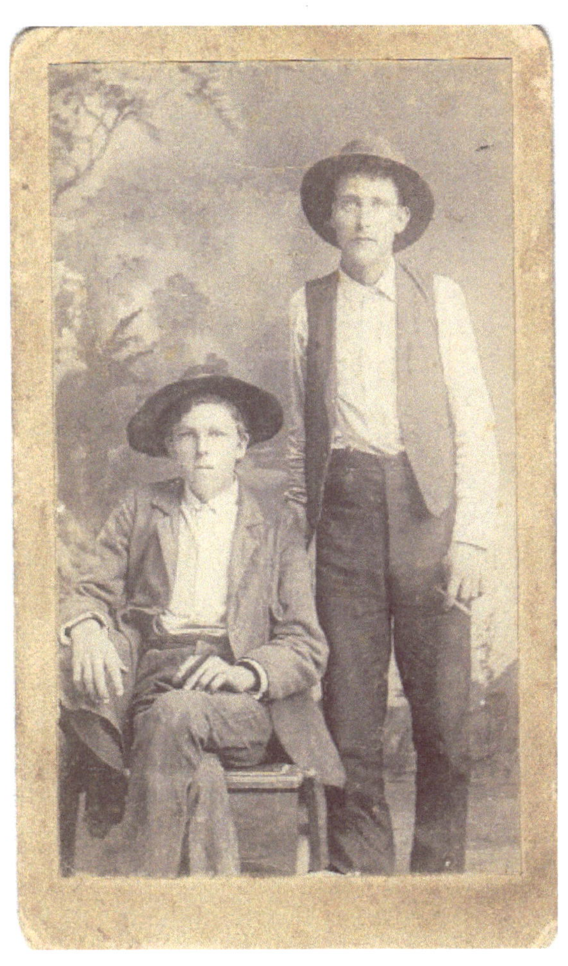

**1. Photo of Mike Meyer/Disfarmer (right) and his younger brother, Charley Meyer (left) taken at Dayton Bowers studio in DeWitt, Arkansas circa 1900. The stamp image below is from the reverse side of the photo.**

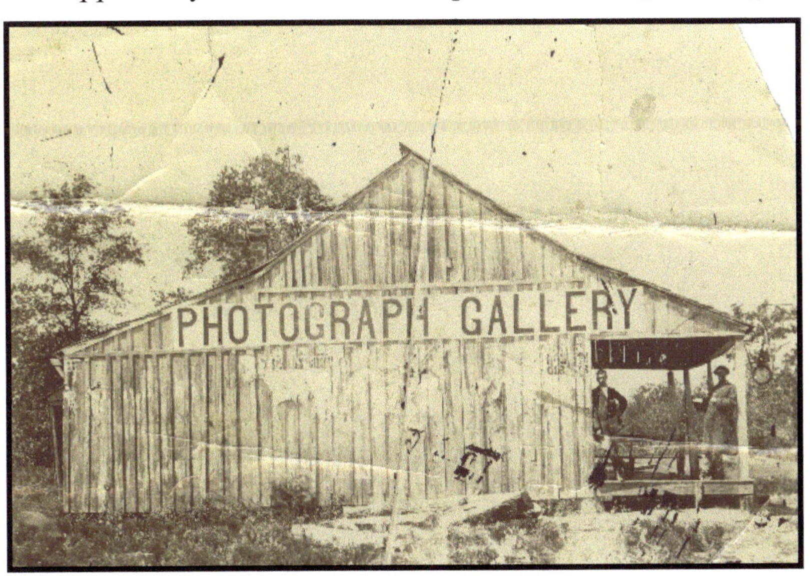


**2. Dayton Bowers' "Photograph Gallery" in DeWitt, Arkansas circa 1890.**

tographs were used in advertising materials in the local
area. A photograph in the book *Images of America ARKANSAS COUNTY*[6] shows the two-story wooden frame home of Mr. Bowers and the caption notes that the house was one of the largest in the city in the 1900 timeframe.

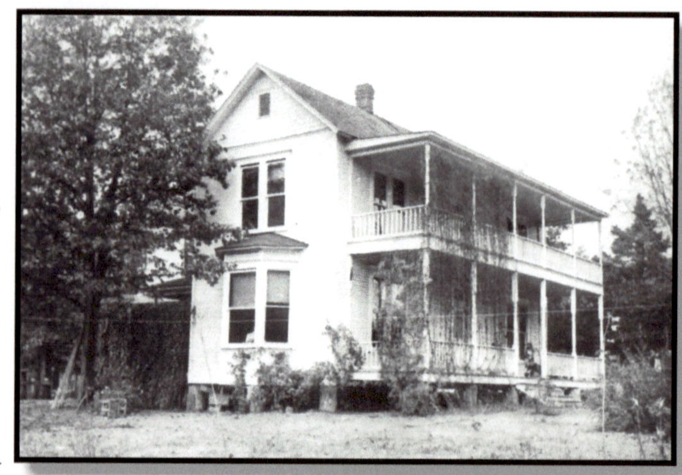

3. DeWitt, Arkansas, home of Dayton Bowers circa 1900.

Disfarmer's home in 1900, was in Keaton Township, southeast of Almyra. That would place his home somewhere between Almyra and DeWitt. Arkansas County has the unique distinction of being the oldest county in Arkansas and the only county with two county seats -- DeWitt in the southern part of the county and Stuttgart in the northern part. Disfarmer's 1900 home lying southeast of Almyra, was less than five miles from DeWitt, Bowers' hometown. I believe that Disfarmer and his brother Charley probably made frequent excursions to the county seat of DeWitt -- a larger town than nearby Almyra. On one of these excursions, Disfarmer and Charley likely stopped in Bowers' Photography Studio and had a portrait made. Two young fellows -- possibly on a Saturday trip to town enjoying freedom from the rigors of farm life were smoking cigars and having fun -- decided to have their photo made to commemorate the occasion. This experience Disfarmer had traveling to town on a Saturday jaunt from the farm for some fun would plant a seed for his eventual vocation as a photographer catering to farm folk taking similar Saturday excursions to the Cleburne County Seat of Heber Springs.

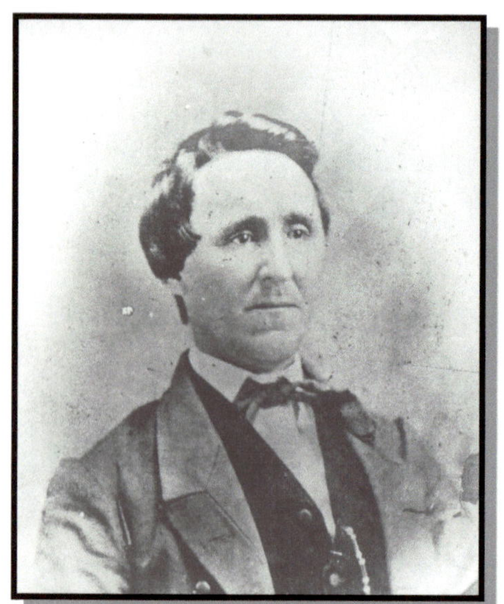

4. Dayton Bowers.

During these Saturday jaunts to DeWitt, Disfarmer undoubtedly became aware that Dayton Bowers, the photographer, was living a very prosperous life compared to the meager lifestyle of many of those scratching out a living from the soil. Its very likely that Disfarmer's family may have known Dayton Bowers from their time in Indiana. Like Disfarmer's family, Bowers moved to Arkansas County from Indiana. Disfarmer's father, Martin Meyer, was a harness maker. Dayton Bowers had once worked as a harness maker in Indiana. An early photo of an unidentified man taken at a photography studio in Crawfordsville, Indiana was donated in a collection of Dayton Bowers photos to the Butler Center for Arkansas Studies by Anna Grace Bowers, the granddaughter of Dayton Bowers. Disfarmer's sister, Mary Ursula (Meyer) Fricker, was born in Crawfordsville, Indiana (see Appendix 2, Timeline Report for Margaretha Weidenhammer).

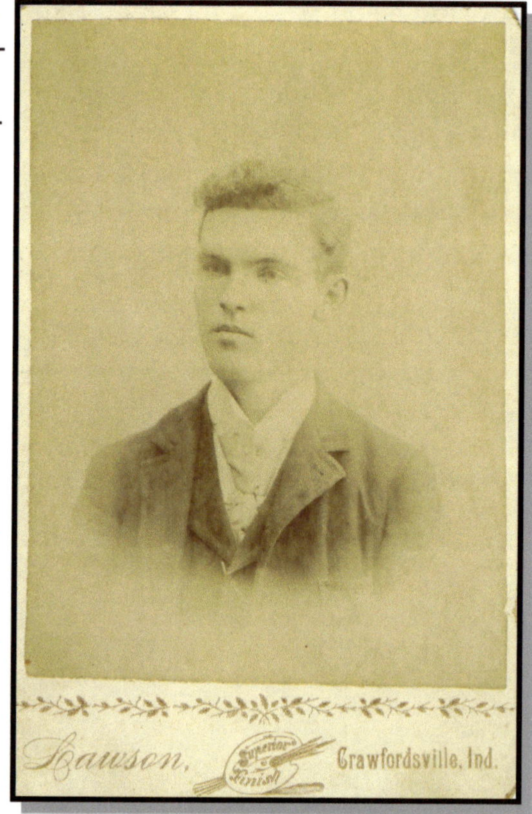


5. Photo of unidentified man taken in Crawfordsville, Indiana from the Dayton Bowers collection given by his granddaughter, Anna Grace Bowers to the Butler Center for Arkansas Studies in Little Rock, Arkansas.

Though circumstantial, the evidence is compelling that Disfarmer had family ties to Dayton Bowers going back to Indiana. Its plausible that Dayton Bowers may have provided some photographic instruction to the young Disfarmer. At a minimum, Dayton

Bowers may have been a role model for the impressionable young Disfarmer. Disfarmer's father died in 1898 leaving the large family without a primary bread-winner. Its possible that Dayton Bowers, due to a long-standing tie to the family, may have become a mentor to young Disfarmer following the death of his father. Mr. Bowers' apparent prominence and financial success in the DeWitt community was no doubt influential on the young and impressionable Disfarmer.

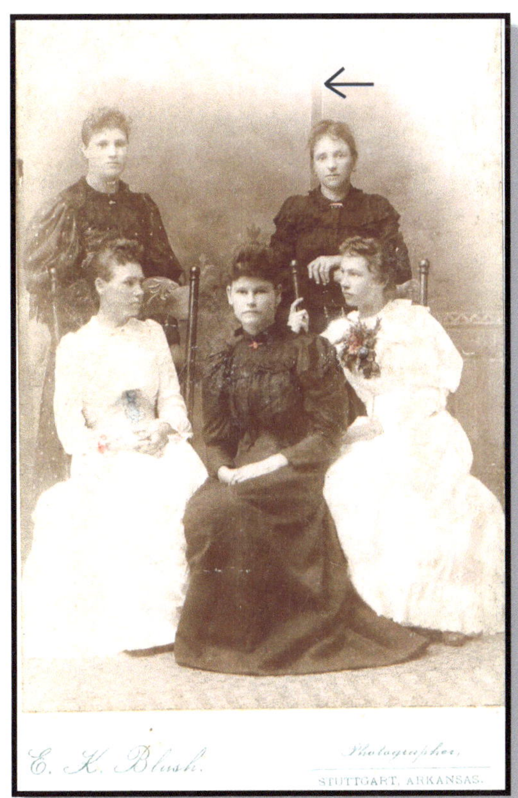


**6. The Payer sisters photo taken by E.K. Blush, Stuttgart, Arkansas, circa 1894. Notice distinct vertical stripe in backdrop similar to that found in many Disfarmer photos.**

## Edward K. Blush

Edward King Blush operated a photography studio from at least 1894 to 1905 in Stuttgart, Arkansas, the northern county seat in Arkansas County. Blush was born in Belleview, Iowa in 1868. He first married Myrtle Simmermacher and the couple had one child together, Claudia, who died early. The couple divorced after Claudia's death. Edward K. Blush then married Rosetta Elizabeth Heinmiller in 1894 in Stuttgart, Arkansas. Blush and Rosetta Elizabeth had two sons born in Stuttgart, Harry King Blush born 1897, and Bert Edward Blush born 1899. The couple moved to Denver, Colorado around 1908 where a daughter, Ethel M. Blush was born in 1908, and another son, Arthur William was born in 1910. Edward K. Blush remained in Denver until his death in 1921.

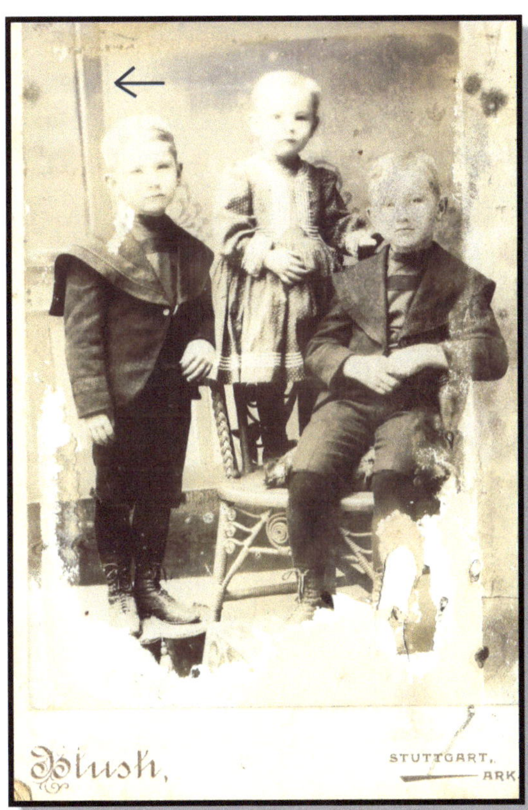


**7. Left to right: William, Jr., Francis and Richard Gettle. Notice distinct vertical stripe in backdrop similar to that found in many Disfarmer photos.**

As noted, Disfarmer was living with his mother on Cleveland Street in Stuttgart in 1910. It is unclear exactly what year Disfarmer moved to Stuttgart from the farm near Almyra. Some intriguing facts suggest connections between E.K. Blush, Mike Disfarmer and George A. Penrose, Disfarmer's eventual Heber Springs photography business partner. A most intriguing of these possible connections can be seen by closely examining the backdrops of a couple of photos made by E.K. Blush in his Stuttgart studio in the late 1890's. Two photos in the family collection of William G. Coleman show a distinctive backdrop that is eerily similar to the now famous backdrop from Disfarmer's Heber Springs studio -- the very distinctive white backdrop with the vertical black stripes (see Chapter 7, photo #5). One of the Coleman Family photos is of the five Payer sisters dated 1894. The other is of a young William, Francis and Richard Gettle. The Payers and the Gettles

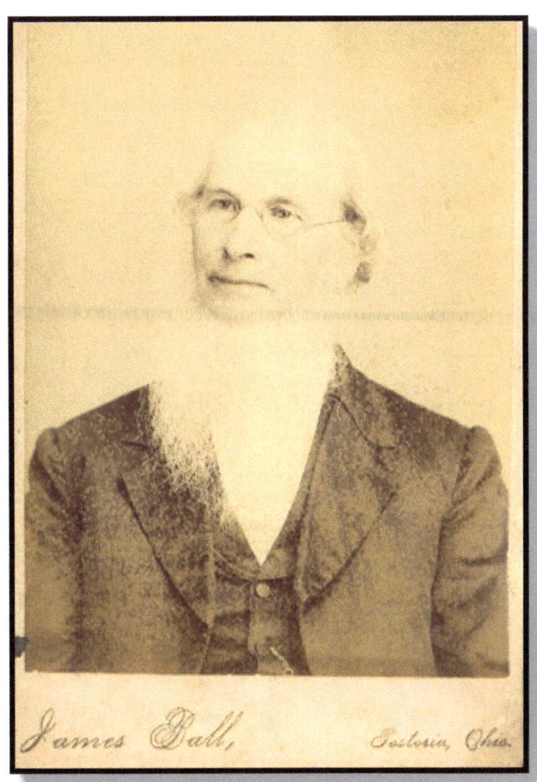


**8. Reverend Edward Kornbaum, Jr.**

were residents of Ulm, Prairie County, Arkansas -- lying just across the county line from Stuttgart. On the backdrop of these two photos, a dark, vertical line is clearly visible. Both photos are clearly marked as being made in the Stuttgart studio of E.K. Blush.

Another intriguing connection between Disfarmer and E.K. Blush involves Disfarmer's future Heber Springs partner, George Albert Penrose and Penrose's wife, Edith Kornbaum. Disfarmer's first photography studio operated under the name of "Penrose & Meyer Photography Studio" in Heber Springs from 1914 to 1920. George A. Penrose married Edith Kornbaum in 1901. A more thorough biography of George A. and Edith Kornbaum Penrose is provided in Chapter 5. According to the 1910 census, George A. Penrose was the head of household and living with him were his wife, Edith (Kornbaum) Penrose and Edith's father, Emanuel Kornbaum. George, Edith and her father were residing in the town of Hunter in Caney Township, Woodruff County, Arkansas in 1910. Woodruff County lies one county north of Prairie County containing the town of Ulm and two counties north of Arkansas County containing the larger town of Stuttgart. Edith (Kornbaum) Penrose had an older uncle, the Reverend Edward Kornbaum, Jr. who lived and died in Stuttgart, Arkansas. Edith had an aunt, Fredericka Doratea (Kornbaum) Payer who lived and died in Ulm, lying just north of Stuttgart. Frederica Doratea (Kornbaum) Payer was the maternal great-great grandmother of William G. Coleman. As mentioned previously, one of the William G. Coleman Family photos of the five Payer sisters was made by E.K. Blush in 1894 and has a distinctive dark vertical stripe in the backdrop similar to many of the unique and highly collectible Disfarmer photos from his classical 1939 to 1946 period.

## Charles W. Buerkle

Charles W. Buerkle operated a photography studio in the town of Stuttgart, Arkansas, for a very brief period from 1906 to 1907 or 1908, according to the data compiled by Ms. D.L. Ewbank. The family photo collection of William G. Coleman also contained a few photographs made by Charles W. Buerkle. Charles W. Buerkle has the distinction of being the son of the founder of Stuttgart, the Reverend Adam Buerkle, the Lutheran minister who purchased the land in northern Arkansas County, recruited German immigrants to settle in the

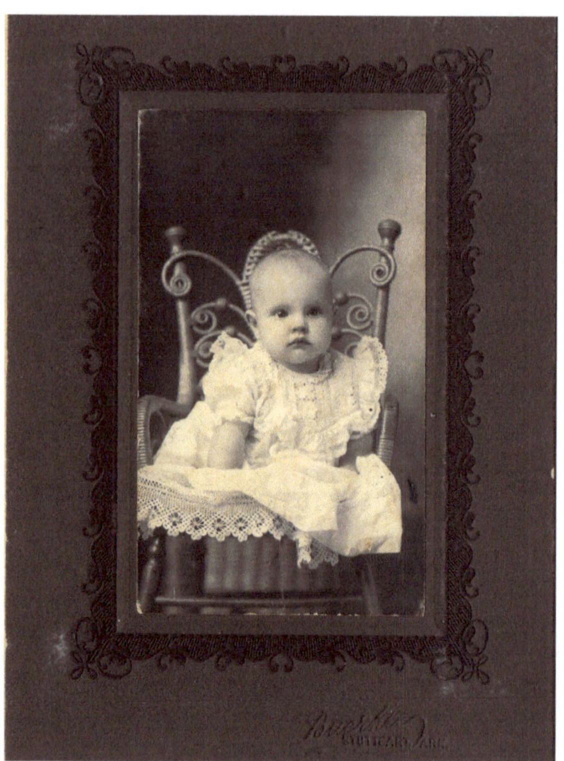

**9. Photo of Eda Clawitter, circa 1905, made at Charles Buerkle's studio in Stuttgart, Arkansas. Note the ornate, wicker high-chair is identical to that shown in a photo of Evelyn Meyer (Chapter 11, #9) tying the Fricker child photo to the Buerkle studio in Stuttgart.**

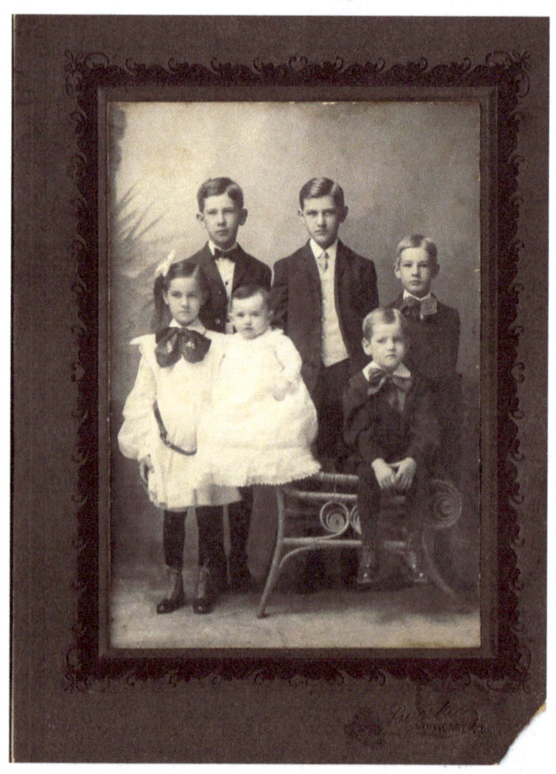

**10. Photo of Gettle children circa 1903, made at Charles Buerkle's studio in Stuttgart, Arkansas.**

area and eventually incorporated the city of Stuttgart. There are no indications of any connections between the Charles W. Buerkle Photography Studio and the work of Disfarmer or his early partner, George A. Penrose. Disfarmer's older brother, Andrew Meyer, did have at least one photo of his baby daughter, Evelyn, made at the Buerkle studio circa 1908 - see photo #9 in Chapter 11 with baby Evelyn sitting in the very ornate wicker high chair shown below on the left.

### Chester W. Vandusen

One other photographer by the name of Chester W. Vandusen was known to have operated a photography business in Arkansas County in the town of Stuttgart from at least 1912 to 1913. No other information is known about the photography of Chester W. Vandusen at the time of this publication.

## Supposition 1: A Photography Venture Enters the Viewfinder

Following the death of his father in 1898, Disfarmer, as the oldest son living at home with his mother, may have felt pressured to provide financially for his mother and remaining siblings that were still living at home – to become the "man of the house." It does not appear that he had the aptitude, desire nor the physical ability to endure the hard work associated with farming. He may have continued to farm for a while, but eventually began to work as a laborer or at various odd jobs like being a night watchman at a local rice mill. On a Saturday excursion to the town of DeWitt, Disfarmer and his younger brother, Charley, stopped in the studio of local photographer, Dayton Bowers, and had the first of many photographs made of the two brothers together. Disfarmer, though he was only about 15 years of age, had his photograph made while smoking a cigar. Disfarmer appears to have been making a statement – "Hey. look at me – I'm a man -- not a boy."

After frequent excursions to the thriving town of DeWitt, Disfarmer became aware that the photographer, Dayton Bowers, had achieved a respectable level of financial success and social status by small town standards. Like many small town photographers though, Bowers was not solely dependent on income from his photography business. Bowers also earned income as a real estate broker and land speculator. Bowers, as a fellow German-American that had moved to Arkansas County from Indiana and had worked as a harness-maker as had Disfarmer's father, may have decided to become a mentor to young Disfarmer. Bowers began to introduce young Disfarmer to the photography business. Its possible that Disfarmer may have begun helping Bowers on a part-time basis with the photography business -- especially on Saturdays when business was brisk with farm families from surrounding communities coming to town for trips to market or for social outings.

Between 1900 and 1910, Disfarmer and his mother decided to sell the farm between Almyra and DeWitt and move to the north Arkansas County seat of Stuttgart. There the pair moved into a house on Cleveland Street. Younger brother, Charley, probably lived in the Stuttgart home for a short time. Disfarmer soon learned that there were two or three photographers operating studios in the larger town of Stuttgart. Disfarmer, having helped Dayton Bowers on a part-time basis, approached the local photographers about a possible apprenticeship or part-time work. Edward K. Blush appears to have accepted his offer and allowed Disfarmer to work either part-time or full-time as an apprentice in his photography studio.

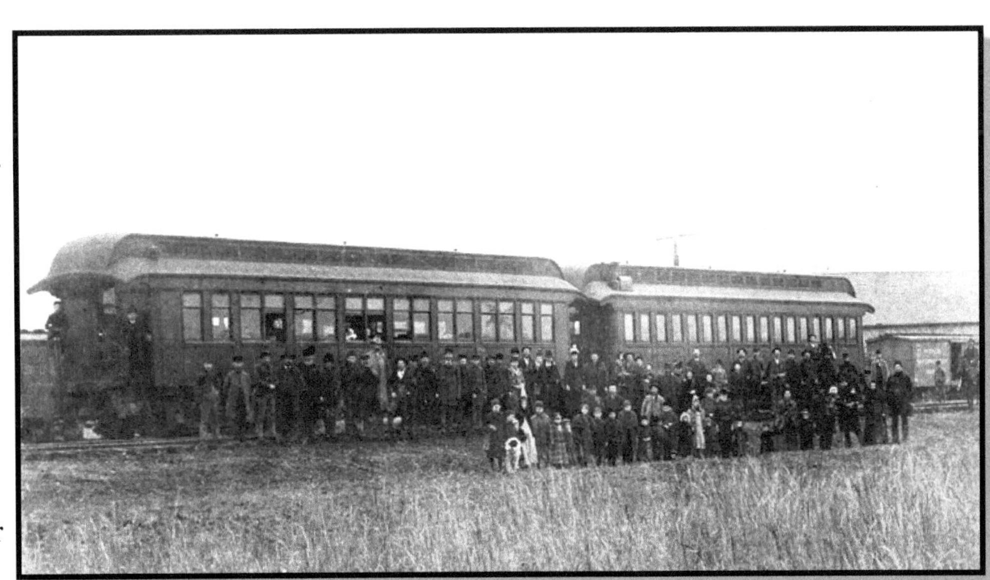

**11. E.K. Blush photo of 40 Iowa families arriving by train to settle near Stuttgart, Arkansas circa 1890.**

From E.K. Blush, Disfarmer learned to construct reversible, movable backdrops, use studio props as well as the techniques and processes associated with taking, developing and contact-printing photographs. Meyer, under Blush's instruction began showing promise as a photographer. It was there that Disfarmer likely learned to construct a backdrop using black tape that is prominent in many of his distinctive photos.

Around 1908, for reasons unknown, Edward King Blush began making plans to move away from Stuttgart. Blush may have offered to sell some of the bulky equipment like backdrops and props used in his photography business to Meyer. According to the 1910 census, E.K. Blush was living in Denver, Colorado and was still listed as a photographer. Meyer had limited capital resources since he was providing financial assistance to his elderly mother and could not make the purchase on his own.

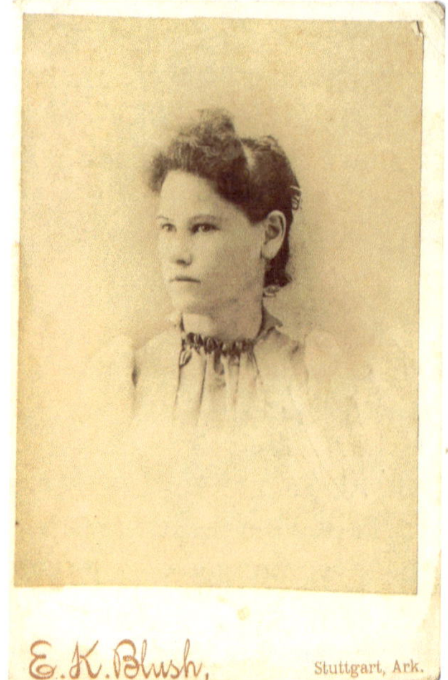


**12. E.K. Blush photo of Ida Payer Gettle circa 1892.**

George A. Penrose likely crossed paths with Disfarmer through visits to Stuttgart to see his wife, Edith's relatives that lived in the area. During one of these photographic sessions at the E.K. Blush studio with the Kornbaum-Payer-Gettle families from the town of Ulm lying just north of Stuttgart or with the Reverend Edward Kornbaum, Jr. Family from Stuttgart, Disfarmer met Edith Kornbaum's husband, George A. Penrose. Penrose was a businessman from Woodruff County lying just north of Prairie County. Whether Penrose sought out or stumbled on the budding photographer, Disfarmer, then known as Mike Meyer, is unclear. What seems abundantly clear is that the confluence of events brought the two men together in the studio of Edward K. Blush in Stuttgart sometime between 1900 and 1908.

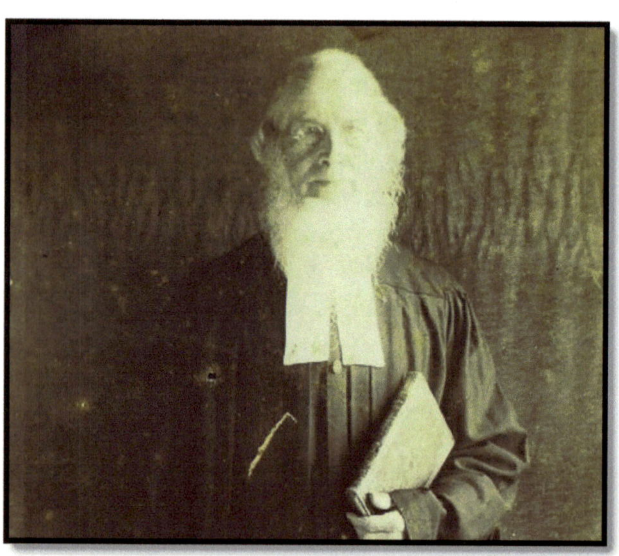

**13. Photo or Reverend Edward Kornbaum, Jr.**

Penrose may have approached Meyer with a business proposition. Penrose would provide the seed capital, business acumen and bookkeeping skills and Meyer could provide the photography know-how. Penrose and Meyer may have acquired backdrops, props or other bulky equipment and supplies from E.K. Blush who was moving to Colorado around 1908.

Disfarmer and Penrose began to lay plans for a new business venture. The decision to open a photography studio in a town such as Heber Springs may have been aided by stiff competition in Stuttgart or the attractive opportunity in the budding town of Heber Springs (discussed more in Chapter 3). In the 1900 to 1914 timeframe, there were three photographers conducting business in Stuttgart alone and a total of four operating on Arkansas County. However in the town of Heber Springs awakening from its slumber at that time was only one photographer, Addison C. Vradenburg, who operated

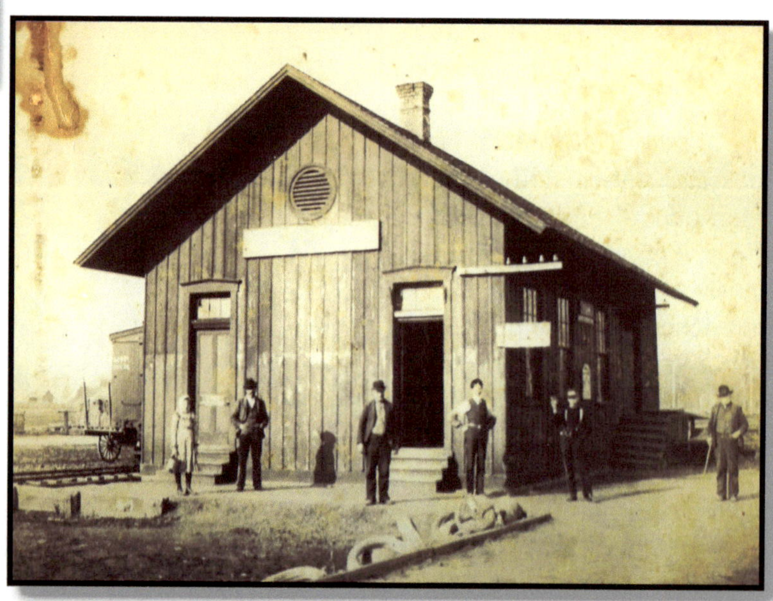

**14. Photo of the Ulm Depot circa 1900 likely taken by E.K. Blush.**

from 1912 to 1913. Perhaps this local competition was part of the reason photographer, E.K. Blush, decided to relocate his studio to Denver, Colorado around 1910. In any event, the next stop for Penrose and Meyer (Disfarmer) was the scenic valley town of Heber Springs, formerly known as Sugar Loaf. Meyer's elderly mother, Margaretha, moved with him to Heber Springs. Moving with Penrose and his wife Edith to Heber Springs was Edith's elderly father, Emanuel Kornbaum.

**NOTES**

[6] Steven and Ray Hanley, Images of America ARKANSAS COUNTY, Arcadia Publishing, 2008, p. 70.

# Chapter IV. Heber Springs: A Brief Introduction

*"If we walk far enough," says Dorothy, "we shall sometime come to someplace."*

- L. Frank Baum, The Wonderful Wizard of Oz

In 1914, Disfarmer and his mother, Margaretha (Weidenhammer) Meyer, would move from the oldest county in Arkansas to its youngest when the pair relocated to Heber Springs, Arkansas, the county seat of Cleburne County. Cleburne County was the last county formed in Arkansas in 1883. The new hometown for Disfarmer would also be his final resting place. Heber Springs today is a quaint town in Arkansas with a population of about 7,100 people. It's the gateway city to Greers Ferry Lake and its main tributary -- the Little Red River. The tourism industry some 100 years after its founding, is a significant source of income for the Ozark foothills community -- finally fulfilling the vision of its founding fathers.

Heber Springs was originally known as Sugar Loaf and was named after the distinctive geological formation called Sugar Loaf Mountain which can be seen many miles distant by those approaching the town from certain directions. Another geologic feature of the town is a grouping of seven (7) distinctive artesian, sulphur springs located in a park in the heart of the city. Early travelers through the area believed the sulphur springs had medicinal properties and could cure many illnesses. These geologic features along with the beautiful, meandering Little Red River attracted the attention of its founding fathers.

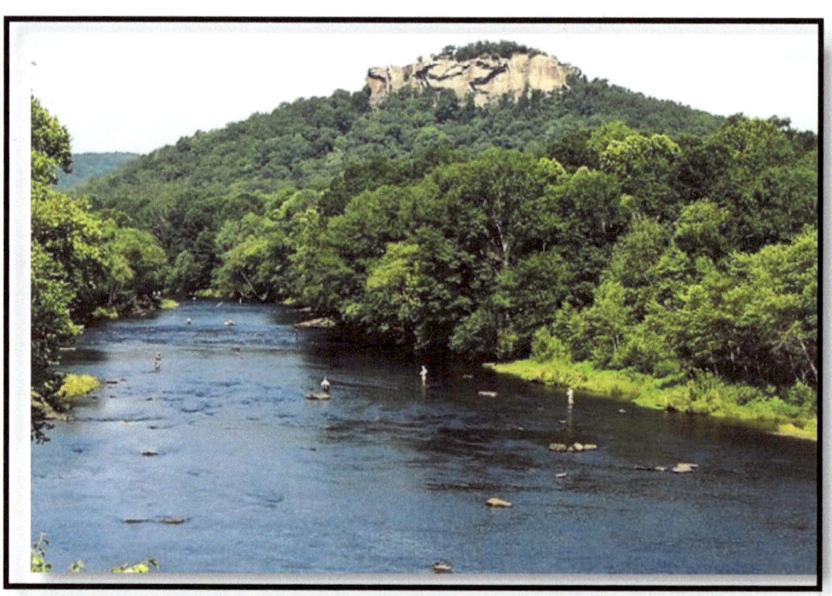

**1. Trout fishermen on the Little Red River with Sugar Loaf Mountain in the background near Heber Springs, Cleburne County, Arkansas.**

The first enterprising soul to take a financial interest in the land surrounding the sulphur springs lying in the shadow of Sugar Loaf Mountain was Judge John T. Jones. Jones acquired sole title to about 600 acres around the springs in 1851 with the intention of developing the plot into a health resort. However, Judge Jones appears to have been long on vision and short on initiative. The land languished undeveloped for about 30 years. Around 1880, the Jones property came to the attention of Max Frauenthal, a successful merchant of German-Jewish descent who was born in Bavaria, Germany. In an interesting twist of fate, Disfarmer and his mother also had ancestral roots in the southernmost German state of Bavaria. In 1881, Max Frauenthal purchased the plot of land on which the town of Heber Springs now sits from Judge Jones.

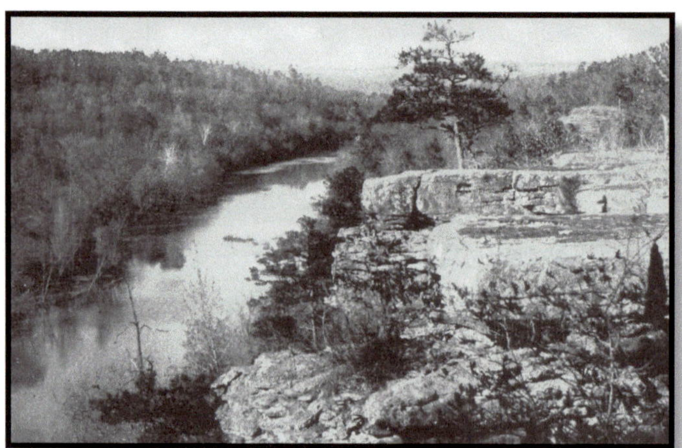

**2. The Little Red River flowing by Sugar Loaf Mountain, Heber Springs, Arkansas.**

A town was incorporated and Frauenthal sold shares to 10 other investors, most of whom were acquaintances from Conway, Arkansas, where he was residing at the time of the purchase. The town first went by the name of Sugar Loaf. Some time passed and an application was made for a post office at Sugar Loaf. The U.S. Post Office rejected the name because another Arkansas town had secured the name first. Frauenthal then selected the name of Heber for the post office which was the name of Judge Jones' son, Dr. Heber Jones, a well known physician from Memphis, Tennessee. Its believed that Dr. Heber Jones may have urged Frauenthal into developing the town as a health resort based on the suspected medicinal qualities of the sulphur springs. An 1886 booklet about the medicinal qualities of the springs claimed, "The sulphur springs are a sure cure for dyspepsia, headache, biliousness and hundreds of other ailments."[7]

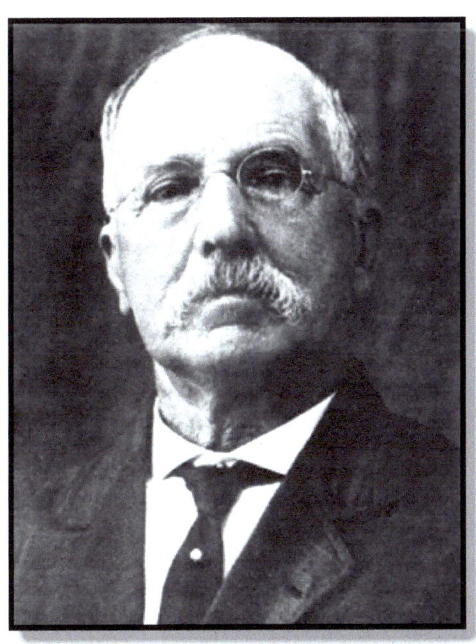

**3. Max Frauenthal, founder of Heber Springs, Arkansas.**

Frauenthal was likely acquainted with the famous Baden-Baden bath springs in his native Germany. He also undoubtedly knew that within the State of Arkansas, there were two other cities with a regional and national reputation as places where people with various illnesses and physical infirmaries could go to take the cure by bathing in and drinking the mineral waters. Those towns being Hot Springs to the southwest and Eureka Springs to the northwest. Being the entrepreneur that he was, Frauenthal developed a plan to execute on the vision that Judge Jones and Dr. Heber Jones shared for the sulphur spring oasis near the scenic Sugar Loaf Mountain and Little Red River.

The young, resort town grew slowly. The rocky, hilly terrain that made it attractive was also a barrier to its growth. Heber Springs was not located on any major road connecting to any of its neighboring population centers. As the saying goes, you had to be going there to get there. It certainly was not easy to get to the little town by horse and buggy. Even after Model T's became more common in Arkansas in the early 1900's, the town still lay at the end of an all-day journey over unpaved, hilly roads from its closest larger cities of Little Rock or Memphis.

A fortuitous event occurred in 1909 that was expected to make the Jones and Frauenthal vision finally become a reality -- the Missouri and North Arkansas Railroad (M&NA) finally connected the sleepy Ozark foothill town to the thriving trade centers of Kansas City, St. Louis, Memphis, and Little Rock providing twice-daily passenger service during the week. The much-anticipated and long-awaited lifeline to the outside world had finally arrived. Initially, the arrival of passenger train service in 1909, appears to have had its expected affect:

*"Tourists flocked to Sugar Loaf Springs and filled the eleven rooming houses and hotels that were built to serve them. Doctors sent patients to Heber Springs to drink the mineral water for relief from nervous disorders and stomach ailments. Main Street thrived with a*

BLACK SULPHUR SPRING, HEBER, ARK.

COPYRIGHT 1910, BY E. G. SPELLMAN

**4. Black Sulphur Spring, Heber, Arkansas, circa 1909. The name of the town was changed to Heber Springs in 1910.**

*movie house, an open–air skating rink, an ice cream parlor, a bowling alley, and other diversions. Fishing and picnics on the Little Red River were popular among residents and summer visitors."*[8]

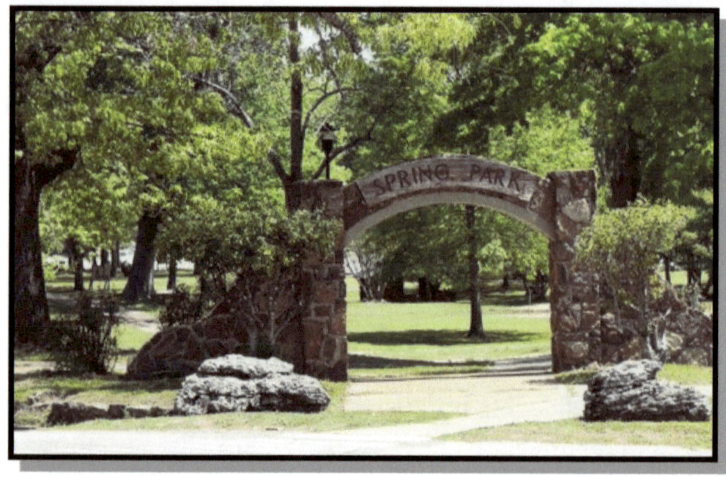


**5. Today's entrance to Spring Park, Heber Springs, Arkansas.**

For a period of time, the town went by the name of Sugar Loaf Springs and the post office was called Heber. However, in 1910, both the town and post office were renamed to Heber Springs in an attempt to attract more visitors.

The M&NA has the unique honor of being the most expensive railroad ever built in Arkansas based on construction cost per mile. It also took years to connect the segments of the line that finally formed a continuous ribbon of steel that connected Helena, Arkansas on the Mississippi River just south of Memphis with Joplin in Southwest, Missouri. The lengthy and costly construction project was due to the rocky, rugged terrain and numerous rivers crossed by the M&NA on its route across the foothills and the Boston Mountain Range of the Ozarks. The rocky route is the perfect metaphor for the rocky history that would eventually play out for the M&NA.

Powell Clayton, the first Reconstruction governor of Arkansas, was a key promoter of the M&NA, and lead a group of risk-taking investors. The gutsy investors in the railroad had a *Field of Dreams*[9] vision for the M&NA -- "if we build it, they will come." It was a high stakes roll of the dice. The delusional investors believed that the railroad infrastructure was the catalyst needed to spark an economic boom across the hills of Northern Arkansas. The mild climate and natural resources of the area along the right-of-way combined with the promise of speedy and economical rail transportation would attract farmers, loggers, miners, proprietors and all types of potential settlers looking for a new place to call home. The icing on the cake would be the tourists and short-term travelers coming from the mid-America cities in search of rest, relaxation and rejuvenation in the towns of Eureka Springs and Heber Springs.

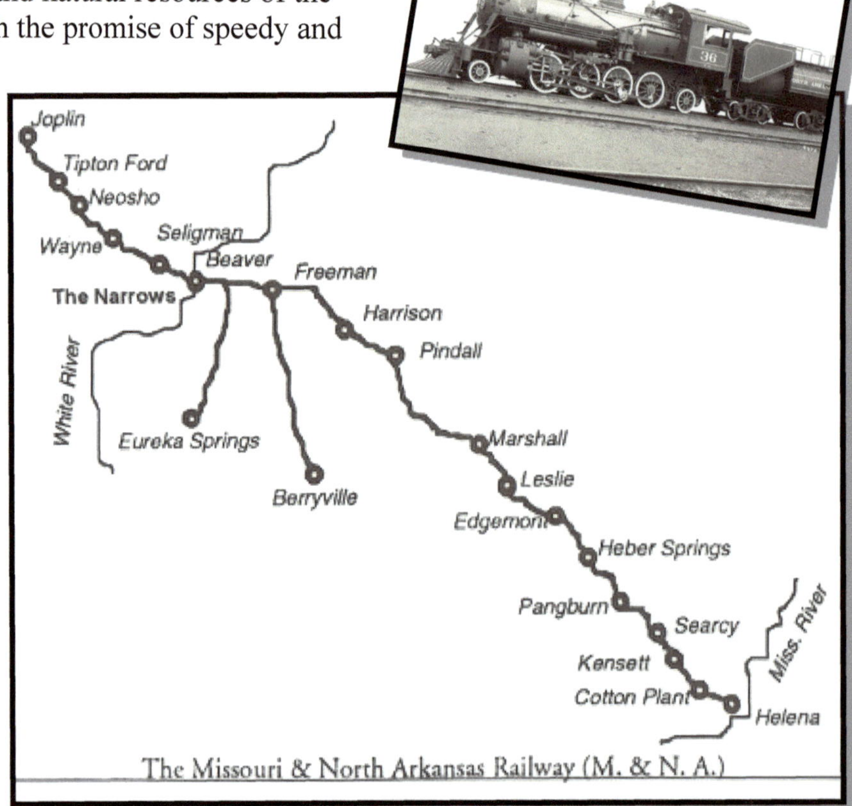


**6. The Missouri & North Arkansas Railway (M&NA) map and one of its steam locomotives (insert) circa 1912.**

It was a high-stakes gamble that never really paid off for the investors. However the owners pulled out all the stops in an attempt to generate a return on their investment. As part of its early marketing effort, the M&NA began publishing a public relation magazine called the *Oak Leaves*. This early company-magazine was targeted at individuals in an attempt to attract them to settle in one of the communities served by the M&NA. The magazine was a cover to cover advertisement promoting the communities located along the railroad right-of-way. It contained articles and pictures about each community along the route highlighting the many qualities and natural resources intended to attract settlers looking for a new place to call home.

A copy of the *Oak Leaves Special Edition 1912* is particularly insightful regarding Heber Springs. On the back cover of the 1912 edition was a full-page ad promoting the towns of Eureka Springs and Heber Springs as "the place to spend your vacation."

> *"The waters are famous for their curative properties. The climate is ideal; the scenery is unsurpassed. The pleasure seekers' paradise; no mosquitoes; no malaria. Where sleepless nights are unknown....Heber Springs has several kinds of sulphur waters which are noted for their curative properties. Round trip all year tourist tickets are on sale daily from all points."*

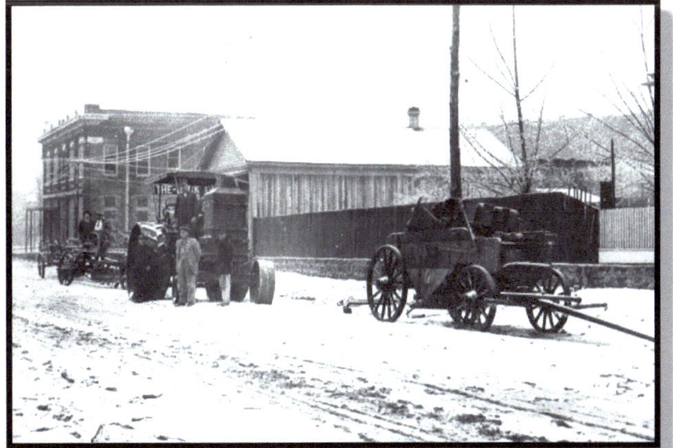

**7. View of 3rd Street in Heber Springs circa 1910.**

Inside the magazine were three (3) pages devoted to the promotion of the idyllic community of Heber Springs -- two pages of narrative with one full page of black and white photographs of the town and its springs. Following is a brief excerpt from the special edition magazine:

> *"Heber Springs have a reputation for healing qualities. About nine springs rise within a small compass, each of their qualities differing from the others, including black and white sulphur, chalybeate and freestone. The springs are said to be a panacea for many ills, and are especially recommended for chronic malarial diseases."*

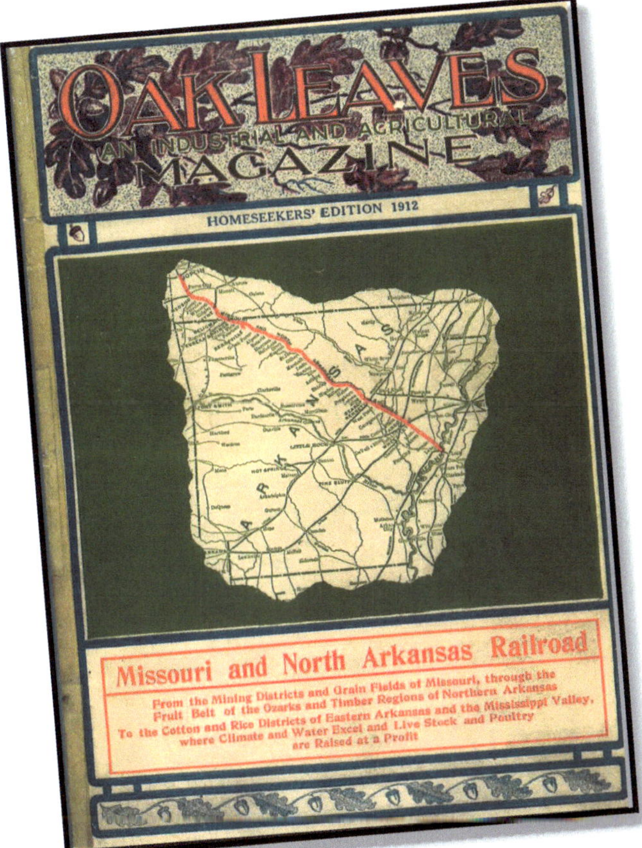


**8. M&NA Oak Leaves Magazine, Homeseekers' Edition 1912.**

In the ten acre Spring Park in the center of town, are seven (7) major mineral springs that are enclosed in concrete and covered with an open-sided structure. These seven springs are: 1. White Sulphur, 2. Arsenic, 3. Chalybeate, 4. Red Sulphur, 5. "Eye" Spring, 6. Black Sulphur and 7. Freestone.

According to the *Oak Leaves* magazine, in 1909, when the railroad first completed passenger service to Heber Springs (Sugar Loaf Springs), the population was only 600 citizens. By 1912, the population had mushroomed to 2,500 -- a quadrupling in size in a mere three (3) years. This statement appears to have been a bit of marketing hyperbole. Following is the Heber Springs U.S. Population Census by year[10]:

| | |
|---|---|
| 1890 - 322 | 1940 - 1,656 |
| 1900 - 552 | 1950 - 2,109 |
| 1910 - 1,126 | 1960 - 2,265 |
| 1920 - 1,675 | ... |
| 1930 - 1,401 | 2010 - 7,165 |

As noted by the census, the population in Heber Springs in 1900 was 552 so the *Oak Leaves* 1909 population figure of 600 seems plausible. However, according to the 1910 census the population was 1,126 and by 1920, the population had only arisen to 1,675 so the *Oak Leaves* estimate of 2,500 seems to be inflated by as much as twice. The marketers appear to have taken a little creative license in promoting the impact of rail service on the local demographics. Nevertheless, the population does appear to have doubled between 1900 and 1910. Its certainly plausible that the M&NA Railroad may have played a significant role in this outcome. A doubling of the population in a mere three year time is worthy of note but is obviously much less dramatic than the quadrupling in size published by the *Oak Leaves* spin-doctors.

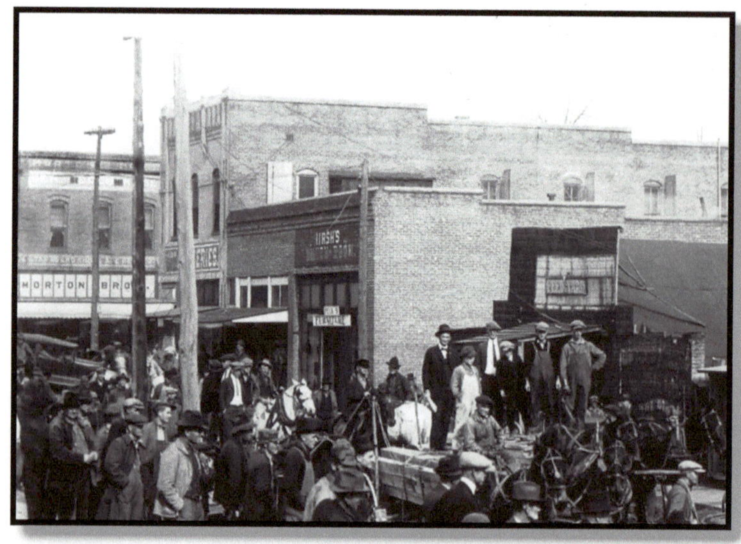

**9. View of 3rd Street in Heber Springs, Arkansas, circa 1920.**

As alluded to earlier, the M&NA had a checkered and rocky history. At some point, the M&NA was re-branded by its customers to the "May Never Arrive" for its dismal service record. The M&NA was frequently late and off-schedule causing its passengers and shippers of freight great inconvenience and discomfort as well as economic hardship. On August 5, 1914, an M&NA train collided with a Kansas City Southern train near Joplin, Missouri killing 38 people. Both companies shared in the settlement with the families of the deceased, but the reparations wiped out the M&NA treasury. In 1921, an employee strike shut down the railway for several months and garnered national attention as one of the longest railroad strikes in U.S. history. These events were major setbacks to the already tarnished image of the undercapitalized railroad.

Then came the 1929 stock market crash followed by the Great Depression which dealt major financial blows to the already shaky rail line as well as the local economies of Heber Springs and Cleburne County. Changes in ownership and reorganizations of the struggling railroad occurred during the 1930's and 40's but the deck was stacked against it. The railroad finally closed its doors in 1947. Eventually, most of its tracks were removed leaving little sign that the much-maligned railroad had ever existed in the hills, valleys and river delta of Northern Arkansas and Southwestern Missouri.

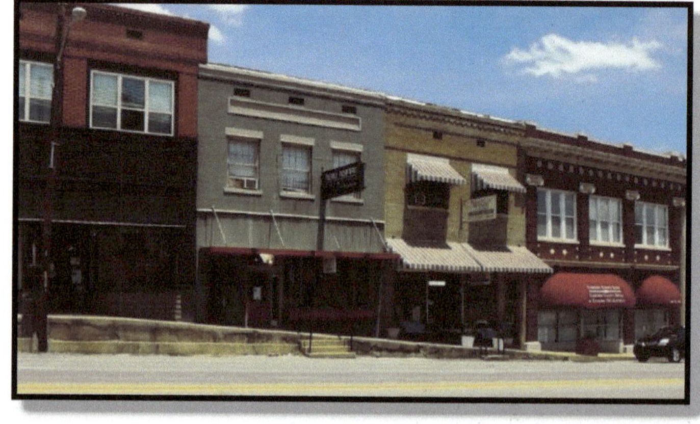

**10. Today's Main Street, Heber Springs, Arkansas, Cleburne County.**

## NOTES

[7] "Heber Springs (Cleburne County)", The Encyclopedia of Arkansas History & Culture, last updated 3/1/2012, The Butler Center for Arkansas Studies, Central Arkansas Library System, Little Rock, Arkansas, <http://www.encyclopediaofarkansas.net/encyclopedia/entry-detail.aspx?entryID=853>.

[8] Heber Springs (Cleburne County).

[9] Field of Dreams, 1989 20th Century Fox film, directed by Phillip Alden Robinson, starring Kevin Costner, Amy Madigan, James Earl Jones and Ray Liotta, produced by Lawrence and Charles Gordon.

[10] Heber Springs (Cleburne County)..

# Covered Springs in Spring Park, Heber Springs, Arkansas

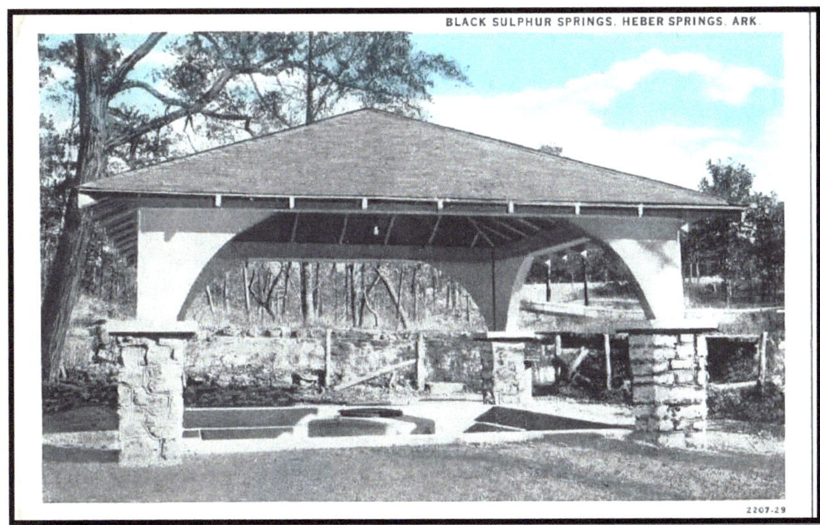


11. Black Sulphur Springs, Heber Springs, Arkansas.

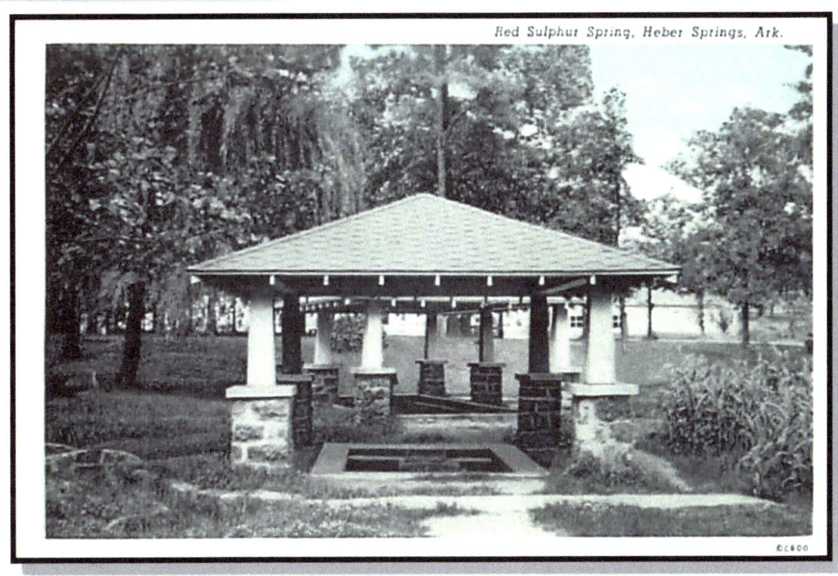


12. Red Sulphur Springs, Heber Springs, Arkansas.

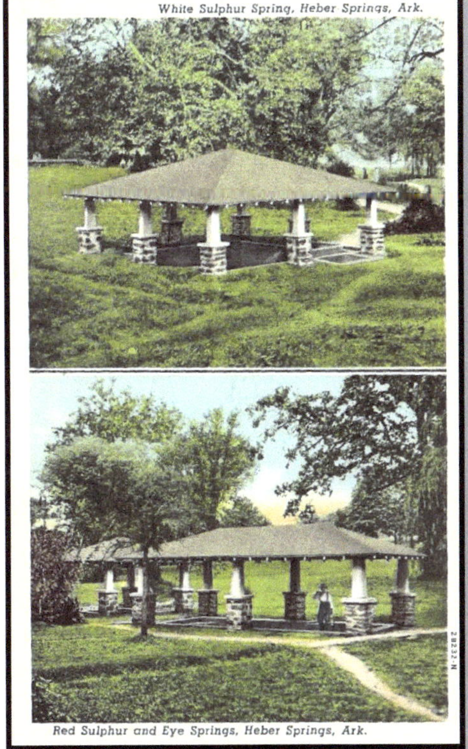


13. White Sulphur Springs, Heber Springs, Arkansas.

14. Red Sulphur and Eye Springs, Heber Springs, Arkansas.

# Chapter V. Penrose & Meyer Photographers: 1914 to 1920

*"You have some queer friends, Dorothy,' she said.*
*The queerness doesn't matter, so long as they're friends,' was the answer"*

— L. Frank Baum, The Road to Oz

From a newspaper article that covered the strange 1939 court proceeding in which Mike Meyer legally changed his name to Mike Disfarmer, we know that Disfarmer and his mother, Margaretha, moved from Stuttgart to Heber Springs, Arkansas, on January 8, 1914.[11] Disfarmer appears to have relocated from Stuttgart to Heber Springs with the deliberate intention of entering a partnership with George Albert Penrose to operate a photography studio in the young but rapidly growing town.

No previous tie or connection between Meyer or his mother and the community of Heber Springs has been found. Meyer's sister, Anna, and her husband, Dave Goodrich, were living in Heber Springs according to the 1920 U.S. Census. However, Dave Goodrich's WWI draft registration reveals that he was still residing in Arkansas County in 1917. So it appears that Anna (Meyer) Goodrich, her husband, Dave, and daughter, Ione, moved to Heber Springs after 1917 to be near her brother, Mike, and her mother, Margaretha. Anna was Mike's next older sister by three years and the two had numerous photos taken together suggesting they had a close relationship.

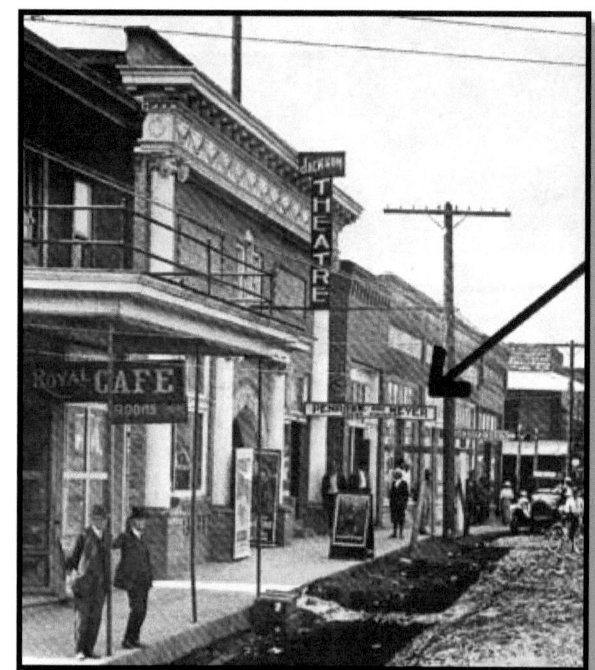

**1. The Penrose & Meyer Photography Studio next to the Jackson Theater, circa 1916.**

It's safe to assume that Disfarmer's newfound partner, George A. Penrose, relocated from Hunter, Woodruff County, the second county north of Arkansas County, to Heber Springs in 1914 – the same time as Disfarmer. Penrose appears to have been the business mind behind the small enterprise and most likely provided the seed capital required to fund the photography studio during its start-up phase. The Penrose & Meyer Photography Studio was housed next to the Jackson Theater on Main Street in Heber Springs from 1914 until about 1920.

Little has been known or published about George Albert Penrose – the other half of the partnership. Some researchers have speculated that Penrose was a photographer himself and that maybe he provided instruction to Disfarmer. The facts simply do not support that hypothesis.

George A. Penrose and his twin brother, Thomas, were born in Ohio in 1870 to their parents, William Orestus Penrose and Eliza Jane Greenwalt. Between 1880 and 1900, the Penrose clan moved from Ohio to Woodruff County, Arkansas. According to the 1900 census, George was single at age 28 and was living with his father, William O. Penrose, and his mother, Eliza Jane, in Dent Township, Woodruff County, Arkansas. George and his twin brother, Thomas, were the oldest boys. Living with the twins in their father's home were his older sister, Sarah, his younger sister, Anna, and two other brothers, Howell Orestus and William. George's father, William O. Penrose and all his siblings were apparently born in Ohio. George's mother, Eliza Jane Greenwalt, was born in Pennsylvania.

George's occupation in 1900 was listed as a sawmill engineer in his father's sawmill. His father is listed as the owner of the sawmill and his brother, Tom, is listed as a machinist. In Woodruff County in the early

1900's, sawmill businesses in the area made barrel staves and railroad ties. The Penrose sawmill may have turned out one or both of these products.

According to the April 11, 1901 edition of the Fremont Courier in Fremont, Ohio, George, 30, from Marietta, Ohio, married Edith Kornbaum, 25, who was from Gibsonburg, Ohio.[12] Edith was the daughter of Emanuel Kornbaum, who was born in Germany, and Elizabeth, who was born in Ohio. Emanuel was the son of the Reverend Edward Kornbaum, Sr., a Lutheran minister. As was mentioned in Chapter 3, Edith was the niece of Edward Kornbaum, Jr., a Lutheran minister who lived in Stuttgart around 1900. Fredia Kornbaum Payer, was Edith's aunt and lived in Ulm, just north of Stuttgart. Edith's aunt, Fredia, and various other Kornbaum Payer-Gettle family members were subjects of several photos taken by E.K. Blush in Ulm and Stuttgart, Arkansas circa 1894 to 1910. The Kornbaum family connection is a compelling linkage between George A. Penrose, Mike Disfarmer and E.K. Blush, the Stuttgart photographer.

By the 1910 census, George, 39, and his wife, Edith, 34, were living on Brooks Street in the town of Hunter, Caney Township, Woodruff County, Arkansas. Living next door to the couple were Edith's father, Emanuel Kornbaum and her mother Elizabeth. Also living next door to George in the same household was his father and mother, his sister, Sarah, and two of his brothers, Thomas and Howell. All three of these siblings were in their 30's, still unmarried and living at home with their parents. On the same street a few doors down was George's youngest brother, William Joseph, 32, who was then married and had two daughters of his own.

Uhr von der St. Josephs - Kirche aus statt. ... St. Joseph's ... bten Eltern

Fremont Courier
4/11/1901 p4 c2

— Heiraths-Licenzen wurden gelöst von Samuel Miller, 22 Jahre, und Estella L. Overmyer, 21 Jahre, beide von Rice Township. Rev. Bowman. George A. Penrose, 30 Jahre, von Marietta, O., und Edith L. Kornbaum, 25 Jahre, von Gibsonburg. Edward E. Murphy, von Columbus, O., 22 Jahre und Marie M. Miller, 24 Jahre, von Fremont.

**2. Wedding announcement from the German language edition of the April 11, 1901, *Fremont Courier* in Fremont, Ohio.**

In 1910, George Penrose was no longer working as a sawmill engineer. His occupation in the 1910 census was listed as a bookkeeper at a mercantile store. His father and his brother William, Jr. were listed as farmers in 1910. Apparently the sawmill that his father owned in 1900 had either been sold or had gone out of business. Between 1901 and 1914, George A. Penrose likely met Mike Meyer while visiting his wife's relatives that lived in and around Stuttgart, Arkansas, and the two decided to form a partnership to operate a photography business in Heber Springs.

According to the 1920 census, George A. Penrose, 49, his wife Edith (Kornbaum) Penrose, 44, and Edith's father, Emanuel Kornbaum, 78, were living on Sugar Loaf Street, in the town of Heber Springs, Arkansas. George's occupation was listed as a photographer in a studio. Living on the same street was Penrose's partner, Mike Meyer/ Disfarmer and his mother, Margaretha. Disfarmer's sister, Anna, and her family lived across the street from Disfarmer.

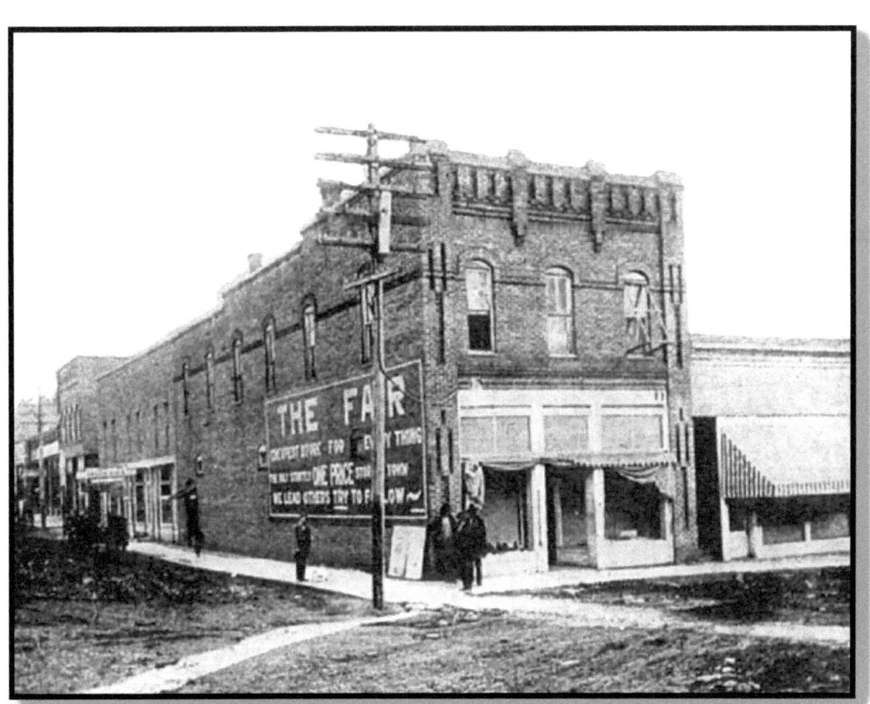

**3. Early photo of Main Street, Heber Springs, Arkansas.**

A fire broke out in the Jackson Theater in 1921. It has been previously reported that the fire caused the photography studio to go out of business and the partnership to dissolve. However, according to Dr. Mickey Barnett, a member of the Cleburne County Historical Society who has spent years researching Disfarmer, the Penrose & Meyer Photography Studio ceased doing business circa 1920 before the theater fire in 1921.

Immediately following the closing of the Penrose & Meyer Photography Studio in Heber Springs and dissolution of the partnership, Penrose and his wife, Edith, moved to Davenport, Iowa. There they enrolled in and attended the Palmer School of Chiropractic (see Vignette on Palmer School of Chiropractic) with intentions of becoming chiropractors. To become a chiropractor, the school required three years of six months study each year. Both Georges and Edith Penrose appear as members of the graduating Class of 1923 in the Palmer School yearbook, the *Pisiform*, at the famous chiropractic school. The timeline is consistent with the dissolution of the Penrose and Meyer partnership occurring around 1920.

In the 1930 census, George, 59, and Edith, 54, were living on First Street in Lordsburg Village, Hidalgo County, New Mexico. Both are listed as Chiropractors in the 1930 census. In the 1940 census, George, 69, and Edith, 64, were living on Orange Avenue in Paonia, Delta County, Colorado. George's occupation was still listed as a Chiropractor in Private Practice. No occupation is listed for Edith so it is presumed she was retired.

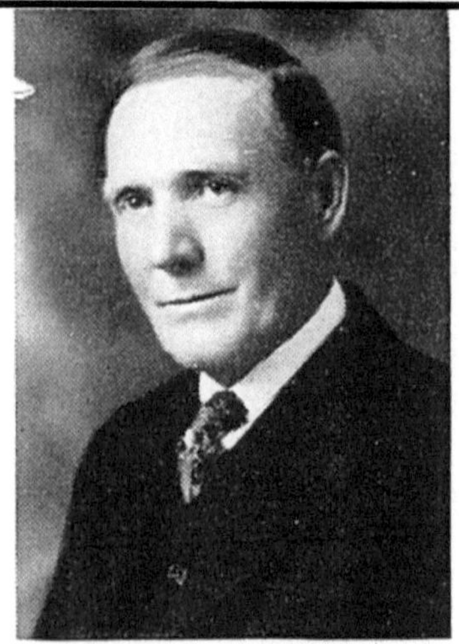

**Penrose, George A.**
**Hebersprings, Ark.**
Spinograph, U. C. A., 100% Club, Texas Alumni.
"Generous amounts of tact, humor, unselfishness and patience."

**4. Palmer School of Chiropractic 1923 yearbook photo. George is a member of the United Chiropractic Association (U.C.A.). It is unclear why he is listed as a member of the Texas Alumni group since he had no known connection to Texas.**

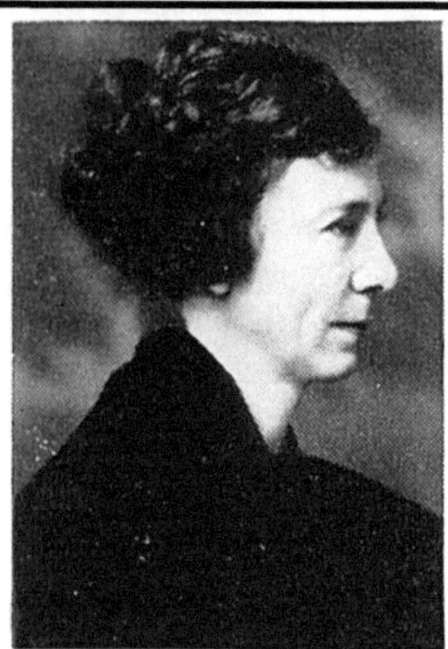

**Penrose, Edith L.**
**Hebersprings, Ark.**
U. C. A., 100% Club, Texas Alumni.
"Sweet prompting unto kindest deeds are in her very looks."

**5. Palmer School of Chiropractic 1923 yearbook photo. Edith is a member of the United Chiropractic Association (U.C.A.). It is unclear why she is listed as a member of the Texas Alumni group since she had no known connection to Texas.**

George A. Penrose died in 1960 in Grand Junction, Mesa County, Colorado and is buried at Hotchkiss, Delta County, Colorado, in Riverside Cemetery along with Edith K. Penrose who died in 1958 and her father, Emanuel Kornbaum. Even though George was some 14 years older than his former partner, he outlived Disfarmer by a year.

## Supposition 2: Penrose & Meyer Focus on Heber Springs

The Missouri and North Arkansas Railroad (M&NA) railroad had a junction at the town of Wheatley, Arkansas in Woodruff County, the county in which George A. Penrose resided in 1910. The junction in Wheatley was where the M&NA interconnected with the St. Louis Southwestern "Cotton Belt" Railroad that ran through Stuttgart, Arkansas, the then current home of Mike Disfarmer, northward to St. Louis. The M&NA completed its much anticipated connection to the town of Heber Springs in 1909. The M&NA Railroad provided passenger and freight service to the difficult to access town of Heber Springs nestled in a valley of the Ozark Mountain foothills.

It's likely that George A. Penrose, the future Disfarmer partner, may have picked up a copy of the *Oak Leaves Special Addition 1912* in which he read about the rapidly growing town of Heber Springs which was cashing in on its medicinal springs and scenic surroundings and its early 20th Century, state-of-the-art railway connection to its surrounding urban neighbors. Being an astute businessman, Penrose heard opportunity knocking in the up-and-coming town of Heber Springs. If only he could come up with an idea for a business venture to capitalize on the events unfolding in Heber Springs. Enter Mike Meyer. Fate brought the two men together in the town of Stuttgart.

The town of Heber Springs was built around seven, unique mineral springs long believed to have medicinal qualities. The town was also located near the scenic Little Red River and the distinctive Sugar Loaf Mountain. The newfound access via passenger rail to major cities like St. Louis, Memphis and Kansas City created a heightened expectation that the sleepy town would become a tourist destination finally cashing-in on its founding fathers vision.

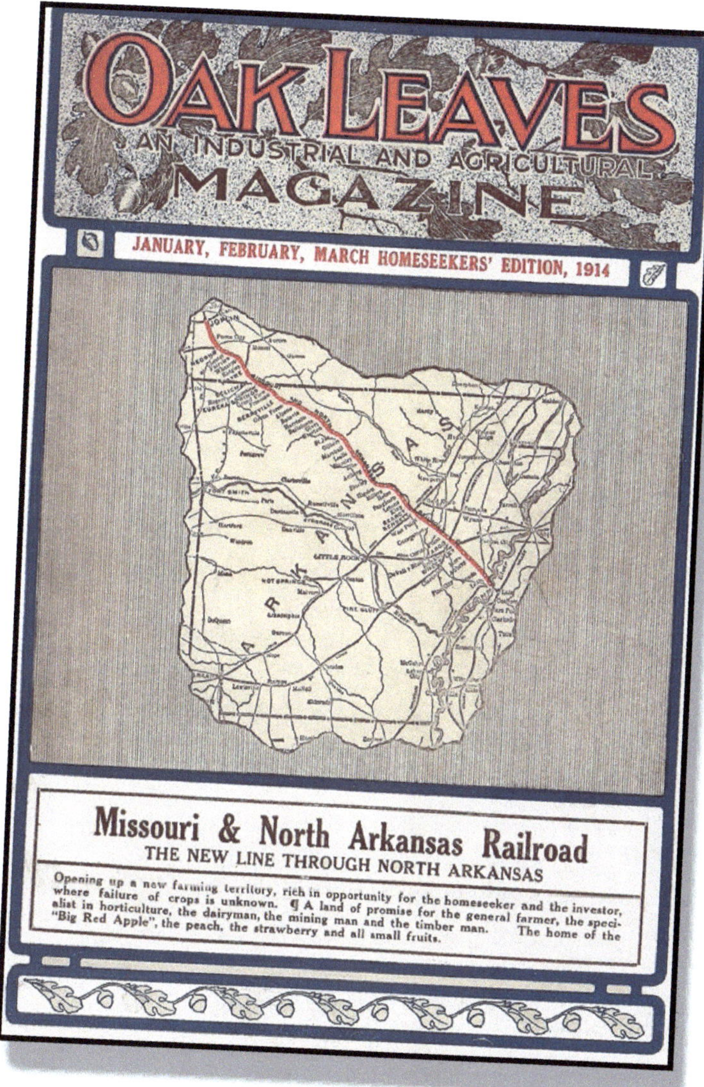

6. Cover of M&NA Oak Leaves Magazine, January, February, March Homeseekers Edition, 1914.

Penrose shared his vision with Meyer that the town of Heber Springs would become a boomtown due to the recent completion of passenger train service. The town was surely attractive to tourists seeking the medicinal benefits of the mineral springs and the other attractive draws of the scenic Little Red River and the Ozark foothills. Also, Penrose and Meyer may have felt there was too much competition in the photography business in Stuttgart since two or three other photographers were operating there at the time. Stuttgart was not a destination for tourists. Heber Springs on the other hand had only one photographer and was a rapidly growing town -- possibly the fastest growing town in the State at that time.

Maybe they were both ready for a change in scenery and were enticed by the more attractive scenery offered in Heber Springs – hills, trees and mineral springs versus the Mississippi Delta lowlands and the natural grass prairie of Woodruff, Prairie and Arkansas counties. Perhaps George wished to put some distance between himself and his family. George's twin brother, Thomas, died in 1910 at the age of 40. Possibly George did not see eye-to-eye with his father's political views – George was a capitalist and his father, William O., was a prominent socialist (see the Vignette: William Orestus Penrose). Meyer also may have desired to put some distance between himself, his family and his farming roots.

Besides their contributions to the partnership, Penrose and Meyer had much in common that may have led them to team up in a photography business. Both men had fathers that served in the Union Army during the civil war – Penrose's father joined in Ohio and Meyer's father joined in Indiana. Both men's families moved from the Midwest to the Arkansas Delta region. George's wife, Edith, was a first generation American of German descent. Meyer's mother was a first generation American of German descent. Both men had to provide financial support to elderly parents who spoke German and English – George to his wife's father and Meyer to his mother. Neither man fathered any children. Undoubtedly, these commonalities initially established rapport between the two further fueling the willingness to enter a business venture.

The two men formed the partnership and laid plans to open the photography studio in Heber Springs. Meyer and his mother likely purchased special one-way tickets on the Cotton Belt railway connecting with the M&NA in Wheatley with a final destination of Heber Springs. The M&NA offered special fairs to new settlers which allowed ticket holders to bring along personal possessions at no charge as they moved to their new homes along the railway. Meyer and his mother loaded their belongings on the train and departed Stuttgart on January 8, 1914. Next stop -- Heber Springs.

The Penrose & Meyer Photography Studio opened as planned in Heber Springs in 1914. Penrose was 43 and Meyer was 29. The new business appears to have been successful lasting beyond the five-year mark -- a key milestone for any start-up enterprise. Many Penrose & Meyer photographs exist that were taken during that time and are in the hands of collectors and relatives of the subjects. Many of these photographs are stamped on the back with "Penrose & Meyer Photography Studio / Heber Springs, Arkansas."

The partnership did not last. Even though Penrose and Meyer had much in common, the partnership was nearing the end of its life at the seven year mark -- circa 1920. Was it the "seven year itch" or was it a situation similar to the Beatles -- ego clashes or creative differences about the future direction of the partnership – that led to the break-up? In Chapter 9, I will suggest a theory on what led to the partnership dissolution.

Penrose, being the enterprising soul that he was, had an exit strategy. George was planning to become a chiropractor – a new profession that was booming around 1920. And it was open to women as well so Edith, with no children to care for, could help double the couple's income. Arkansas in 1915, became one of the first three states to pass a law allowing chiropractors to ply their trade. Perhaps Penrose became acquainted with a chiropractor in Heber Springs between 1915 and 1920, that may have peaked his interest in the new profession. It's likely that a chiropractor would have set up shop in the young town that was attracting visitors seeking cures for various ailments.

Perhaps Penrose read a print ad about the Palmer School of Chiropractic (see the Vignette: Palmer School of Chiropractic) offering great economic potential for those joining the new profession. Or perhaps Penrose heard a promotional spot on the newest form of mass media communication catching fire -- the radio. The owner of the Palmer School, B.J. Palmer, acquired radio station WOC in Davenport Iowa in 1922. WOC became one of the first and most successful radio stations West of the Mississippi and undoubtedly, the new medium was used by the marketing genius, B.J. Palmer, to promote the school.



**7. 1922 print ad promoting The Palmer School of Chiropractic in Davenport, Iowa.**

Penrose and his wife Edith attended the Palmer School of Chiropractic in Davenport, Iowa and graduated from the school around 1923. In 1922, the school's enrollment was over 3,000 students. Shortly after graduation, George and Edith opened a chiropractic practice in Lordsburg, New Mexico. New Mexico passed a law permitting the licensing of chiropractors in 1921. Perhaps this was the catalyst that led Penrose and his wife, Edith, to move to Lordsburg and to open a practice in that western state far from family and friends. George and Edith never returned to Arkansas. Both died and were buried in Colorado.

## Vignette: William Orestus Penrose

William Orestus Penrose, the father of George A. Penrose, was a well-known member of the Socialist Party of Arkansas and of America in the early 1900's. He was born in 1847 and died in 1933. In 1903, the Socialist Party of Arkansas chose William O. Penrose as its nominee for Governor. Penrose received 1,364 votes compared to 91,991 votes received by the winning candidate, Jeff Davis, a Democrat. Penrose was one of only two delegates from Arkansas to the 1904 Convention of the Socialist Party of America held in Chicago and one of six delegates from Arkansas to the 1908 Chicago convention. Eugene V. Debs, the Socialist Party's candidate for President in 1900, 1904, 1908, 1912 and 1920 visited Arkansas several times during the early 1900's and no doubt met with W.O. Penrose on those trips.

William O. Penrose, who was a successful businessman, had a meteoric rise in politics as well.

> *"The Arkansas Socialists decided on William O. Penrose as their nominee for governor. Penrose had not appeared before as a prominent Socialist leader in the state, but his nomination was a sound one. He as a successful businessman, a lumberman who operated a large sawmill in Woodruff County. The enthusiasm for Penrose was best expressed by the "Office Boy" when he said: 'Say have you read Penrose's letter of acceptance to the Socialists of the state. It's a dandy! He don't mince any words telling you why you have to live on sour molasses and corn bread half of the time. . . . Askes [sic] you to vote for him? Oh, no! He just asks you to study the question, and if you believe as he, then vote for principles!'."*[13]

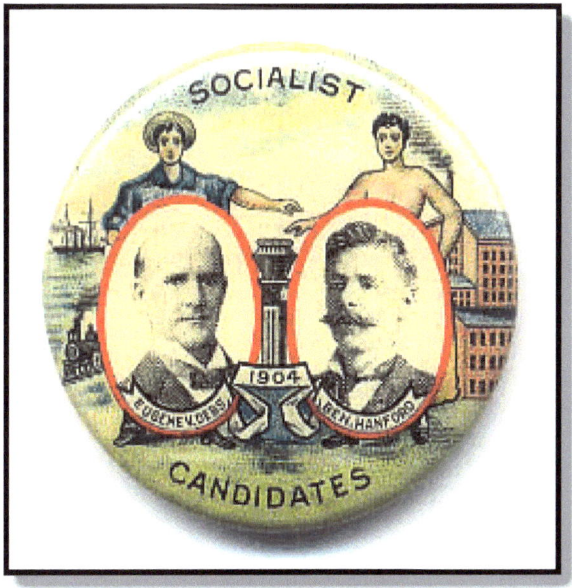


**8. Political button: Socialist Party candidates for the 1904 Presidential Election – Eugene V. Debs for President, Ben Hanford for Vice-President.**

Apparently, George inherited his father's leadership skills, integrity and ambition. Because of Penrose's rise to prominence in the Arkansas Socialist Party and in honor of his nomination as its candidate for Governor, the town in which Penrose's sawmill was located had its name changed in May, 1904, from Meredith to Penrose, Arkansas.

## Vignette: Palmer School of Chiropractic

The Palmer School of Chiropractic in Davenport, Iowa was founded in 1897 by Daniel David "D.D." Palmer. D.D. Palmer is known as the "Founder of Chiropractic." The Palmer School was the first school of chiropractic in the world. During the early 1900's, the chiropractic profession was being attacked by the medical profession and the American Medical Association for practicing medicine without a license. Many chiropractors were being charged and jailed in various states for practicing healing without a medical license.

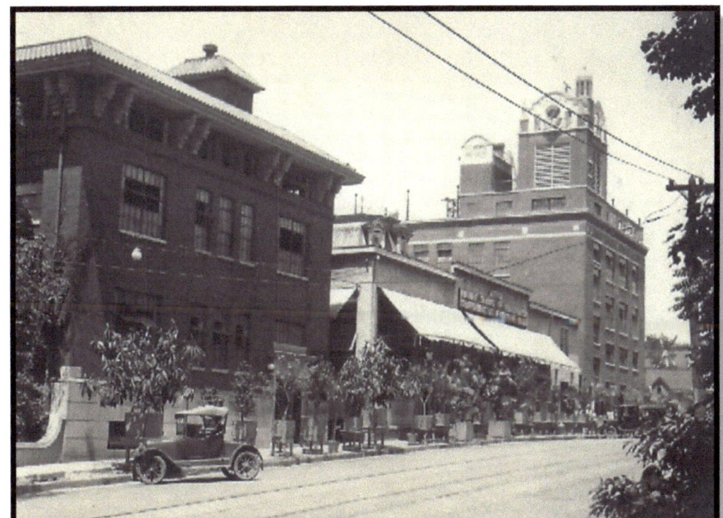

**9. 1920 photo of The Palmer School of Chiropractic, Davenport, Iowa.**

The "Founder of Chiropractic," D.D. Palmer was charged and jailed in 1901.[14] D.D. Palmer's son, B.J. assumed responsibility for the school in 1904 following the conviction of his father. B.J. Palmer is considered the "Developer of Chiropractic" because he "greatly expanded the scope of the school and laid the foundation for campus and the profession as it exists today."[15]

After his release from jail, D.D. Palmer formed the Universal Chiropractic Association (UCA) which raised money and provided legal defense to its members to fight attacks by the medical profession. States began to pass legislation and establish licensing boards allowing chiropractors to ply their trade legally and without threat of law suits and jail time. In 1913, Kansas and North Dakota followed by Arkansas in 1915 were the first three states to issue chiropractic licenses.[16] By 1923, 27 states had enacted chiropractic laws.

The Palmer School is still in business today and is turning out graduates in chiropractic. The name of the school was changed to Palmer College of Chiropractic in 1961 and later became accredited under the leadership of Dr. David D. Palmer the son of B.J. Palmer and grandson of D.D. Palmer. The college now has branch campuses in California and Florida. Its graduates are awarded the Doctorate of Chiropractic Degree.[17]

## NOTES

---

[11] "Mike Meyer Petition to Change Name to Mike Disfarmer," filed March 29, 1939, Cleburne County Circuit Court.

[12] "Wedding Announcements," Fremont Courier, (German Language Edition) [Fremont, Ohio], April 11, 1901, from the Rutherford B. Hayes Presidential Center, Spiegel Grove, Fremont, Ohio, <www.rbhayes.org/index>.

[13] G. Gregory Kiser, "The Socialist Party in Arkansas, 1900-1912," The Arkansas Historical Quarterly, Vol. 40, No. 2 (Summer, 1981), pp. 119-153, Published by: Arkansas Historical Association, <http://www.jstor.org/stable/40027669JSTOR, Socialist Party in Arkansas, 1900-1912>.

[14] "Chiropractic History," Citizendium, the Citizen's Compendium, last modified 11/1/2010, <http://en.citizendium.org/wiki/Chiropractic_history>.

[15] Chiropractic History.

[16] Joseph C. Keating, Jr., Ph.D., Carl S. Cleveland III, D.C., Michael Menke, M.A., D.C., Chiropractic History: A Primer, Association for the History of Chiropractic (2005): 1 - 23.

[17] "Palmer College of Chiropractic," Wikipedia, the free encyclopedia, last modified on April 10, 2013, <http./en.wikipedia.org/wiki/Palmer_College_of_Chiropractic>.

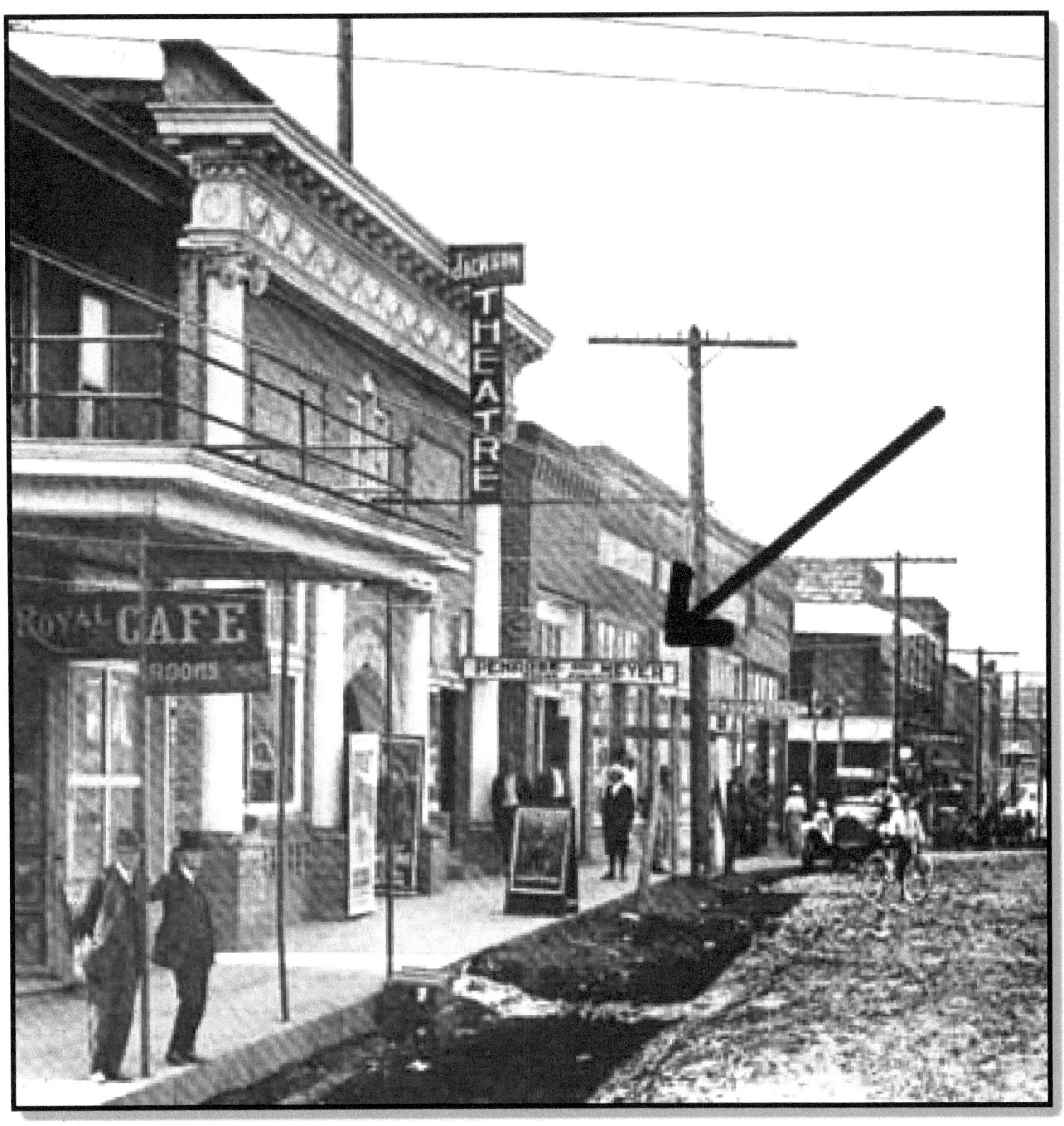


**10. Enlarged view of the entrance to the Penrose & Meyer Photography Studio located next to the Jackson Theater on Main Street, Heber Springs, Arkansas.**

# Chapter VI. The Meyer Photography Studio: 1921 to 1938

*"You people with hearts,' he said once, 'have something to guide you, and need never do wrong; but I have no heart, and so I must be very careful."*

— L. Frank Baum, The Wonderful Wizard of Oz

After the dissolution of the Penrose & Meyer partnership circa 1920, Meyer appears to have moved the photography studio to the back porch of his home at 109 Sugar Loaf Street where he and his mother were living according to the 1920 Census. His occupation was still listed as a photographer. Meyer was 35 and middle aged and his mother, Margaretha, was 70. The business then operated as "The Meyer Photography Studio" as some of the surviving photographs from this time period are stamped on the backside.

Meyer's home was very near Spring Park from which the town of Heber Springs draws its origin and name. It has been reported that Meyer frequently took photos of people visiting the mineral spring-laden park near his home -- the subjects posing in front of the covered springs. This certainly seems plausible given his home / studio's close proximity to the park and the drawing power of the mineral springs. Meyer would develop the photos in his makeshift dark room on the back porch of the old home.

The house was a sizable, wood-frame structure with a white clapboard exterior and shingled roof. It had an out-building similar to a small barn. Margaretha (Weidenhammer) Meyer, in keeping with her farming roots, was raising chickens, rabbits and vegetables in her backyard. Mother Meyer sold eggs and vegetables out of her house to her neighbors. And fortuitously, as did many houses in the area at the time, the house either came with or Meyer constructed a storm cellar adjacent to the home.

Heber Springs, Arkansas is at a higher-than-average risk for tornadic activity.[18] Since there was no weather service providing the populace with advance storm warning, most families would rush to the storm cellar at the first sign of an approaching storm. Its likely that Meyer and his mother fled to their storm cellar on Thursday, November 27, 1926 when a large and destructive tornado struck the town of Heber Springs. The house at 109 Sugar Loaf Street was destroyed by the "Thanksgiving Tornado," an EF-4 tornado -- the most destructive tornado ever to strike the town (see Vignette: Heber Springs Early Twentieth Century Tornados). Thanks to the storm cellar, the pair were spared from injury.

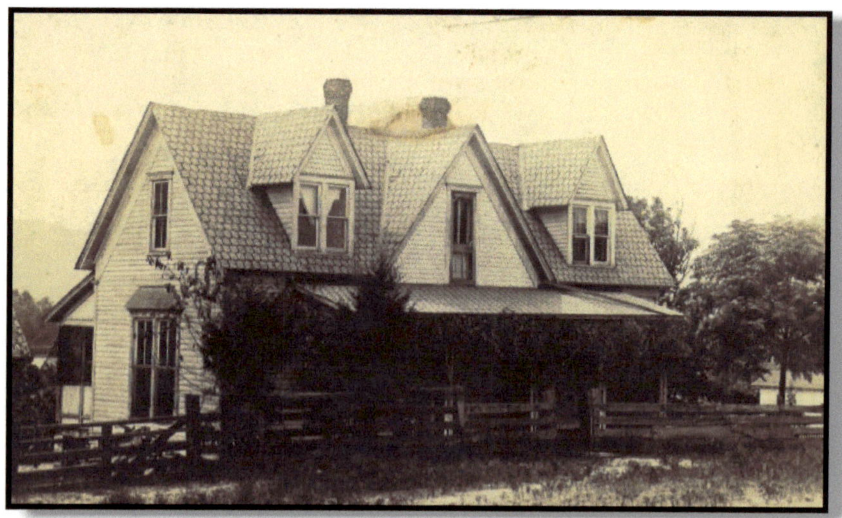

**1. The Heber Springs home of Mike Meyer and his mother, Margaretha (Weidenhammer) Meyer. The photo was made prior to the 1926 Thanksgiving tornado that destroyed the home.**

This was not the first time Meyer and his mother had been exposed to this violent act of nature common in this part of the country where warm, moist air streaming up from the Gulf of Mexico collides with cooler, drier air moving down across the Great Plains. Only a couple of years after the Meyers moved to Heber Springs, on June 7, 1916, a tornado struck the town killing 22 people and causing considerable destruction of property. The vivid details of an encounter with such violent natural events are forever etched into the memories of those surviving these horrific storms. As will be seen later, the 1916 and 1926 tornadoes became indelibly etched into Meyer's memory, as well.

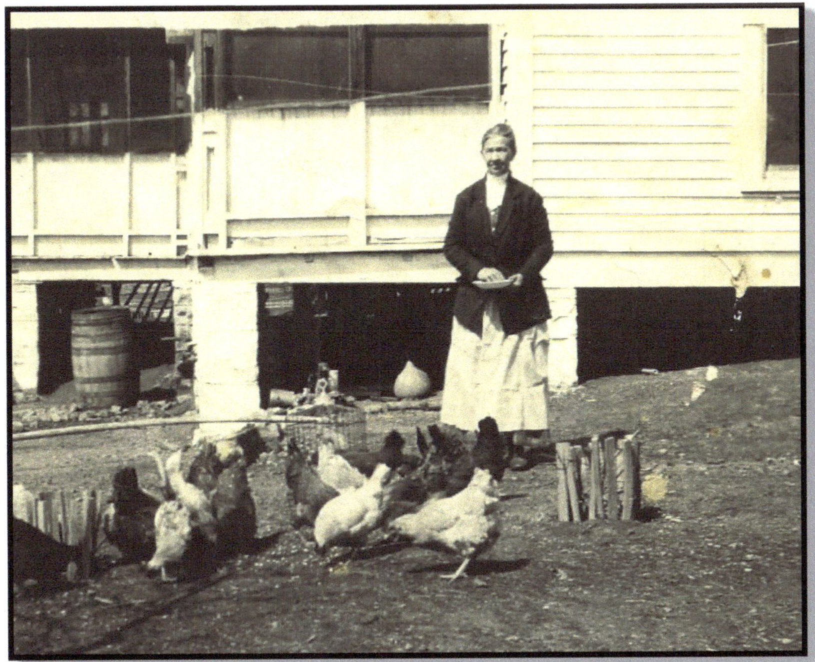

**2. Meyer's mother, Margaretha, feeding chickens behind their home on Sugar Loaf Street in Heber Springs, Arkansas. The back porch visible in the photo is where Mike had his second studio in Heber Springs. This photo was likely made by Meyer.**

Meyer's nephew, Roy Fricker, must have visited Meyer's home shortly before it was destroyed by the 1926 Thanksgiving Tornado. Fricker, born in 1912, would have been about 14 at the time. In a brief biographical sketch, Fricker wrote that "Uncle Mike" constructed a home-made radio while living on Sugar Loaf Street. This event provides us with some keen insights into Meyer's persona and helps us answer another significant question about Meyer that has previously been the source of much conjecture. According to Roy, "Uncle Mike" constructed a home-made radio and then placed the speakers on the front porch of his home so that sounds emanating from the radio could be heard by his neighbors. Meyer claimed he placed the speakers on the front porch because it was too loud. His nephew speculated that Uncle Mike did this because he wanted to share the radio with his less fortunate neighbors that could not afford a radio.

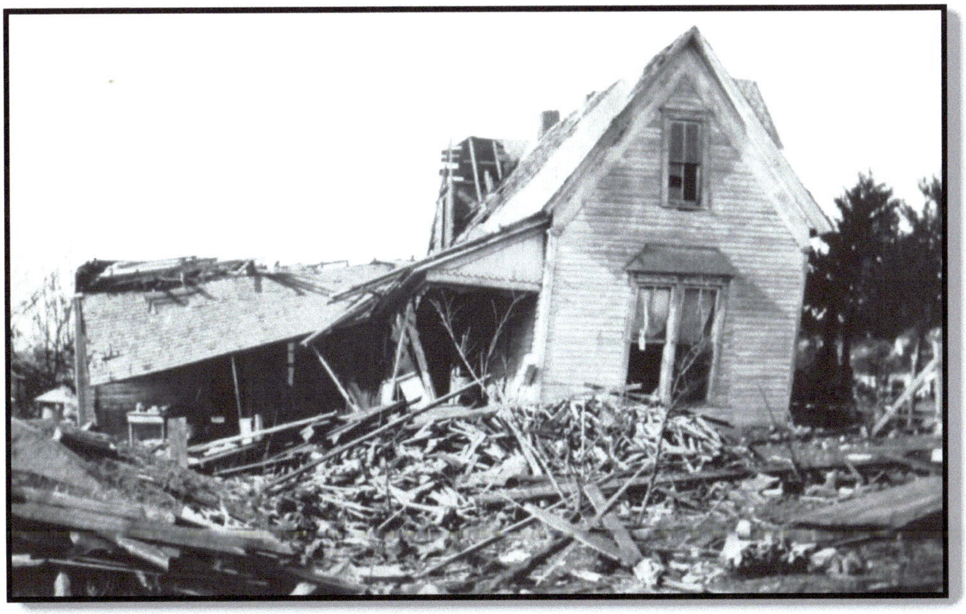

**3. The Meyer home in Heber Springs after the Thanksgiving Tornado of 1926. This photo was likely taken by Meyer.**

Meyer's odd behavior has two plausible motivations: 1) Meyer wanted to flaunt the fact that hc had the money and intellect to acquire the parts and construct such a device on his own or 2) Meyer felt some pity for his less fortunate neighbors and desired to share the entertaining programs offered by this new-fangled technology that was envied by all that did not have enough money to purchase such a luxury.

Fricker ascribed to the latter motivation. I disagree. As I will explain in Chapter 9 in an examination of the psyche of Disfarmer, I assert that the first motivation is likely the more correct driver behind Meyer's odd act of placing the home-made, radio speakers on his front porch for his neighbors to hear. This action by Meyer circa 1926 is somewhat akin to the modern-day scenario where you are sitting at a traffic light and suddenly you hear the deafening rumble of never-ending thunder until you realize that the sound is erupting from the high-wattage stereo system cranked-up to full throttle on a youth's car pulling up next to you. After mentally debating the motivation behind the youth's odd behavior, you conclude that it's a cry for attention -- "Hey everybody, look at me!" Another insight revealed by this first-hand account is that Meyer likely learned to construct the radio and acquired the parts through mail-order, thus demonstrating his ability simply to read and learn about new, technical, subject matters.

Destiny intervened yet again for Meyer. His next and last studio at the northwest corner of the intersection of East Main Street and North First Street[19] in downtown Heber Springs had a distinctive and rather large north-facing skylight design (see Vignette: The Skylight Photography Studio). It is likely that he completed construction of the unique studio on the corner of Main Street and First Street prior to the Thanksgiving Tornado of 1926. I base this assumption on several corroborating facts. First, according to the Arkansas Historic Preservation Program:

> "...Mike Meyer opened his photographic shop one-half block north of Main Street in the late 1920's. The studio, razed after his death, was a small stucco building, approximately 20 X 30 feet, facing east on First Street. It featured a glass skylight on the north. Meyer used natural light for his portraits. He lived in small space in the back of the building."[20]

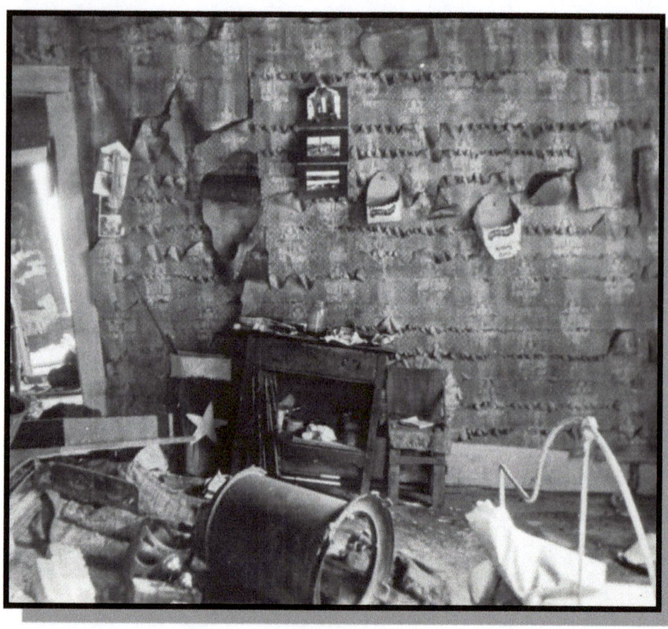

**4. Photo of the interior of the Meyer home in Heber Springs after the 1926 tornado. Meyer likely took this photo.**

Second, it is documented by photos taken at the time that Mike Meyer ventured out shortly after the storm struck to take photos of its aftermath. One well-known photo taken by Meyer after the 1926 storm, shows his home on Sugar Loaf Street that was completely destroyed. The storm cellar near the house is visible in the photo. Clearly, Meyer's cameras, developing equipment and supplies were not destroyed by the tornado. Had Meyer's photography equipment and supplies been in the house at the time of the storm, it is likely that all would have been destroyed along with the home.

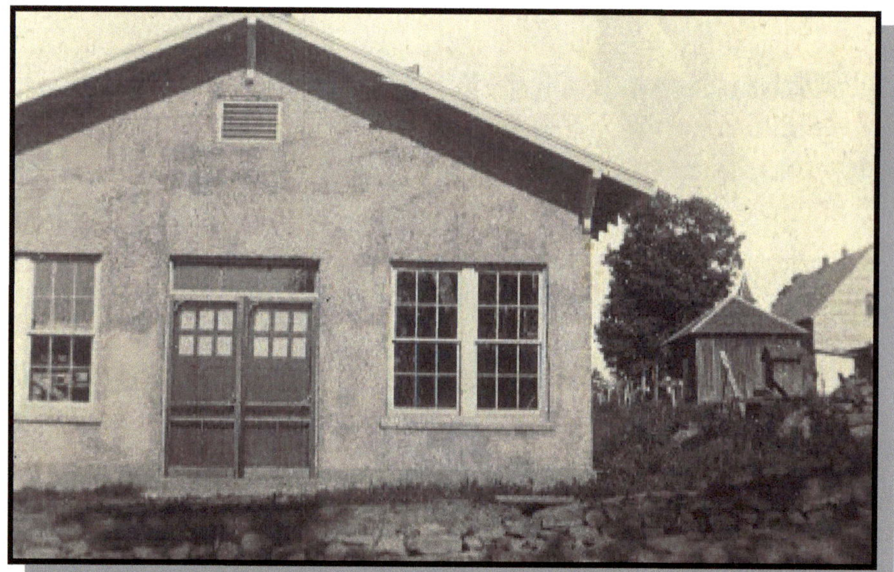

**5. Meyer's Skylight Studio located on the corner of Main and First Streets. This is the east side of the building facing North First Street. The north facing skylight is not visible from this angle however, the tip of the skylight structure appears visible over the eave of the roof.**

Lastly, a photo taken sometime around 1926 or 1927 shows Meyer's mother, Margaretha, standing in the front of the distinctive double doors and stucco covered wall of the Main Street Studio. Roy Fricker, in his brief biographical sketch (see Appendix 1), reported that in 1927, Margaretha Meyer fell in a rabbit hole in her backyard and broke her hip. She remained in her Heber Springs home where she was tended to by her daughter, Anna, who lived across the street and a housekeeper. Margaretha recovered from the first accident but in 1927, again fell breaking her hip. After the second fall, she became and invalid and was moved to the De Valls Bluff, Arkansas home of her daughter, Maggie, and Maggie's husband, Theodore Hursley Minor. Earlier researchers have reported that the destruction of the family home by the tornado caused Margaretha to move to De Valls Bluff. However, the story of her injury sustained in a fall combined with her age is certainly a more plausible explanation behind her needing to move in with her daughter who could provide her with better care during her convalescence. These facts also match the biographical sketch written by Harry Neukam, another of Disfarmer's nephews (see Appendix 1).

The photo showing Meyer's mother standing at the entrance to the newly constructed studio on Main Street strongly suggests that the studio was completed before she moved to De Valls Bluff in 1927. Since the Meyer home in Heber Springs was destroyed by a tornado in late 1926, its highly likely that the new studio was completed before the tornado -- in time for Meyer to have moved the contents of his studio from the back porch of the Sugar Loaf Street home to the newly constructed studio on Main and First Street, sparing the precious photography equipment from an untimely ruin. It also appears likely that Meyer's mother may have lived in the newly constructed studio for a short time following the tornado.

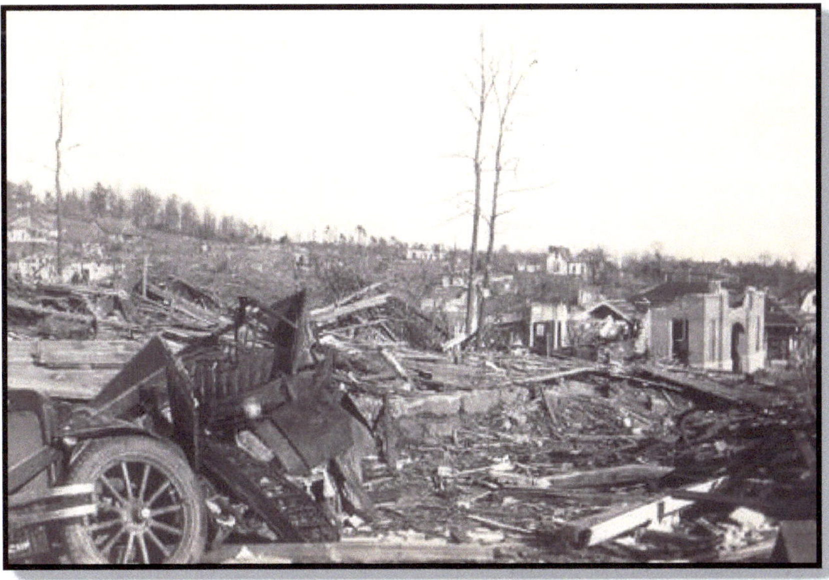

**6. Photo taken by Mike Meyer of the destruction of the town following the 1926 tornado. This photo appeared in the local *Heber Springs Times and the Headlight* newspaper.**

In 1927, Margaretha Meyer, with whom Mike Meyer had lived under the same roof since birth in 1884 -- some 43 years -- moved to live with her daughter, "Maggie," in De Valls Bluff, Arkansas. Mike became the sole occupant of the studio at East Main and First Street where he was residing according to the 1930 U.S. Census. Meyer entered a new and uncharted phase of his life after his mother moved away in 1927 -- life alone separated by considerable distance from any living relative.

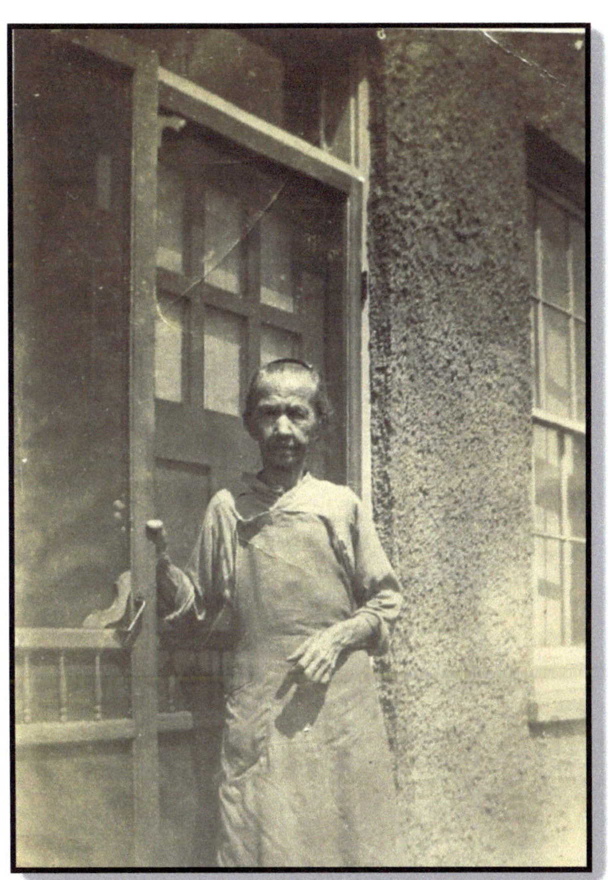

**7. Margaretha (Weidenhammer) Meyer, Mike's mother, standing at the main entrance to the skylight studio. This photo was taken by Meyer circa 1026.**

During the Meyer Photography Studio phase, Meyer took photos both in and out of his studio. Roy Fricker noted that Meyer owned a "Ford Model T" automobile (see Vignette: Ford Model T) which was most likely purchased at O.B. Robbins Motors in Heber Springs. It has been reported that Meyer would frequently load his camera in the back of his "Tin Lizzy" and ride around the countryside taking photographs. In some of these photographs, Meyer's distinctive "shadow" can be seen in the foreground of the photo with his hat or hood on his head as he snaps the photo. Meyer also appears to have been in the business of developing and printing other peoples' photos during this phase. Residents in and around Heber Springs would shoot a roll of film and bring it to Meyer for him to develop and make prints. Meyer had an affinity for a certain paper stock that had a distinctive diamond pattern border. It is often presumed that these diamond bordered photos were made by Meyer. In fact some of the photos were made by Meyer but many were made by others and Meyer simply developed and printed the photos -- often times stamping the photos on the back with "Meyer Photography Studio."

After Meyer's mother moved to De Valls Bluff, he did not totally lose contact with his aging and frail mother. Meyer would load his camera equipment in the back of his T-Model Ford and travel south from Heber Springs to De Valls Bluff in Prairie County to visit his mother, his sister, Maggie and her family. The trip undoubtedly took several hours as the roads were unpaved and hilly and the Model T had a top speed of 40 to 45 miles per hour. While visiting his extended family in and around De Valls Bluff, Meyer would take photographs of his various relatives. Many photos of Meyer and his extended family are presented in Chapter 11. Some of these photos show the distinctive hallmarks of a Meyer photograph - the somber expressions of the ordinary rural people in everyday clothes, the occasional shadow of the hooded photographer in the foreground, many printed on postcard stock or some stamped by the photographer on the backside.

What these family photographs taken by Meyer show us is that until the time of Meyer's name change to Disfarmer, he was somewhat connected with his family. He cared enough about his extended family to maintain contact with them. He was willing to travel several hours to visit his elderly mother, his sister the caretaker, his sister's husband and their children. He cared enough for these relatives to make photographs of them most likely at Meyer's own expense.

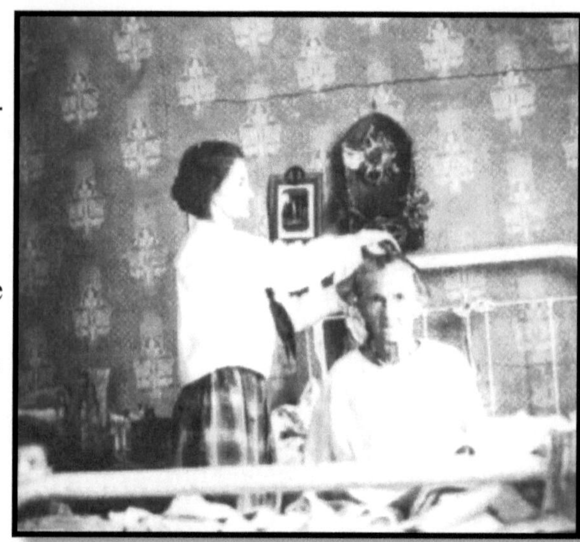

**8. Meyer's mother, Margaretha, having her hair groomed after breaking her hip in a fall in a rabbit hole. She is living in Heber Springs at this time.**

On February 18, 1935, Meyer's mother, Margaretha (Weidenhammer) Meyer, died just shy of her 86th birthday. This was surely a tragic yet life altering event for Mike Meyer. His biological mother whom he had known for a half-century and with whom he had lived and provided a livelihood for most of his life was dead. Meyer was now freed from a heavy burden. On a personal level, Meyer had sacrificed a great deal to provide necessities for his mother which extracted a heavy toll.

## Vignette: Heber Springs' Early Twentieth Century Tornados

According to City-Data.com, the town of Heber Springs, Arkansas is above the state average in tornadic activity and is 285% greater than the overall U.S. average for tornadic activity. In other words, Heber Springs lies in a corridor in which atmospheric conditions favor the development of tornadic activity. On June 7, 1916, a little over two years after Mike Meyer moved to Heber Springs, a major tornado struck the town killing 22 people and injured 54 others. A little over ten years later, on November 25, 1926, Thanksgiving Day, at 5:45 p.m., the town of Heber Springs was struck by an EF-4 tornado -- the most devastating tornado in Cleburne County's history. Casualties included 21 dead and countless injured and homeless. The town sustained considerable destruction with 145 homes, five churches and many businesses lost or heavily damaged. Fortunately, following the horrific 1916 tornado, many of the citizens had built storm shelters adjacent to their homes which surely lowered the death toll that could have resulted. The property damage was 20 to 30 times greater with the 1926 tornado but the death count was one less than the 1916 storm's death count of 22.[21] [22] [23]

## Vignette: The Skylight Photography Studio

The northwest corner of the intersection of East Main and First Streets in Heber Springs, Arkansas is currently occupied by a very typical looking bank building but from 1926 to 1960, it was the location of very atypical structure. That structure was the Meyer / Disfarmer Photography Studio with its very prominent, north-facing skylight. The design of the studio was surely a strange and eye-catching sight for the rural folks venturing into the small town on a go-to-market Saturday. No doubt many visitors were drawn to the odd-looking studio itself and decided to get a keepsake photograph while there.

Some researchers have identified the studio address as "102 North First Street" but the 1930 U.S. Census lists Mike Meyer's address as "106 North East Main Street." Main Street in Heber Springs runs almost due east and west and First Street crosses perpendicular to Main with North First Street beginning on the north side of Main. A close examination of a few rare photos of the studio taken after it was abandoned reveals some insights. In a close up shot of the double front-door entrance, the street number "102" is clearly visible over the doors. Interestingly, both front-doors had an array of window panes in each panel and the glass panes appear to have been made of recycled glass plate negatives with the images of former customers clearly visible. In another photo of the side of the studio with the prominent skylight clearly visible, a shadow cast by the roof structure suggests the photo was made in the afternoon with the sun in the western sky demonstrating that the skylight was clearly facing north. The double-door entrance is not visible on the skylight side of the studio so the entrance would have to have been on the east side facing North First Street.

Perhaps the studio had dual addresses since it was situated on the corner of the 100 block of Main and First Streets. Perhaps the main entrance to the studio was at 102 North First Street and Disfarmer had a separate entrance to his living quarters at 106 North East Main Street.

The bigger questions regarding the unique studio with the north-facing skylight is why did Disfarmer construct the studio and where did he obtain the design? North-facing skylights were utilized by photographers as early as the 1840's when the daguerreotype process was in vogue and were popular in the northern states as well as Europe throughout the latter half of the 19th Century. The advantages of the north-facing skylight were that it admitted indirect sunlight into the indoor studio providing ample, high-quality illumination prior to the advent of artificial light sources such as electric lights. Oftentimes, these large skylights were fitted with blinds or shades so that the light intensity could be better controlled on sunny days.

It is unclear whether Disfarmer chose to build his skylight studio in the mid-1920's for aesthetic reasons or due to a lack of ample electrical lighting or maybe both. Heber Springs received electricity in 1919. However, its possible the electric utility service was unreliable or too costly. Perhaps, Disfarmer did not like the quality of photographs taken when he and Penrose started out in the Jackson Theater or a bit later when he was operating on the back porch of his mother's home on Sugar Loaf Street.

The basic design for the studio was very likely obtained from *Cassell's Cyclopedia of Photography* edited by Bernard E. Jones and published in 1911 by Cassell of London and New York.[24] This encyclopedia is a virtual bible of photography with an "a to z" topical coverage of all aspects of the art and science of photography in 1911. In a section titled "Studio Design and Construction," over three full pages including almost a full page of illustrations is devoted to alternate skylight designs and clearly explains how to go about constructing such a studio. One such design is referred to as a "ridge-form studio" in which a portion of the roof of the studio, beginning at the ridge and running down to the eave, is covered with glass much like that in a greenhouse. According to the Cassell publication, one of the advantages of the ridge-form studio is its "eas[e] of construction by the ordinary builder." The pitch of the glass roof is recommended to be at an angle of 60° which is the maximum mid-day attitude of the sun on a summer day. Constructing the roof at that angle would prevent the sun from shining over the ridge and directly into the sky lit area of the studio. "The length of the studio may be anything from 20 ft. to 35 ft., less being too short for the use of ordinary portrait lenses for full length figures, and a greater amount being of not much real practical use."

Disfarmer's studio matches the encyclopedia's ridge-form studio design to a "T". As shown in the surviving photos of the studio, a considerable section of the north-facing roof beginning at the ridge and running to the eave was covered in glass. The pitch of the glass roof was very steep – clearly greater than 45° and certainly approaching a 60° pitch. According to the Arkansas Historic Preservation Program, the dimension of the building was approximately 20 by 30 feet.[25]

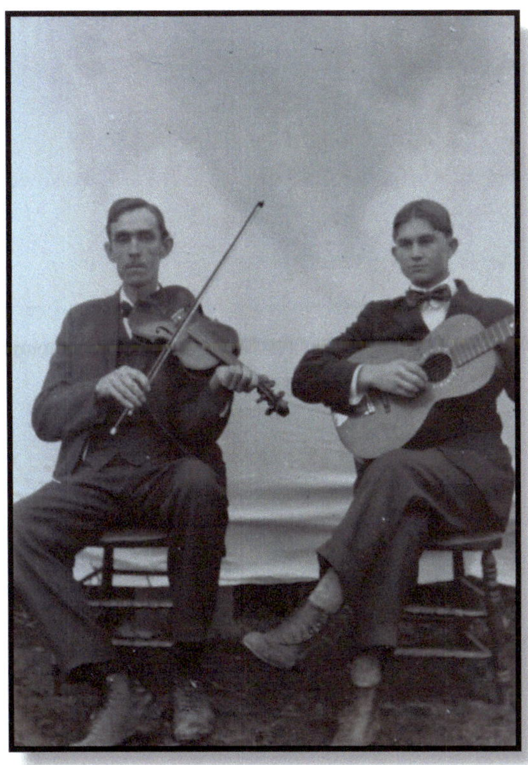

**9. Mike Meyer (left) playing the violin and unidentified man playing the guitar, circa 1929.**

Some researchers believe that George A. Penrose, Disfarmer's former partner was the architect master-mind behind the skylight studio. Penrose may have had some brief construction experience prior to his venture with Disfarmer and may have drawn-up the plans for the unique studio prior to the dissolution of the partnership around 1920. However, we know that Disfarmer was adept at reading publications and then applying newly acquired knowledge to different tasks. From a note Disfarmer wrote to his nephew, we learn that Disfarmer was largely a self-taught violinist having studied violin by mail though he would have preferred hands-on instruction. We also know that Meyer built his own radio set -- likely from a mail-order kit available during the late 1920's.[†]

Regardless of how or why, the good news is that Disfarmer chose to build the unique studio and photographed the local people there for almost 35 years. Part of the appeal of his photos is undoubtedly attributable to the large, north-facing skylight that bathed his subjects in natural light. As described in Cassell's encyclopedia, the natural light helped put the subjects at ease and helped avoid "a screwing up of the eyes, thus giving a false expression..." The soothing effects of natural light on peoples behavior has been embraced of recent by the world's largest retailer which utilizes skylights in its stores to dramatically lower its utility bills but also to enhance the shopping experience by mellowing the mood of its millions of customers. Disfarmer appears to have stumbled onto this side-benefit of natural lighting by sheer accident.

*[The following is a transcription of a postcard (right) written by Mike Meyer to his niece in 1915. Permission to reproduce the postcard was provided by the Cleburne County Historical Society in Heber Springs, Arkansas, which received the postcard courtesy of Henry Wilks, great nephew of Mike Meyer a.k.a. Mike Disfarmer.]*

Heberspings Ark
Dear Niece, Reed [sic] your letter & was glad to hear From you if you have a boy at your House I think I'm his great uncle. grandma is O.K. at this writing. so you have a New Piano. I taken music Lessons by mail. while that way of studing [sic] music is alright, I think it would be Better For you to get Lessons of a teacher. you Know when I took Lessons, I worked and could have no Time to learn of a Teacher at Regular Hours. I Just studied my lessons at night and when I had a chance. Sometimes I worked at the Rice Mill 15 Hours a day, and then I had to save the Lessons till I had time to learn them.
From your uncle Mike

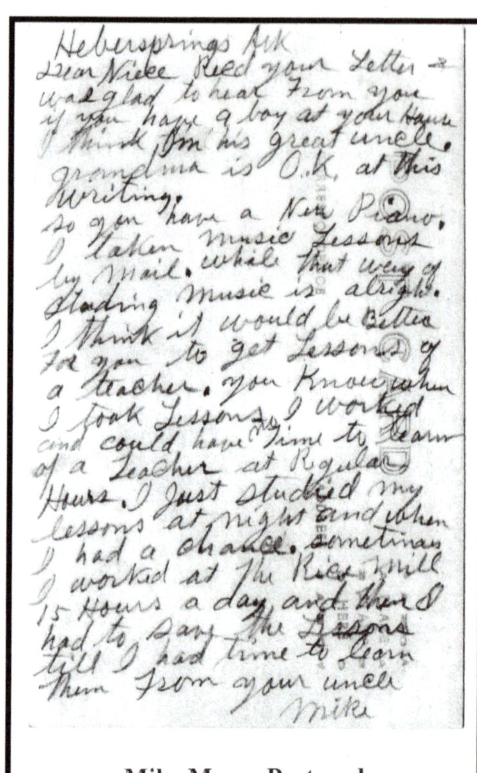

Heberspings Ark
Dear Niece Reed your Letter &
was glad to hear From you
if you have a boy at your House
I think I'm his great uncle.
grandma is O.K. at this
writing.
so you have a New Piano.
I taken music Lessons
by mail. while that way of
studing music is alright.
I think it would be Better
For you to get Lessons of
a teacher. you Know when
I took Lessons, I worked
and could have no Time to learn
of a Teacher at Regular
Hours. I Just studied my
lessons at night and when
I had a chance. sometimes
I worked at The Rice Mill
15 Hours a day, and then I
had to save the Lessons
till I had time to learn
them from your uncle
Mike

**Mike Meyer Postcard**
**Written in 1915 to his niece.**
***Card courtesy of Henry Wilks, great nephew of Mike Meyer aka Mike Disfarmer***

[†] Due to the rapid growth and popularity of radio during the 1920's, several companies such as Atwater Kent, Crosley, RCA and Westinghouse began making and selling radio kits for consumers.

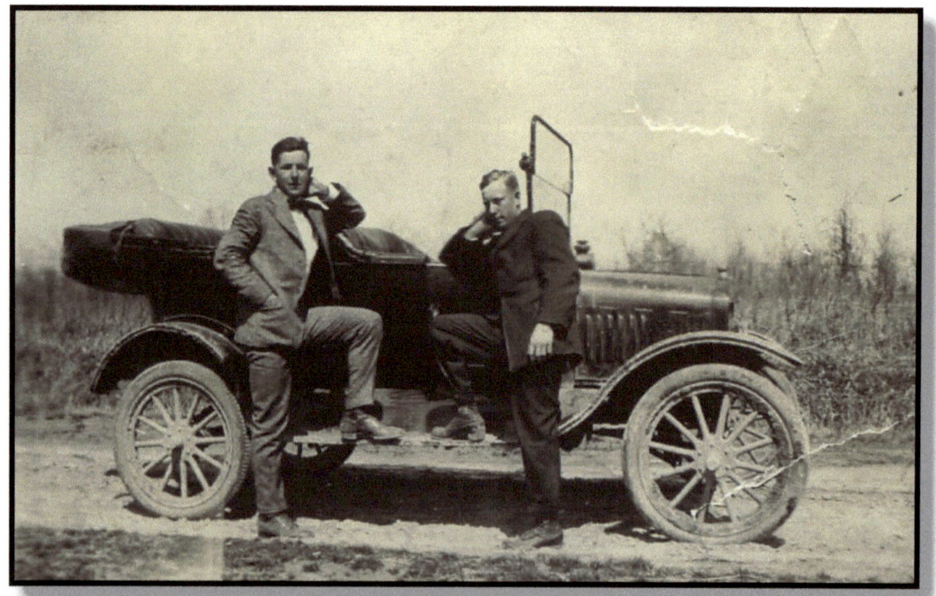

**10. A Ford Model "T" similar to the one owned by Disfarmer. Standing in this photo on the left is an unidentified relative of Disfarmer's, possibly his nephew, Harry Neukam, and a friend (right).**

**Vignette: Ford Model T**

The Ford Model T automobile was mass produced by Henry Ford's Ford Motor Company from October 1, 1908 to May 27, 1927. Fifteen million Model T's were rolled off the assembly line during almost 20 years of production. The Ford Model T, also know as the "Tin Lizzy" or the "T-Model" is considered the first affordable motor car that was accessible to the middle class. In 1909, a four-seat open tourer sold for $850. By the 1920's, due to economies of scale and production techniques, the price had dropped to $260 making it very affordable to many middle class wage earners. A Ford factory worker could earn enough in four months to buy a Model T. The inline, four cylinder engine had a top speed of 40 - 45 mph.[26]

**NOTES**

---

[18] "Heber Springs, Arkansas," Cityt-data.com, 2013, <http://www.city-data.com/city/Heber-Springs Arkansas.html>.

[19] According to the 1930 U.S. Census, Mike Meyer, photographer, was residing at 106 North East Main Street where he likely resided in his photography studio.

[20] "HEBER SPRINGS COMMERCIAL HISTORIC DISTRICT, HEBER SPRINGS, CLEBURNE COUNTY," Arkansas Historic Preservation Program, <http://www.arkansaspreservation.com/historic-properties/_search_nomination_popup.aspx?id=2459>.

[21] <http://www.city-data.com/city/Heber-Springs-Arkansas.html>.

[22] Pris, "A Little Bit of This, a Little Bit of That, and a Whole Lot of Arkansas," Arkansas Ties, Oct. 7, 2006, <http://www.arkansasties.com/WhatsNew/2006/10/1919-tornado/>.

[23] Jessica Baureis, "Devastating Thanksgiving Tornado," TheSunTimes.com, Updated Jun. 29, 2012 @ 11:27 am, <http://www.thesuntimes.com/article/20081125/NEWS/311259982>.

[24] Peter c. Bunnell and Robert A. Sobieszek, Encyclopedia of Photography, Arno Press, Inc., New York, 1974, Reprint of Bernice E. Jones, Cassell's Cyclopedia of Photography, Cassell, London New York, 1911.

[25] HEBER SPRINGS COMMERCIAL HISTORIC DISTRICT, HEBER SPRINGS, CLEBURNE COUNTY.

[26] "Ford Model T," Wikipedia, the free encyclopedia, last modified on 5 June 2013 at 13:02, <http://en.wikipedia.org/wiki/Ford_Model_T>.

# Chapter VII. The Classical Period: Disfarmer Photography Studio / 1939 to 1945

*"Pay no attention to the man behind the curtain!"*

— L. Frank Baum, The Wonderful Wizard of Oz

*"Nobody gets in to see the wizard. Not nobody."*

— L. Frank Baum, The Wonderful Wizard of Oz

The front-page headline of the Thursday, April 13, 1939 edition of the *Heber Springs Times and the Headlight* read, "Photographer Changes Name After Residing Here Twenty-Five Years." The leading line in the article was, "Truth's stranger than fiction." The article continued, "[a]nd there is no fiction stranger and more interesting than the life story of Mike Disfarmer, local photographer, who up until the recent special term of circuit court here was Mike Meyer, manager of the Meyer Studio here."

On March 20, 1939, the photographer Mike Meyer, through his attorney G.P. Houston, petitioned the Cleburne County Circuit Court, to have his name legally changed to Mike Disfarmer (see the Vignette: Origin of the Name Disfarmer). In his petition, Meyer stated "that he was supposedly born near Portersville, Indiana, August 16, 1882 [1884]; that his father's name has never been known to him and neither has his mother's name ever been known to him." Meyer went onto state "that about three years after his birth, he was blown in a tornado to the home of one Martin Meyer and his wife, Margaretha Meyer who lived near Kellerville, Indiana, and with which he lived and made his home until they each departed this life." In his petition, Mike clarified that "the Meyer Family by whom he was reared and their many relatives and kinsmen have on many occasions been embarress [sic] and humiliation; that because of petitioner's status the Meyer family have expressed themselves from time as being desirous to disown him." He reiterated that "knowing himself not to be a Meyer" and wishing to save "the Meyer Family and their many kinsmen from further embarrassment" and "keeping them constantly in fear that he might attempt to inherit" some of the family wealth, that he "decided to petition for a change of name." This was not an overnight decision. In his petition, he stated that he reached this decision "after many years of pondering and meditation."[27]

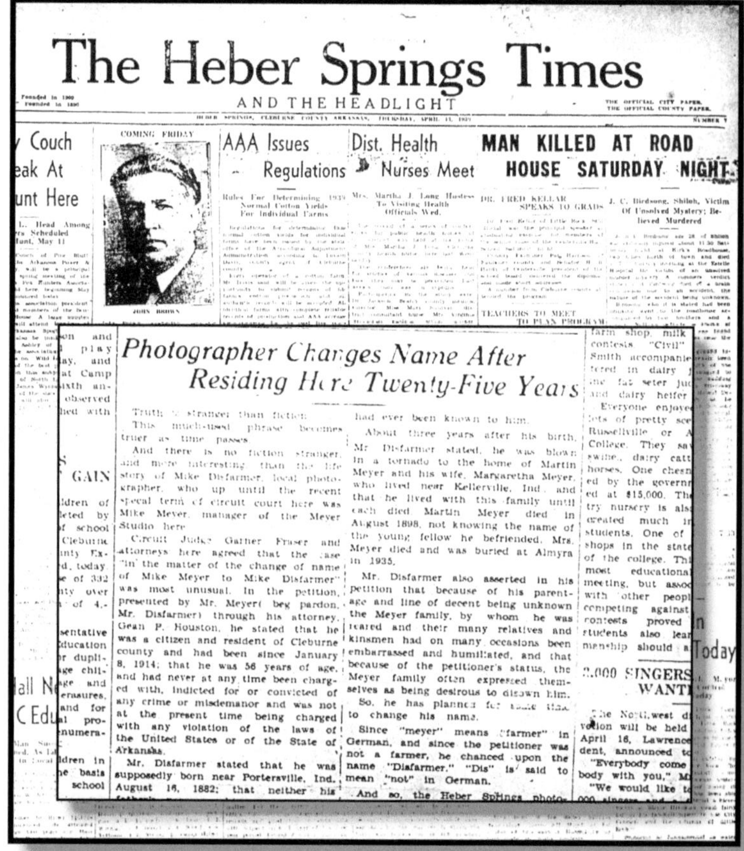

The Heber Springs Times

AND THE HEADLIGHT

AAA Issues Regulations

Dist. Health Nurses Meet

MAN KILLED AT ROAD HOUSE SATURDAY NIGHT

JOHN BROWN

TEACHERS TO MEET TO PLAN PROGRAM

**Photographer Changes Name After Residing Here Twenty-Five Years**

Truth is stranger than fiction.

This much-used phrase becomes truer as time passes.

And there is no fiction stranger and more interesting than the life story of Mike Disfarmer, local photographer, who up until the recent special term of circuit court here was Mike Meyer, manager of the Meyer Studio here.

Circuit Judge Garner Fraser and attorneys here agreed that the case "in the matter of the change of name of Mike Meyer to Mike Disfarmer" was most unusual. In the petition, presented by Mr. Meyer( beg pardon, Mr. Disfarmer) through his attorney, Gean P. Houston, he stated that he was a citizen and resident of Cleburne county and had been since January 8, 1914; that he was 56 years of age, and had never at any time been charged with, indicted for or convicted of any crime or misdemanor and was not at the present time being charged with any violation of the laws of the United States or of the State of Arkansas.

Mr. Disfarmer stated that he was supposedly born near Portersville, Ind., August 16, 1882; that neither his

had ever been known to him.

About three years after his birth, Mr Disfarmer stated, he was blown in a tornado to the home of Martin Meyer and his wife, Margaretha Meyer, who lived near Kellerville, Ind., and that he lived with this family until each died. Martin Meyer died in August 1898, not knowing the name of the young fellow he befriended. Mrs. Meyer died and was buried at Almyra in 1935.

Mr. Disfarmer also asserted in his petition that because of his parentage and line of decent being unknown the Meyer family, by whom he was reared and their many relatives and kinsmen had on many occasions been embarrassed and humiliated, and that because of the petitioner's status, the Meyer family often expressed themselves as being desirous to disown him.

So, he has planned for [illegible] time to change his name.

Since "meyer" means "farmer" in German, and since the petitioner was not a farmer, he chanced upon the name "Disfarmer." "Dis" is said to mean "not" in German.

And so, the Heber Springs photo-

1. Front-page article from the April 15th, 1939, ***Heber Springs Times and the Headlight*** **reporting on the name change of Mike Meyer to Disfarmer.**

This event marked the beginning of what I call the classical period in the photography career of Mike Disfarmer. Judge Garner Fraser issued his order on March 29, 1939, approving Disfarmer's name change and the Meyer Photography Studio legally began conducting business as the Disfarmer Photography Studio. The studio with the north facing skylight was the same. The photography equipment was the same. The developing process was the same. The photographic subjects were the same. However, the photographer was not the same.

Mike Meyer was vanquished being re christened as Mike Disfarmer. Like a phoenix rising from the ashes, Disfarmer was no longer shackled to his past. By this symbolic act of legally changing his name and by disowning any connection with the Meyer clan, he was now reborn as a different person -- a person who would no longer be an embarrassment to any of his living kinfolk.

However, was the name change more than a symbolic act? Did Disfarmer truly feel transformed into a new being? Perception is reality. We have little insight into the statement made in his petition to the court, that he had been an embarrassment to his family and that members of his family had stated on more than one occasion that they would like to disown him. Perhaps, an embarrassing event in Disfarmer's past had been an added catalyst for him and his mother to move to Heber Springs and distance themselves from his other siblings. We will never know the answer to this question. We are left to make suppositions based on the facts at hand.

CIVIL

CLEBURNE COUNTY, ARK.

IN THE CLEBURNE COUNTY CIRCUIT COURT

IN THE MATTER OF THE CHANGE OF NAME OF MIKE MEYER TO MIKE DISFARMER .

PETITION

Comes Make Meyer by his attorney, G. P. Houston, and states to the Court:

That he is a citizen and resident of Cleburne County, Arkansas, and has been since January 8,1914; that he is (56) Fifty-six years of age, and has never at any time been charged with, indicted for or convicted of any crime or misdemeanor and is not at the present time being charged with, or under suspicion of, or indicted for any infractio or violation of the laws of the United States or of the State of Arkan But, on the contrary, has always demeaned and comported himself as a good christain, law abiding person.

Your petitioner states that he was supposedly born near Portersville, Indiana, August 16,1882; that his father's name has never been known to him and neither has his mother's name ever been known to him.

Petitioner states that about three years after his birth, he was blown in a tornado to the home of one Martin Meyer and his wife, Margaretha Meyer who lived near Kellerville, Indiana, and with which

" who is a resident of Heber Spri

who is a Photographer and doing business in said Town in the name of "The Meyer Studio" asks that he be known in the future by the name of Mike Disfarmer, that busi be transacted with him by that name, that all conveyances, instrume papers and transactions between him and the public and individual shall be by the name of Mike Disfarmer.

Your petitioner states that he knows of no person, past or pre by the name of Mike Disfarmer, and that his adoption of such a nam would not be to the detriment of, a disadvantage, cause embarrassme or be a hindrance to any one now living in this community or else

WHEREFORE, it is prayed that an order of this court be made c the name of your petitioner from Mike Meyer to Mike Disfarmer.

G. P. Houston

Attorney for Petitioner.

Petitioner, Mike Meyer states that the above and foregoing statements contained in said petition are true and correct.

Mike Meyer

Petitioner.

Subscribed and sworn to before me this 20th day of March,1939

My commission expires January 14,1943.

Lorene Houston

Notary Public.

**2. Copies of portions of Disfarmer's 1939 petition to the court for his name change from Meyer.**

Disfarmer's mother, Margaretha, with whom, he had cohabitated for much of his adult life, finally died in 1935 at the age of 85. The apron strings were finally cut. Perhaps for Disfarmer, the proverbial apron strings were more like puppet strings (see Chapter 9 for insights into the psyche of Disfarmer). Nearly four years after his mother's death, Disfarmer chose to act on a thought he had been harboring and nurturing for many years, at least since 1936 -- the changing of his name and publicly disowning his Meyer family roots. Oftentimes, when we resist or endure an irritant in our lives for long

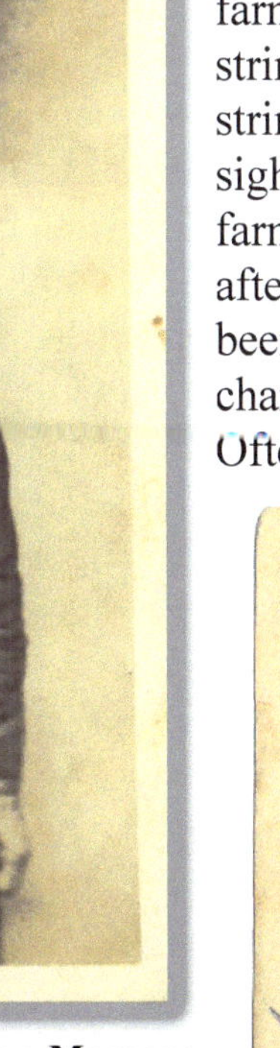

**3. Disfarmer RPPC of his mother, Margaretha (Weidenhammer) Meyer taken in his skylight studio circa 1926 (postcard AZO stamp block with squares in corners dates photo between 1925 and 1940).**

periods of time, we are permanently transformed -- like a carpenter that develops calloused hands from constantly wielding a hammer. Putting on a glove does not make the callous go away. In Disfarmer's mind, all ties that bound him to his painful past were severed once and for all by the simple act of changing his name.

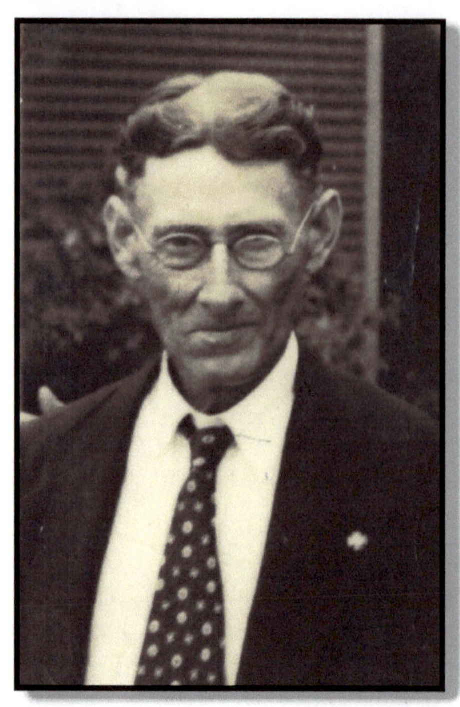

4. Mike Meyer circa 1935 possibly taken at the funeral of his mother.

## Supposition 3: A Unique Combination of Ingredients

Disfarmer could now be who he had always wanted to be. He could now project the image that he had always wanted to project. The residents of Heber Springs and Cleburne County would finally get to know the real Mike Disfarmer. Or would they? Was there still a facade being projected to those he encountered in his daily life? Was he truly different or was it simply his name that was different? The answer is intuitively obvious but, in Disfarmer's mind, he had been transformed by the name change. Perhaps, the local townsfolk, after reading the "believe it or not" tale in the newspaper, became a bit more leery of the strange man who had lived in their midst for 25 years. By his free-will act of changing his name and sharing a strange reason for the change, had revealed his mental state to the public who had been left to speculate beforehand. The odd-acting town photographer was truly odd.

As a result of this very public act along with the front-page publicity, its possible that Disfarmer's interactions with the community at-large became even more strained. Perhaps the Heber Springs residents began to mock Disfarmer or further limit interactions with him. In a small town, they undoubtedly gossiped behind his back about his bizarre court appearance. A story shared with me by Dr. Barnett, a lifelong resident of Heber Springs and prominent member of the Cleburne County Historical Society and noted expert on Disfarmer, seems to support my supposition that Disfarmer had a strained relationship with the local citizenry. Dr. Barnett shared that in researching the names of the subjects of the glass plate negatives recovered from the Disfarmer Studio after his death, that the researchers were unable to identify any resident of Heber Springs as being one of the photographed subjects -- that the subjects were from the surrounding county or other locales.

Its possible Disfarmer became more reclusive and withdrawn after being ridiculed or shunned by the townsfolk. Its probable he began to spend more time in his studio rather than venturing out to take photographs. Its likely that Disfarmer's studio interactions with his customers became more stilted. Disfarmer may have become more absorbed in his photography and less concerned with the impressions he made on the subjects of his photograph sessions. The end result -- Disfarmer was not concerned with providing his customers a great experience. He was singularly focused on delivering his customers a quality photograph in exchange for the small sums of hard-earned money they tendered.

We have all had professional photo sessions with a local photographer to preserve our families images at various points in our lives. These portrait sessions may have been to commemorate special occasions or for inclusion in the church directory. These photo shoots are generally the same regardless of who is behind the camera. First, we are ushered into a semi-dark room and placed in front of a backdrop in front of two or three bright lights that are shining uncomfortably into our eyes. We watch our step so as not to trip on the draped backdrop or the electrical chords running to and fro. We are then posed on stools of differing heights or other props and cajoled into tilting our heads and twisting our torsos in almost contortion-like maneuvers. Finally, we are asked to smile and not blink while the photographer makes small-talk with us in an attempt to make us more relaxed. The end result is that we are anything but relaxed. The setting is unsettling. Instead of feeling comfortable, we feel very uncomfortable. No matter how hard he tries, its unlikely that the well-intentioned photographer could ever obtain his desired result -- to make us appear natural -- in such an unnatural setting.

In stark contrast, a portrait session with Disfarmer during his Classical Period was a completely opposite experience for his subjects. The subjects arrived at the studio in their everyday attire -- some wore their nicer things -- for many, their nicer things and everyday things were one and the same. They were then ushered by Disfarmer from the small, fenced-off waiting area into the main studio which was virtually devoid of props or equipment. They were positioned in front of a minimalist backdrop that was more like a wall -- it did not drape outwards onto the floor. There were no bright lights and electrical chords to step over. The lighting was natural, indirect sunlight coming from the overhead, north-facing skylight. (Anyone who has ever stood in a room with a skylight can attest to how natural and relaxed one feels -- the lighting is almost mood-altering.) The subjects were shown where to stand by the aloof, automaton-like photographer. There was no banter, cajoling, instruction or small-talk. Disfarmer did not attempt to make the subjects feel relaxed. They were not coaxed to pose or smile. He simply let the subjects be who they were -- unadulterated and natural. Disfarmer then moved behind the camera -- opened the shutter -- paused -- then closed the shutter. The subjects were often unaware that their photo had been taken.†

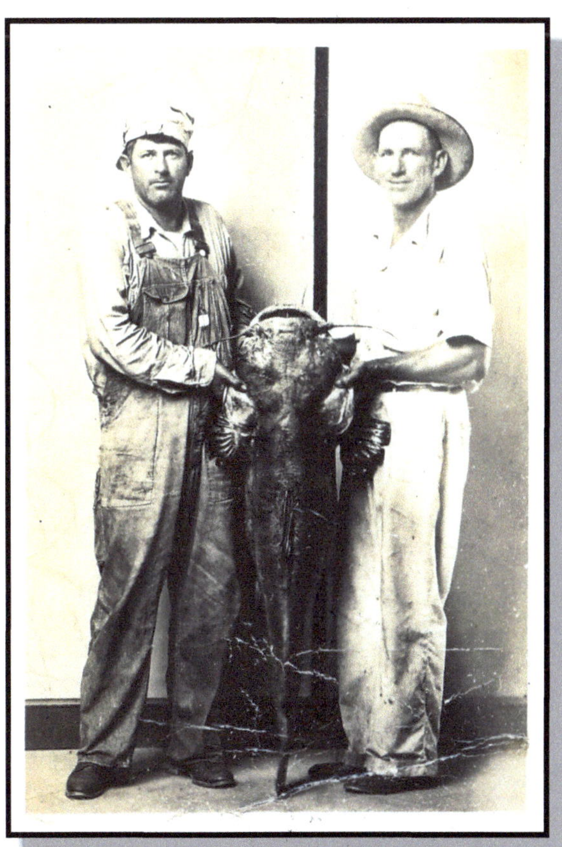

5. Disfarmer photo of two men holding a large catfish they caught. This photo was taken in the Disfarmer skylight studio and shows the light background with the distinctive dark vertical stripe.

Who were these daring souls that felt compelled to stroll into the hermit-like photographer's oddly shaped studio? It appears that they were not residents of the town but dwellers from the surrounding countryside. These people lived a very hardscrabble life -- scratching out a living from the soil and other natural resources afforded them in the Ozark Foothills. A near fatal blow would be delivered by the Great Depression that was so devastating in its effect on the local economy (see the Vignette: The Great Depression's Impact on Cleburne County). Then came World War II -- yet another hardship placed on these resilient people. The war was a "good news, bad news" story for the county residents. It provided the residents with another source of income but it took many young men away from their loved ones -- some never to be re-united this side of heaven.

REGISTRATION CARD—(Men born on or after April 28, 1877 and on or before February 16, 1897)

SERIAL NUMBER U-431 | 1. NAME (Print) Mike — Disfarmer (First) (Middle) (Last) | ORDER NUMBER

2. PLACE OF RESIDENCE (Print) Heber Springs Cleburne Ark. (Number and street) (Town, township, village, or city) (County) (State)

[THE PLACE OF RESIDENCE GIVEN ON THE LINE ABOVE WILL DETERMINE LOCAL BOARD JURISDICTION; LINE 2 OF REGISTRATION CERTIFICATE WILL BE IDENTICAL]

3. MAILING ADDRESS Heber Springs, Arkansas [Mailing address if other than place indicated on line 2. If same insert word same]

4. TELEPHONE (Exchange) (Number) | 5. AGE IN YEARS 59 DATE OF BIRTH Aug. 16 1882 (Mo.) (Day) (Yr.) | 6. PLACE OF BIRTH Supposedly in Daviess (Town or county) Indiana (State or country)

7. NAME AND ADDRESS OF PERSON WHO WILL ALWAYS KNOW YOUR ADDRESS Bishop Manson Heber Springs

8. EMPLOYER'S NAME AND ADDRESS Self

9. PLACE OF EMPLOYMENT OR BUSINESS Heber Springs Cleburne, Ark. (Number and street or R. F. D. number) (Town) (County) (State)

I AFFIRM THAT I HAVE VERIFIED ABOVE ANSWERS AND THAT THEY ARE TRUE.

D. S. S. Form 1 (Revised 4-1-42) (over) 16—21630-2 Mike Disfarmer (Registrant's signature)

6. Mike Disfarmer's WWII draft registration card circa 1941. Disfarmer incorrectly listed his birth year as 1882 when in fact he was born in 1884, making him approximately 57 years of age.

It was these salt-of-the-earth people that scraped together their pennies and sought out the quirky town photographer. Despite their stark realities, they were desirous of preserving their moment in time through photographic images that could be shared with their loved ones for posterity. Some had a more poignant intent to capture their image as a leave-behind with loved ones as they departed for the war knowing they may never return. Others wanted to capture their images to mail a keepsake to a loved one serving their country overseas. Regardless of the motive, the hard-to-come-by money was well spent and never begrudged because these ordinary people could now preserve their place in time -- a small bit of immortality on earth.

A unique combination of ingredients came together in the small, rural town of Heber Springs from 1939 to 1946 - Disfarmer's sunlit, minimalist studio, his glass-plate technology, his unique, off-putting persona and his post-depression era, pastoral subjects. The alchemy of blending together these rare ingredients yielded pho-

† Based on personal accounts provided by Disfarmer's assistant, Bessie Utley, other photographic subjects, family recollections and based on reviewing various photographs made in Disfarmer's skylight studio.

tographs with a purity and simplicity unmatched in modern photography. The black and white photographs provide a window into the soul of common people under uncommon circumstances. On viewing these photos in quiet and solitude, one cannot help wondering and speculate about the true-life experiences of those people reflected in the two-dimensional image. To view more of Disfarmer's photos, see *Links to Disfarmer Photos* at the end of this publication.

## Vignette: Origin of the Name Disfarmer

The origin of the name "Disfarmer" is not mentioned in Mike Meyer's petition to the court for a legal change of his name. His petition to the court did state "that he knows of no person, past or present by the name of Mike Disfarmer." Nor did the contemporary article from the local newspaper mention the origin of his new surname. However, a story has been commonly attributed to Disfarmer as the reason he selected his surname replacement for Meyer.

Disfarmer was a second generation American of Germanic descent. He allegedly claimed that "Meyer," in German, meant "farmer" and the prefix "dis" meant "not." And since he was "not a farmer," Disfarmer was an appropriate surname. Dictionary.com confirms that the prefix, "dis" means "lack of / not" as in "dishonest." According to About.com, the meaning behind the German surname "Meyer" or variations thereof, is "steward of landholder" or "leaseholder." In post-Civil War Arkansas, sharecropping or tenancy farming was a common system whereby the landholder or owner would provide all the capital while the tenant farmer would provide the labor in exchange for a share of the crop, usually one-half. In that sense, Disfarmer's claim that "Meyer" meant "farmer" was not far-off the mark.

After the death of his father when the family resided on a farm in Arkansas County, Disfarmer likely had the opportunity to demonstrate his prowess as a farmer. However, facts suggest that Disfarmer never embraced farming as an occupation. He and his mother moved to the town of Stuttgart sometime after his father's death where Disfarmer worked for a brief time as a night watchman at the local rice mill. I have been unable to confirm the authenticity of the story attributed to Disfarmer as the source of his new surname but, anecdotally, the story seems plausible.

## Vignette: The Great Depression's Impact on Cleburne County

At the time of the 1929 stock market crash, most people in Cleburne County lived on small farms and were less impacted by the onslaught of the Great Depression. However, in 1930, a severe drought destroyed crops across the county causing many people to look for other means of providing for their families. Many turned to the timber industry or lumber mills for income. As the Great Depression wore on, many local businesses cut-back employment or closed altogether. Many county residents sought work through social programs like the Works Progress Administration (WPA) and the Public Works Administration (PWA). In 1933, more than 1,200 Cleburne County families had received governmental relief aid. Despite these programs, many county residents found themselves out of work. Adding to the economic hardships for the county residents, tourism dropped significantly in the 1930's. There were no paved roads in the county until 1940 so Heber Springs was unable to attract automobile travelers. Fewer and fewer visitors were arriving on the Missouri and North Arkansas Railroad (M&NA) due to its own unreliability, its financial woes as well as the economic impact of the Great Depression and the increased reliance on automobiles. The M&NA finally ceased service to Heber Springs in 1945.[28]

**NOTES**

[27] "In the Matter of the Change of Name of Mike Meyer to Mike Disfarmer," Petition, Cleburne County Circuit Court, March 20, 1939.

[28] "Heber Springs Commercial Historic District, Heber Springs, Cleburne County," Arkansas Historic Preservation Program, <http://www.arkansaspreservation.com/historic-properties/_search_nomination_popup.aspx?id=2459>.

# Chapter VIII. Decline and Death: 1946 to 1959

*"Everything has to come to an end, sometime."*

— L. Frank Baum, The Marvelous Land of Oz

The end of World War II marks the beginning of the last phase of Disfarmer's life. Disfarmer was 62 years of age in 1946. In terms of his photographic work, the period from 1946 until his death in 1959, is the least remarkable. Perhaps with the local GIs returning from Europe and the Pacific, the women, children, moms and dads who had often been the subjects of Disfarmer's photographs just before and during the war, no longer felt the need to have photos made to send oversees to Joe. Perhaps the world was changing too fast and the small town photographer with his old school technology was no longer relevant. Perhaps families found it was easier and more desirable to make their own photos of their families at home or, while traveling in the family automobile on fun trips. Whatever the reason, Disfarmer's career was in decline.

It has been reported by local townsfolk that Disfarmer began consuming more beer and ice cream -- two of his favorite vices -- and eating less food. The always reclusive Disfarmer became even more isolated and withdrawn. His finances were likely in decline as well. The confluence of bad health habits, advancing age, declining income and increasing isolation undoubtedly took their toll on his physical and mental health. Metaphorically, like the imaginary tornado that dropped him on the Meyer's Indiana home doorstep, Disfarmer was now spiraling to his death.

In 1958, about one year before Disfarmer's death, he was visited on two different occasions by the last of his relatives to see him alive. These visits are well substantiated and have very different outcomes. Rather than clearing up some of the enigma surrounding the relationship between Disfarmer and his family, these encounters simply add to the controversy.

One of the last groups of Disfarmer's relatives to see him alive was that of his sister, Margaretha "Maggie" (Meyer) Minor/Klinger, Maggie's daughter and Disfarmer's niece, Martha (Minor) Price/Eanes, Martha's son and Disfarmer's great-nephew, John Price, and John's wife, Lillian Mae (Gardner) Price. This encounter between Disfarmer and this quartet of relatives was told to me during a January, 2013 phone interview I had with John Price, Disfarmer's great-nephew. In about 1958, Disfarmer's sister, Maggie, who lived in De Valls Bluff, had grown increasingly concerned about her brother, Mike, since she and the family had not heard from him in sometime. Maggie arranged for her grandson, John Price, to drive her to Heber Springs to visit her estranged brother, Disfarmer. John Price was serving in the military at the time and was stationed at the Little Rock Air Force Base.

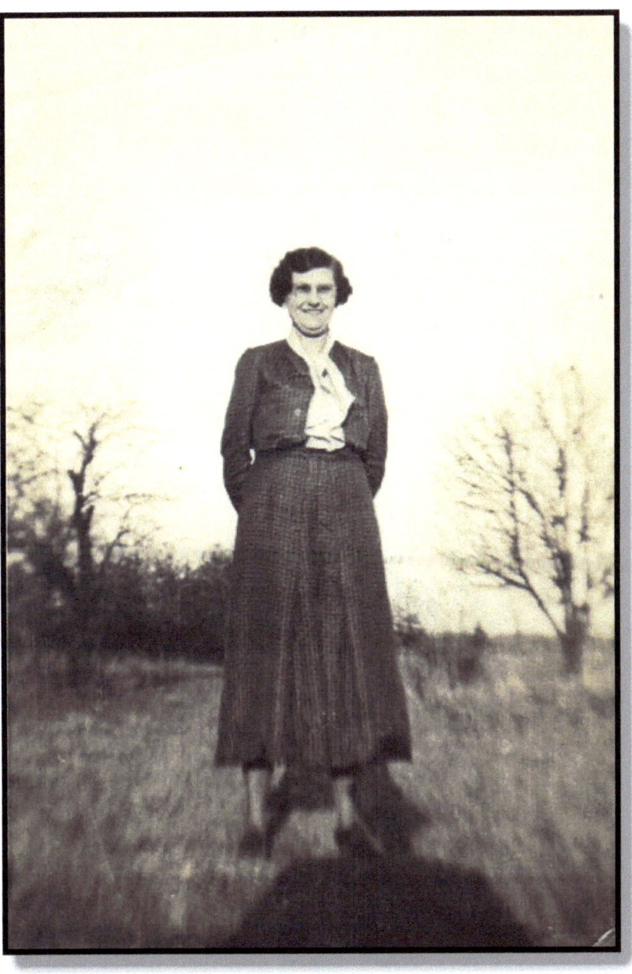

**1. Margaretha "Maggie" (Meyer) Minor, Disfarmer's sister circa 1932. This photo was taken by Disfarmer near De Valls Bluff, Arkansas - note Disfarmer's shadow in foreground.**

The four concerned relatives - John, his wife, mother and grandmother - loaded into John's automobile and drove to Heber Springs.

Mr. Price told me that the four visitors arrived unannounced and walked into the front door of the Disfarmer Photography Studio off Main Street in Heber Springs. Disfarmer was in the studio and met them at the door. Disfarmer was surprised and caught off guard by the arrival of the unexpected guests. As John Price describes the scene, Disfarmer had a sort of waiting area just inside the front-door that was separated from the main studio by a picket-fence like structure that had a gate to allow people to enter the studio area. When Disfarmer encountered his sister and the other relatives that he had not seen in sometime, he quickly opened the gate in the room divider and hurriedly moved across the room -- putting as much distance as possible between him and his relatives. Then Disfarmer nervously proclaimed that he had no relatives and that they should all leave his studio immediately. Disfarmer apparently repeated this statement more than once -- that he had no relatives, that he was not a Meyer and that he had been blown by a storm into the lives of the Meyer family. Maggie, Disfarmer's very own flesh-and-blood sister and the other three relatives remained in the studio for about ten minutes, then turned and left never to see Disfarmer alive again.

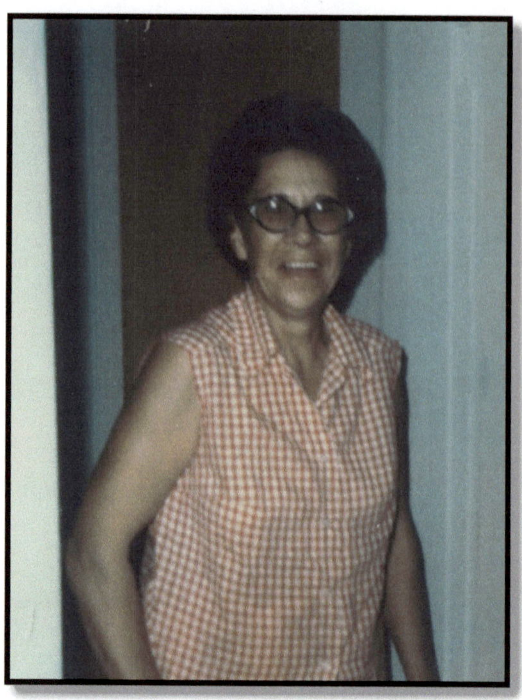

**2. Disfarmer's niece, Martha (Minor) Price / Eanes circa 1965.**

The other story about a family visit paid to Disfarmer in the Fall of 1958 is documented by Louise and Roy Fricker in Appendix 1, page 80. According to this account, Roy and Louise drove to Heber Springs to see Uncle Mike. Louise notes that Uncle Mike did not converse with her very much and she would entertain herself by looking at the many photos that he had hung on the walls of the studio while Roy and Uncle Mike visited. Louise does not indicate how long the visit lasted. She wrote that when they were ready to leave, that Disfarmer did something out of the norm and walked outside to where their car was parked. She said that Mike would usually remain inside the studio. Ms. Fricker also noted that Disfarmer did something else that was highly unusual – he shook both their hands in the parking lot while saying goodbye. Louise explains that since Cleburne County was "dry" meaning the sale of beer and liquor was against the law, that Roy always brought beer to give to Uncle Mike since he liked beer. She says that Roy handed a couple of cans of beer to Mike and he took one in each hand. Roy then asked Uncle Mike if Roy could make his picture with a camera he brought on the trip. Disfarmer consented. So Uncle Mike then placed both hands behind his back so the beer was out of sight and Roy snapped his photo. This photo appears to be the last photo made of Mike Disfarmer before his death. Perhaps Disfarmer knew that the end was near for him and decided to say goodbye to Roy and Louise by following them to the parking lot and allowing them one last photo.

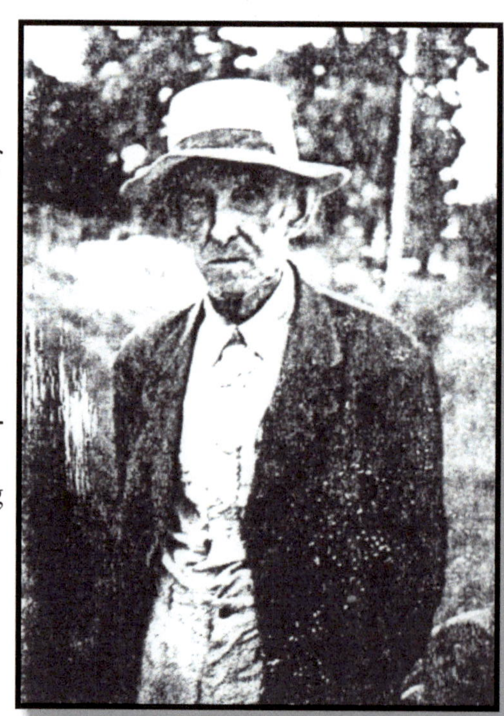

**3. Mike Disfarmer photo taken in the Fall of 1958 by Roy Fricker – believed to be the last photo taken of Disfarmer.**

The starkly contrasting behavior exhibited by Disfarmer during these encounters with his family from De Valls Bluff is at first baffling. Why would he give the cold shoulder to his sister and niece in one instance but then act more cordial with his nephew, Roy. Todd Minor, the third removed nephew of Disfarmer offers a plausible explanation. When I discussed this situation with Todd, he commented that the beer was likely the key. Todd noted that Roy Fricker, a beer drinker himself, apparently always took beer to Uncle Mike. Given Disfarmer's appetite for beer, he certainly would not alienate himself from family bearing such a gift. I suspect that Disfarmer had a stronger bond with Roy Fricker, his nephew, than he had with his sister. It appears that Roy enjoyed having a beer or two with Uncle Mike. This suggests that Roy was not judgmental of Disfarmer's lifestyle whereas it appears that Disfarmer's sister, Maggie, was more religious and frowned on the consumption of alcohol. Maggie's attitude about religion and alcohol may have made it much easier for Disfarmer to turn his back on her when she made her final visit to his Heber Springs studio.

In early August, 1959, Lesby Davis, an acquaintance of Disfarmer's, while visiting with Cartel Haywood, owner of the grocery store across Main Street from the photography studio, inquired whether he had seen Disfarmer recently. Mr. Haywood noted that he had not seen Disfarmer in a few days. The two men decided to check on Disfarmer so they walked across Main Street to his studio and "forced the door open."[29] They found Disfarmer dead behind a counter lying on some newspapers. It appeared that had been dead for several days.[30] Disfarmer's date of death is listed as August 5, 1959.

Some researchers have suggested that Disfarmer died penniless and was buried by the County as an indigent. It has also been reported that the local mortician decided it appropriate to purchase a simple headstone to mark the grave of the eccentric photographer who had lived in worked in their community for some 45 years. In fact, Disfarmer was not a pauper after all. Before his death, Disfarmer had appointed his brother, Charley, to be the Administrator of his estate. At his death, Disfarmer's estate before expenses amounted to $18,146.80. His brother, Charley, who was living in California, asked that the court to name another administrator. U.S. Hensley, President of Arkansas National Bank of Heber Springs was appointed. From the gross estate, the court appointed administrator and legal fees were paid, his debts were settled, his burial expenses and taxes were paid, leaving a net estate of $14,850 to be disbursed to his heirs. The proceeds of Disfarmer's estate went in equal parts to his sister, Maggie, in De Valls Bluff, Arkansas, his sister, Anna, and his brother, Charley, both living in California, and the families of his deceased brother, Andrew, and his deceased sisters, Barbara and Mary, all residing in Arkansas.[31] This story was confirmed by Todd Minor in a telephone conversation with Delphus Klinger, the son of William Klinger, the second husband of Maggie (Meyer) Minor / Klinger. According to Delphus Klinger, the house currently standing on the farm once owned by Theodore Hursley Minor was built in 1959 by Maggie (Meyer) and her second husband, William Klinger, with $2,475 received from the Estate of Mike Disfarmer.

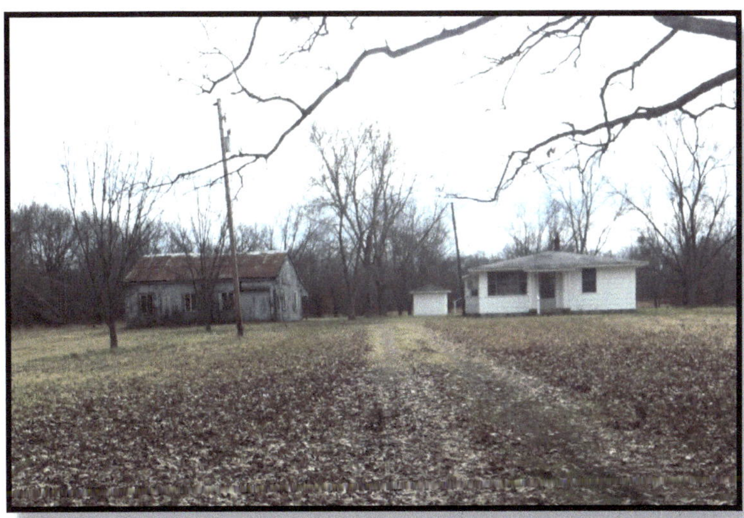

**4. This white, concrete block house (right) now sits on the land once occupied by the home of Maggie (Meyer) and her first husband, Theodore Hursley Minor, where Disfarmer's mother, Margaretha (Weidenhammer) Meyer, lived her final few years. According to Todd Minor and James C. Minor, Jr., the house above was built in 1959 by Maggie (Meyer) and her second husband, William Klinger with $2,475 received from the Estate of Mike Disfarmer.**

At the Disfarmer estate sale, Joe Albright, a former mayor of Heber Springs, a realtor and photography buff, hoping to acquire some camera equipment for his collection, purchased the contents of Disfarmer's studio including 4,000 glass plate negatives for a grand sum of $5.00 (only 3,000 were ultimately salvaged). While rummaging through the glass plates, Albright found $8,000 in savings bonds and several hundred dollars in cash.[32] It is unclear if this money was included in the Disfarmer estate before settlement with the heirs.

There was no fanfare at Disfarmer's death -- no large outpouring of grieving friends and relatives. And that is where the story would have ended except for a twist of fate and a byproduct of the glass plate photography technique used by Disfarmer – that being the longevity of the negatives. Although of questionable value at the time, Albright held onto the plates and did not destroy them. These plates were eventually purchased by Peter Miller in the early 1970's who showed them to Julia Scully, then editor of *Modern Photography* magazine. Miller and Scully published a couple of books showcasing Disfarmer's work and orchestrated a key exhibition. And as they say, the rest is history. Disfarmer's reputation as one America's most significant portrait photographers was sealed. His legacy did not die with him in 1959, but will live on in perpetuity due to the significance of his work in documenting the lives of rural people during a historically significant period -- 1939 to 1945 -- the post-depression, pre-war and war era, a period which is marked by a scarcity of such insightful photographs.

*"As a matter of fact, we are none of us above criticism; so let us bear with each other's faults."*

— L. Frank Baum, The Marvelous Land of Oz

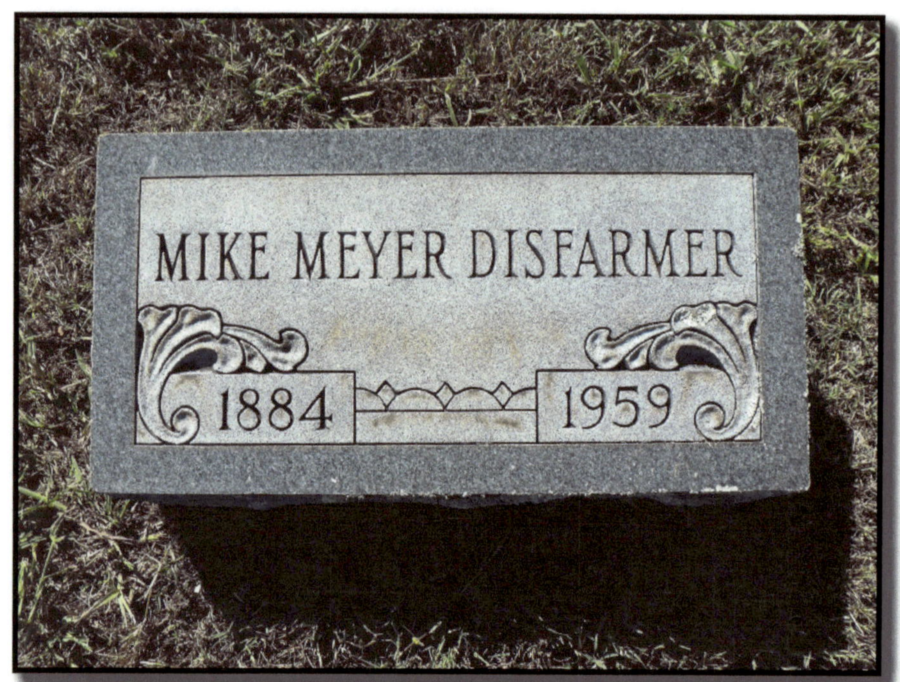


**5. Disfarmer's grave marker in a Heber Springs, Arkansas cemetery.**

**NOTES**

[29] Louise Fricker, "Disfarmer Biographical Sketch," Appendix 1, page 84.

[30] Julia Scully and Peter Miller, Text by Julia Scully, Disfarmer: The Heber Springs Portraits 1939 - 1946, Thomas Todd Company, 1976.

[31] Louise Fricker, pp. 83-85.

[32] According to a first-hand account by Todd and James Minor, Jr., Disfarmer did not trust banks after having lived through the Great Depression.

# Chapter IX. Man Behind the Camera: A Psychological Profile

*"I am Oz, the Great and Terrible,"*
*spoke the Beast, in a voice that was one great roar.*
*Who are you, and why do you seek me?"*

— L. Frank Baum, The Wonderful Wizard of Oz

*"Narcissists can have a wonderful façade, much like the Wizard in the Wizard of Oz. He was just a lonely little man behind a curtain with fabulous illusions, smoke and mirrors."*[33]

— Dorothy McCoy, Narcissistic Personality Disorder

Two things have been widely written about Disfarmer since the discovery of his photographs in the early 1970's: 1) the purity and quality of his photographic portraits of ordinary, working-class people during a historically significant period and 2) his odd, idiosyncratic, gruff, hermit-like persona. The question often raised by researchers and fans alike is, "How can someone with such apparent disdain for people take such insightful and thought-provoking photographs?" Surely, we misunderstand the man behind the camera. Surely, Disfarmer is not the "town crackpot" that scares the local children. It certainly must be that researchers and others trying to learn about Disfarmer have come to incorrect conclusions about the man.

The images developed from the negatives of his life must be out of focus. The two images we have of Disfarmer just do not mesh -- one image we have is based on the perceived empathy projected by his work -- the other being the image of the "town odd-ball" we have based on his life in Heber Springs. Disfarmer has been likened to the "Boo Radley" character in the novel *To Kill a Mockingbird* by Harper Lee. This moniker has stuck like glue.

In the Harper Lee novel, the neighborhood children, having never really seen Boo Radley, imagine that he is a monster that kills and eats small animals with his bare hands. When Scout finally meets the real Boo after he saved her brother's life, she gains a new appreciation for Boo as a nice man or guardian angel. Many fans of Disfarmer have held onto a vision that this surely must be the case with Disfarmer.

Perhaps people having not known the real Disfarmer would find that he was truly a nice person that really liked people. Surely, people just misunderstood him because he was reclusive and hermit-like. Perhaps he was simply a photographic genius that had eccentricities like many other well-known geniuses and that he had poor people skills. I will now attempt to shine a light on the man behind the camera so that we can truly gain insight into this photographic "wizard."

Remember as a child having traced a picture by connecting the numbered dots? When enough of the dots are connected, a child will quickly shout out the character's true identity. My insight into Disfarmer is much like a "connect-the-dots" drawing. As we connect the dots on the abstract picture in front of us, at some point we can surmise that we have a match to the only real identity that fits the pattern of dots. I have presented the dots on the abstract page thus far -- now I will attempt to connect the dots.

### The Little Man Syndrome

Many of us are familiar with the narcissistic personality. In the pop song "Your So Vain," Carly Simon succinctly describes a classic narcissist whom many believe to have been Mick Jagger, the lead singer of the iconic rock band, the Rolling Stones. What most of us may not know is that there is a clinical personality disorder called "Narcissistic Personality Disorder" or NPD which is an unhealthy variation of narcissism. "People with these [narcissistic personality] disorders have intense, unstable emotions and a distorted self-image."[34] Those suffering from NPD have a highly inflated sense of self or an intense feeling of superiority but this appearance is a facade for deep-seated insecurities and low self-esteem. One hallmark of those suffering from NPD is a total lack of empathy for others combined with the guilt-free ability to take advantage of others solely to fulfill their own selfish needs.

One of the several NPD sub-types defined by David M. Allen, M.D.[35] is the "little man syndrome."[36] Dr. Allen notes that "the little man syndrome" is "...seen primarily in males, but as gender equality has evolved, it is beginning to be seen more and more, in a slightly different form, in females." He goes onto note that "[g]ender role conflicts once again are the main culprit."

Dr. Allen lays out circumstances that can lead to the development of the NPD "little man syndrome":

> *"In this situation, a mother who may have been taught as a child to be dependent on men and defer to men for most major decisions has married a man who is inadequate in some way. She may describe him as "never there for me." He may be a poor provider due to a general unwillingness to work hard, a serial philanderer, a hound dog hanging around her door (apologies to Lieber, Stoller, and Willie Mae "Big Mama" Thornton), or may even desert the family altogether.*
>
> *She then apparently turns to her son to take care of her in all the ways his father did not. However, the son fails in this role for two reasons. One, he is probably too young and simply lacks the capabilities to look after her; he probably needs his mother to take care of him. Second, and more importantly, the mother seems to resent his attempts at looking after her and subverts them. The reason for this is that she really is not - nor does she really want to be - as dependent as she may appear to be. The more the son tries to meet her needs, the more the mother emasculates him.*
>
> *The double message in this situation is that the mother will build up the ego of her son at first (which leads to his apparent grandiosity) but then she figuratively castrates him. She acts like what therapists used to call a help-rejecting complainer.*
>
> *A striking example involved the case of an elderly woman who broke her hip after a fall in the bathroom and could not get up. Her son was right in the hallway next to the bathroom, but the bathroom door was locked. She refused to open it so her son could help her, however, explaining that she "did not want to bother" him."*[37]

The profile presented by Dr. Allen fits neatly with the pattern of disjointed dots presented by what we know about Disfarmer's life. We don't know much about the relationship between Disfarmer's mother, Margaretha, and his father, Martin Meyer. Nor do we know whether Disfarmer's father exemplified any of the "husband" traits described by Dr. Allen. We do know that Martin uprooted his large family in 1892 and moved them a great distance from Indiana to Arkansas to take up farming in an unfamiliar place and culture. Shortly thereafter in 1898, Martin Meyer died at the age of 52 leaving his large family without a patriarch and primary bread-winner. Margaretha was left as the head-of-household in a new land with primary responsibility of caring for a farm and large family. Unlike many other women thrown into such circumstances, Margaretha Meyer chose not to re-marry for economic self-preservation or for love.

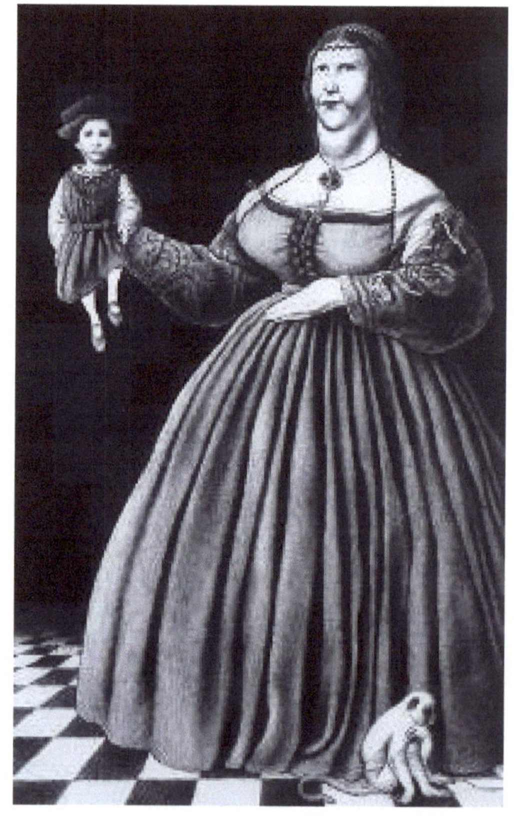

**1. Illustration from Psychology Today.**

Disfarmer, age 14, being the oldest male son living at home at the time, suddenly found himself becoming the "man of the house." According to Dr. Allen and other psychologists, the adolescent stage is critical in the development of a person into normal adulthood. Circumstances suggest that Disfarmer may have felt pressure from his mother to become the main provider for the family. He appears ill equipped to assume such responsibility. Disfarmer did not have a predilection for farming. We do not know his educational status but its likely he only finished the eighth grade. One researcher has reported that Disfarmer worked for a while in Stuttgart helping in the rice fields and as a night watchman at a rice mill.[38] The untimely death of his father and the impact this had on Disfarmer's journey into manhood was no doubt dramatic and life-altering.

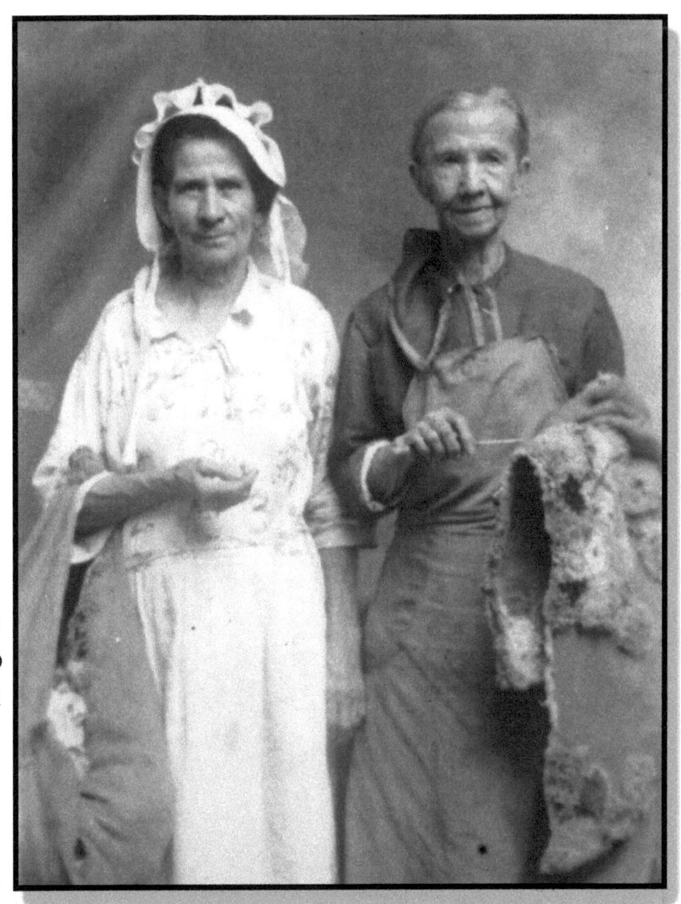

**2. Disfarmer's mother, Margaretha (Weidenhammer) Meyer (right), with an unidentified friend (left) circa 1922. Photo was made by Disfarmer in his home studio.**

We do not know about the true nature of the relationship between Disfarmer and his mother. What we do know is that Disfarmer was never married and lived with his mother for over 45 years until age and health forced her to move in with her daughter some two counties removed from Heber Springs. Was Margaretha domineering? Was she beholden to her son for his protection of her but was she also resentful and unwilling to be dependent on him? Did she feed his ego by encouraging him in his photographic endeavors but then turn around and make disparaging comments? We are left to speculate on the true nature of their relationship.

From a review of known photographs of Disfarmer throughout his life, we find no pictures of him with any known love interests or "significant others." We do see Disfarmer in various photos with his sister, Anna, his cousin, Pearl, or his brother, Charley (see Chapter 11). In most photos taken in his early adulthood, Disfarmer is nattily attired in the fashion of the day -- usually sporting a fashionable hat. From these photos, we can clearly see that Disfarmer liked to stand out and be the center of attention. Also, recall the story related in Chapter 6 about the home-made radio and a possible motive attributed to Disfarmer of seeking attention from his neighbors for his ability to build and own the hottest technology of the day. These facts strongly suggest that Disfarmer suffered from the NPD trait of needing to project a grandiose image.

From the demise of the "Penrose & Meyer Photography Studio" partnership, we can glean additional insight into the Disfarmer psyche from the failed business venture. A caption beneath the photo of his former partner, George A. Penrose obtained from the Palmer School of Chiropractic 1923 yearbook, states "Generous amounts of tact, humor, unselfishness and patience" were George's attributes. For George's wife, Edith L. (Kornbaum) Penrose from the same yearbook, we learn that she was "[s]weet prompting unto kindest deeds are in her very looks." Both of these insights paint a picture of a middle-aged couple that surely must have been desirable, decent people with which to have been in partnership. Yet the partnership was dissolved after seven years. I propose that Disfarmer's personality was the wedge that splintered the partnership.

Next, we have the "fact is stranger than fiction" account of his name change from Meyer to Disfarmer which occurred about two years after his mother's death. Was this dramatic event triggered by Disfarmer's NPD-driven need to change his identity? Could he no longer tolerate living as Mike Meyer, the son of a farmer following the death of his co-dependent mother? The puppeteer was dead -- he was finally freed to be "reborn" as Mike Disfarmer, the photographer.

Shortly after his mother's death and a full three years before he legally changed his name, he apparently wrote letters to several of his nieces and nephews, informing them that he was not truly their uncle. One of these letters is in the possession of Toba Tucker.[39] In the letter dated January 29, 1936 to his nephew, Disfarmer relayed the bizarre story he would later use in his court pleading for the name change. He was not born a "Meyer" but was blown by a tornado to the doorsteps of the Meyer family home in Indiana.

The letter contained embellishments to the far-fetched story which were not included in his 1939 court pleading. Disfarmer wrote that the real uncle was carried away and killed by the same tornado that blew him to the Meyers. According to the Richard D. Woodward's account:

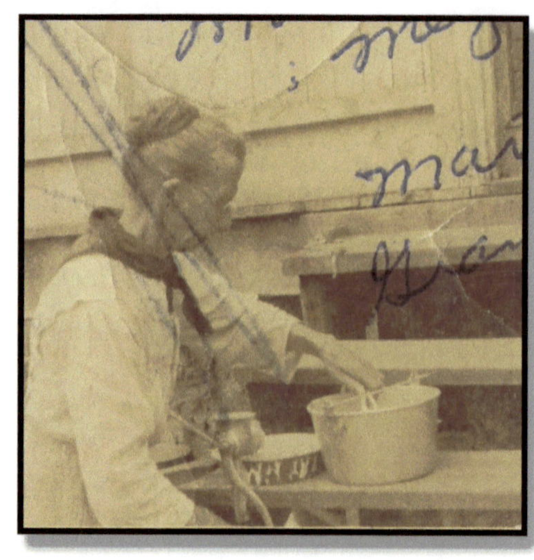

**3. Disfarmer's mother, Margaretha (Weidenhammer) Meyer, making sausage on a her back porch in Heber Springs circa 1925**

> *"'The remains of this other Mike Meyer were found—'a little piece of his dress, little pieces of bones'—and given to his real mother 'who called it her little Mike and huged [sic] it and wept.' She then put this bundle into a big doll, 'played with it and huged [sic] and loved it and called it her little Mike.' The bundle was supposed to be buried with Meyer's grandmother (a woman named Margretha [sic] Weidenhammer). The photographer Mike Meyer was never told about this secret, however, and so burned the bundle and the doll and 'threw the Ashes into the Ditch in front of my studio.'"*[40]

This facet of the story has uncanny overtones of the profile described by Dr. Allen for the "little man" as being like a puppet or doll being manipulated by the mother figure.

During the "Disfarmer Photography Studio" phase, his interactions with his photographic subjects is well documented. People, primarily "out-of-town" residents of the county, would show up at the Main Street studio on a Saturday trip to town and decide to have their photos made. Surely the patrons had heard or knew from prior visits that the photographer was odd-acting and unfriendly. Children were undoubtedly intimidated by this gruff, little man. He would simply show the subjects where to stand, not spending any time on posing them. He did not tinker with the lighting. He would not cajole them into smiling. He did not adjust their clothing or suggest they wear their Sunday clothes, if they had any, as opposed to their everyday work clothes. Disfarmer would simply step behind the camera and with little or no warning -- he would abruptly snap the photo.

One of the hallmarks of the NPD "little man syndrome" is quite evident in this description of Disfarmer's studio behavior -- that being a lack of empathy for other people. These accounts of Disfarmer's interactions with his subjects in the studio suggest he had no desire to provide a positive experience for his customers. His long-time assistant, Bessie Utley, is reported to have said Disfarmer never provided any sort of thank you to his customers. Another hallmark trait of those suffering from NPD, is the ability to exploit people in the fulfillment of personal gratification. These negative traits associated with NPD may actually have been long-term positives for Disfarmer, the photographer.

This lack of empathy and exploitive behavior likely contributed to Disfarmer's legacy as a photographic genius. Disfarmer likely was not concerned in the least about how his subjects appeared in his photos. Disfarmer was singularly focused on snapping the photo, developing and printing the photo and getting paid.

The genesis for my connecting the dots of Disfarmer's life to the "little man syndrome" was triggered by the first-person account relayed to me by John Price, Disfarmer's great-nephew, that is described in greater detail in Chapter 8. Briefly, in about 1958, Disfarmer's sister, Maggie; Maggie's daughter, Martha; Martha's son, John and John's wife, Lillian Mae; drove in John's car to Heber Springs to check on Maggie's estranged brother, Disfarmer. On seeing his sister, niece and grand-nephew, Disfarmer moved quickly across the room, placing distance and a physical barrier between him and his relatives. He repeatedly told the unexpected visitors that he did not have any relatives and recounted the bizarre story told in his motion to the court requesting a name change. Disfarmer told his relatives to leave and they left, never to see him again.

Prior to my conversation with Mr. Price, I was in the same camp as many others that surely the bizarre story of Disfarmer's name change and his odd behavior must have been fabricated. However after hearing a first person account from a relative who was present in the same room with Disfarmer during this surreal, face-to-face encounter between Disfarmer and his blood kin, I became persuaded that following the death of his mother, Disfarmer underwent a dramatic transformation. This first person account from John Price and confirmed by his wife, Lillian Mae, who was also present at the odd encounter with Disfarmer, leaves but one answer -- Disfarmer's true mental state that had been somewhat suppressed for years fully surfaced following the death of his mother. The likelihood that Disfarmer was suffering from the NPD "little man syndrome" helps connect many of the dots in the picture puzzle of his life. This clinical condition would explain many of Disfarmer's actions both as a person and as a photographer.

Following is a brief listing of other famous visual and performing artists who are suspected of being narcissists:

| | | |
|---|---|---|
| Pablo Picasso | Paul Gauguin | Charlie Chaplin |
| Peter Sellers | Joan Crawford | Marlon Brando |
| Lee Liberace | | |

And the following quotes provide additional insights into Narcissistic Personality Disorder:

*"I don't care what you think unless it is about me."*
— Kurt Cobain. Lead Singer of *Nirvana*

*"The greater the artist, the greater the doubt. Perfect confidence is granted to the less talented as a consolation prize."*
— Robert Hughes

*"It is far better to be feared than loved."*
— The red queen in Alice in Wonderland

*Half the harm that is done in this world*
*Is due to people who want to feel important*
*They don't mean to do harm*
*But the harm does not interest them.*
*Or they do not see it, or they justify it*
*Because they are absorbed in the endless struggle*
*To think well of themselves.*
— T. S. Eliot

*"A sociopath is one who sees others as impersonal objects to be manipulated to fulfill their own narcissistic needs without any regard for the hurtful consequences of their selfish actions."*
— R. Alan Woods [2013]

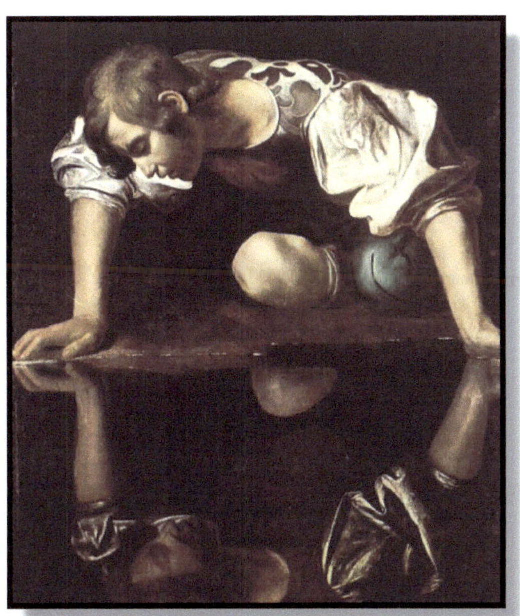

**4. Painting of "Narcissus" by Caravaggio.**

*"The mother gazes at the baby in her arms, and the baby gazes at his mother's face and finds himself therein...provided that the mother is really looking at the unique, small, helpless being and not projecting her own expectations, fears, and plans for the child. In that case, the child would find not himself in his mother's face, but rather the mother's own projections. This child would remain without a mirror, and for the rest of his life would be seeking this mirror in vain."*
— Donald Woods Winnicott

## NOTES

---

[33] Personality Blog, Narcissistic Personality Disorder, Published on 14 August 2008 by Dorothy McCoy.

[34] "Narcissistic Personality Disorder," WebMD Medical Reference, American Psychological Association: "Personality." Reviewed by Joseph Goldberg, MD on May 31, 2012; © 2012 WebMD, LLC., <http://www.webmd.com/mental-health/narcissistic-personality-disorder>.

[35] David M. Allen, M.D., is a Professor of Psychiatry at the University of Tennessee, and author of several books on personality disorders and dysfunctional families.

[36] David M. Allen, M.D., "The Family Dynamics of Narcissistic Personality Disorder and of Psychosomatic Illnesses / How can you be grandiose and feel inferior simultaneously?", Psychology Today, published October 17, 2011 by David M. Allen, <http://www.psychologytoday.com/blog/matter-personality/201110/the-family-dynamics-narcissistic-personality-disorder-and-psychosomat>.

[37] David M. Allen, M.D.

[38] Julia Scully and Peter Miller, Disfarmer: The Heber Springs Portraits, 1939-1946, 1976, p. 2.

[39] Richard Woodward, Disfarmer: A Biography, <http://disfarmer.org/Disfarmer520Bio.htm>.

[40] Richard Woodward.

# Chapter X. Cameras, Equipment, Supplies and Technique

*"A baby has brains, but it doesn't know much. Experience is the only thing that brings knowledge, and the longer you are on earth the more experience you are sure to get."*

— L. Frank Baum, The Wonderful Wizard of Oz

The Eastman Kodak Company was the Apple Inc. equivalent in the late 19th and early 20th centuries, George Eastman was its Steve Jobs and Rochester, New York was its Silicon Valley. (See the Vignette: Rochester Camera and Lens Companies.) In Rochester, George Eastman founded the Eastman Dry Plate Company in 1881 which became the Eastman Kodak Company in 1889. And just like Jobs, Eastman was an inventor of new technologies but it was his marketing genius[41] that allowed the company to become such a powerful and dominant consumer brand for approximately 100 years. Eastman, through his own inventions or through the inventions of others which he often acquired and then successfully marketed, brought photography to the masses. (See the Vignette: The Eastman Kodak Company.) What was once a technology available only to elite, wealthy gentlemen or to serious professionals like Matthew Brady, suddenly became accessible to literally millions of middle class people, including women and children.

These early, 20th Century, amateur photographers that were cult-like users of Eastman's products became known as "Kodakers." Mike Disfarmer himself appears to have been one of those "Kodakers." He truly embraced several of the Kodak break-through technology products on which he built and sustained his small-town photography business. Disfarmer also appears to have standardized on the use of very limited set of tools in his trade from which he never deviated. This allowed him to become very proficient in the use of cameras, glass plates, papers and developers. Because of the remoteness of Heber Springs where his studio was located, he likely ordered cameras and accessories; glass plates; developing chemicals and photographic paper stock via mail order from the Eastman Kodak Company. Following is brief overview of the elements of Disfarmer's commercial photography business when known as well as some speculation on those elements that are not known with certainty.

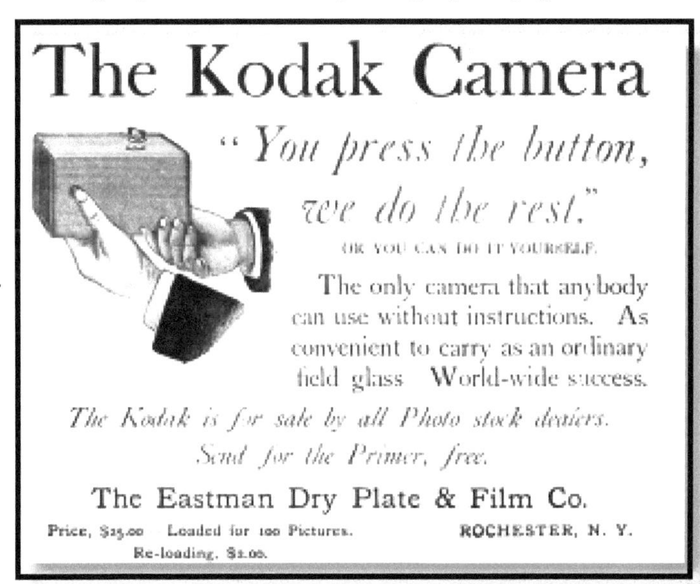


**1. An 1880's ad promoting the brownie type camera that came pre-loaded with a 100 exposure roll of photographic paper that was returned by mail to the company for processing. The company would then reload the camera and return via mail to the customer.**

**Cameras**

Known:

- Kodak No. 3-A Folding Brownie Camera Model A (see cover photo self-portrait of Disfarmer); manufactured from 1909 to 1915 (variations in the Folding Pocket Kodak "F.P.K" line were sold until 1934); pictures 3 ¼" x 5 ½"; original price: $10-$12 (later models priced from $20.00 to $109.50 depending on features), approximately 114,000 made.[42]

The No. 3-A Folding Brownie camera and its sister variant the Folding Pocket Kodak ("3A FPK") were like the Apple iPhone® of its day. The 3-A Folding Brownie and FPK lines were Eastman Kodak's postcard format camera lines meaning that the 3 ¼ by 5

½ inch negative it produced could be contact printed directly onto the back of Kodak AZO postcard stock photo paper. The format was first introduced in 1903 and continued to be marketed until 1934 under several different model numbers. As the result of new legislation, real photo postcards became a cheap, relatively fast way for the masses to send personal photos and brief messages to distant friends and relatives. (See the Vignette: Real Photo Postcards.) The Golden Age of postcards lasted approximately until the end of World War I due to a loss of postcard stock and silver from Germany and due to the arrival of the telephone.

Some of the features of the 3-A camera that made it unique and attractive to buyers were:[43]

- The Automatic shutter was equipped with a pneumatic release which prevented camera shake. Other shutter options were available at varying prices.
- It could accept roll film – Kodak 122 film was first introduced for use in this camera.
- A Combination Back accessory was available at a cost of $3.50 which adapted the camera to accept glass plates and also provided a ground glass focusing screen on which to compose and focus the image on a much larger screen as opposed to the tiny finder.
- Some versions came with a Bausch & Lomb Optical Company Rapid Rectilinear lens or a top of the line version came with the Zeiss Kodak Anastigmatic lens.
- It came with a red or black bellows and was made of a wood body with a metal lens panel covered with imitation leather; later versions were a state-of-the-art aluminum and wood body covered with heavy seal grain leather with wood accents.
- It had two tripod sockets allowing horizontal and vertical time exposures.

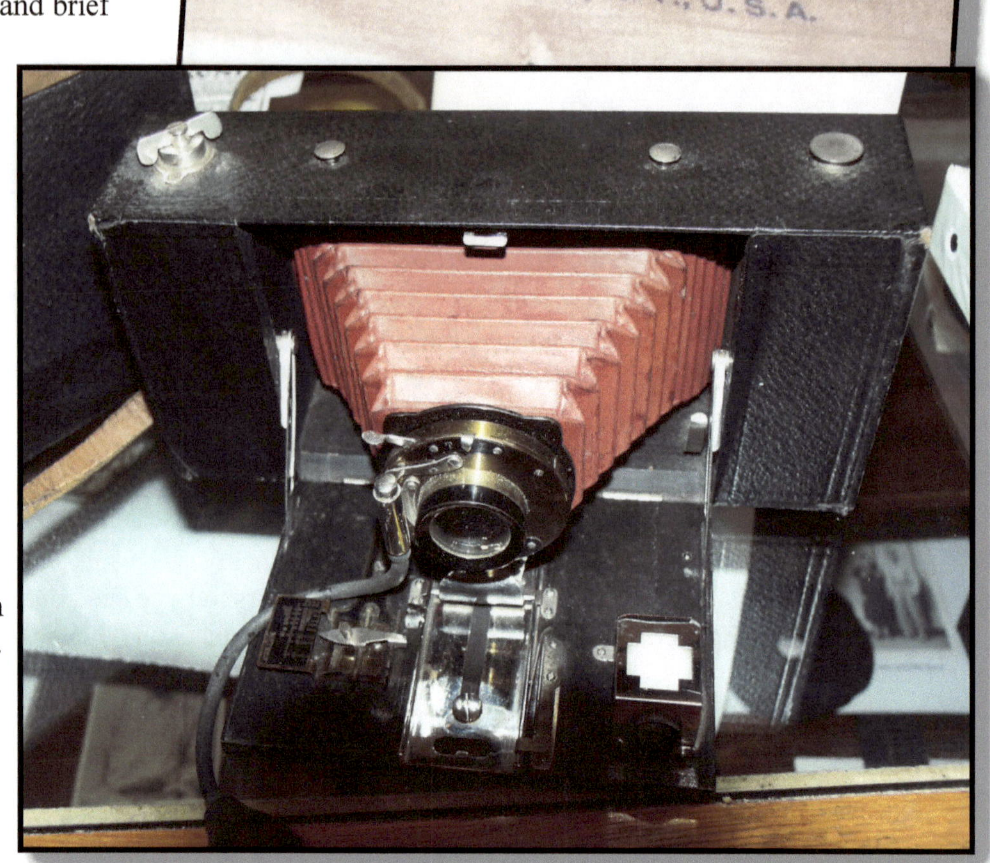


**2. Disfarmer's Kodak No. 3-A Folding Brownie camera. This camera is on display in the Cleburne County Historical Society's Museum in Heber Springs, Arkansas.**

## Supposition 4a: Possible Cameras

According to Louise Fricker, Disfarmer had "a large camera he had made, mounted in the partition between the studio and the dark room where he developed his own negatives."[44] Little else is known about this studio camera however, its unlikely that Disfarmer actually constructed such a camera.

In a June, 2013 telephone conversation with Mr. Greer Lile, a well-known professional photographer and owner of a photography museum in Little Rock, Arkansas, he speculated that Disfarmer may have utilized either a Premo or Auto Graflex camera in his studio work. Mr. Lile assisted Ms. Toba Tucker when she relocated to Heber Springs, Arkansas, to work on her book, *Heber Springs Portraits: Continuity and Change in the World Disfarmer Photographed.*

Following are some examples of the Premo and Auto Graflex cameras that may have been used by Disfarmer in his studio:

- Kodak Premo No. 8 Camera (Rochester Optical Company was acquired in 1903 by George Eastman for $330,000[45]); manufactured from 1913 to 1922, accommodated both glass plates and film; made in 3 sizes: 4" x 5", 3 ¼" x 5 ½", 5" x 7"; priced from $18.50 to $26.00.[46]
- Kodak Premo No. 12 Camera (Rochester Optical Company); manufactured from 1912 to 1921 accommodated both glass plates and film; pictures 2 ¼" x 3 ¼"; priced at $51.50.[47]
- Kodak Auto Graflex Camera (Folmer & Schwing Manufacturing Company was purchased by George Eastman in 1905); manufactured from 1908 to 1923, designed to accommodate the regular Graflex plate holders or the Graflex magazine plate holder which was able hold twelve glass plates; made in 3 sizes: 3 ¼ " x 4 ¼ " inches, 4" x 5", and 5" x 7"; priced at $114.00 in 1914.[48]

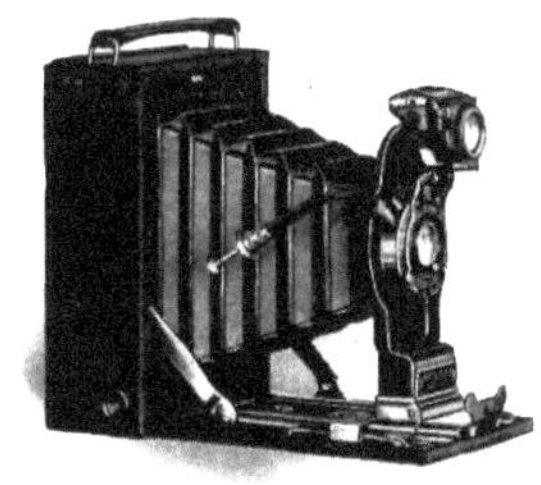


**3. Print ads from early 1920s *Kodakery* magazines promoting cameras made by companies acquired by Eastman Kodak.**

## Dry Glass Plates

## Supposition 4b: Reliance on Glass Plates

- Kodak Seed Dry [Glass] Plates, single coated, 3 ¼" x 5 ½" , price per dozen: $0.75.
- It is unknown if Disfarmer ever utilized roll film in his photography business.

A common question by those interested in Disfarmer and his photography is why he continued to rely on glass plates and the associated cameras that could accept those plates for use as negatives throughout his career? No one knows the answer to this question for certain. We are left to speculate. The most obvious answer is that he had mastered or felt comfortable with the cameras, glass plates and associated processes. It's also plausible that Disfarmer felt that glass plates were superior to roll film. Disfarmer's thinking may be best reflected in the familiar homily – "if ain't broken, don't fix it."

Another common question about Disfarmer is why the glass plate negatives recovered from his studio only date from about 1939 to about 1945? A couple of viable explanations may best be found in a 2001 article by Sandy Barrie[49] regarding the lack of survival of old glass plate negatives. The first explanation offered by Barrie is that "[i]t was standard studio procedure from the 1900's on to cull negative files every five or so years, throwing out old negatives taken at least five or more years earlier..."[50] "Most photographers from the 1900's were very commercially motivated. If it did not make money, then it was not kept."[51] Glass plates could be costly and

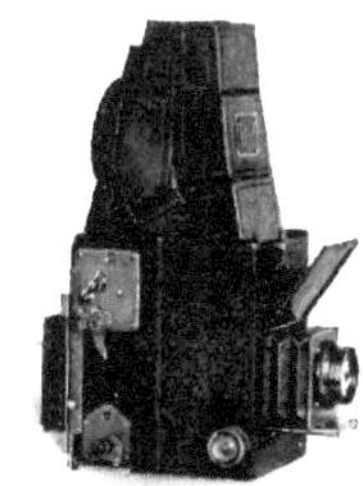

bulky to store. If the photographic subjects could not afford or did not often return for reprints, which is likely the case with Disfarmer's customers, then it made little economic sense to hold on to glass plate negatives that were more than about five years old.

Barrie offers another more plausible explanation for why no pre-1939 glass plate negatives were recovered from Disfarmer's studio. These facts also help support Ms. Julia Scully's assessment that part of the appeal of Disfarmer's photos from this time period is the relative scarcity of such photos. "The main and great destruction of photographic images happened during WWI, during the great depression and then again in WWII."[52] Before 1919, Germany was the main source of photographic silver and World War I caused silver shortages. During World War II, almost all silver was used in the war effort for silver soldering, military reconnaissance and X-ray film. Film for photo studios was highly rationed and established studios were rationed to less than half of their pre-war quotas. To recover silver for the war effort, Kodak and other such companies "would buy back old negatives for 'melting down".[53] Barrie goes on:

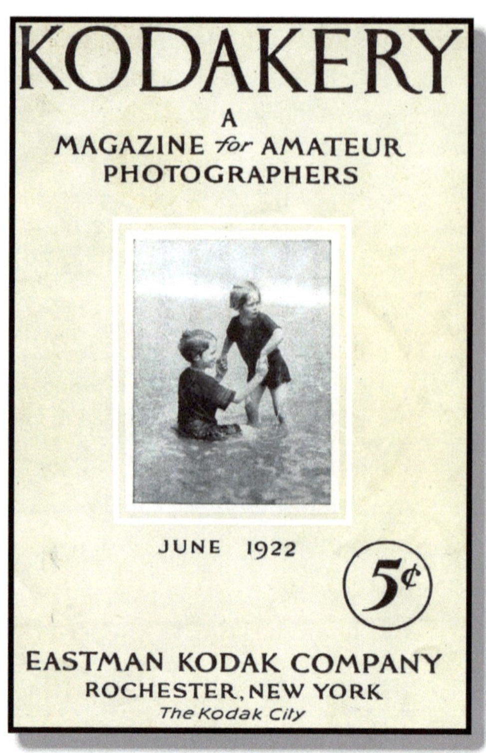


**4. Above: Amateur photographers magazine published by Kodak. Below: Velox paper ad from *Kodakery* magazine.**

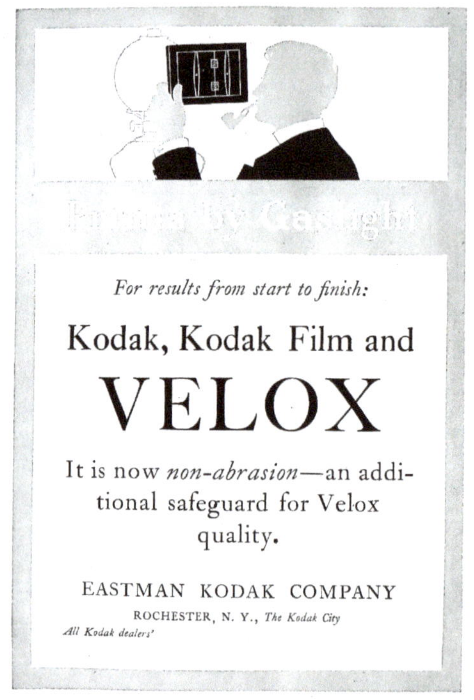


"*But selling of negative files hit a high point during the great depression, when photographers found that the old negatives were about all they could sell for their silver content, and almost no customers could afford to buy reprints anyway. I have hundred[s] of great stories about that era, and many have been published. One owner of a silver recovery firm in the great depression in America published this story in the 1960's where he remembers buying negatives of Abraham Lincoln and other Civil War negative files to melt down!*"[54]

### Photographic Paper

Known print paper preferred by Disfarmer:

- Velox Paper, 3 ¼" x 5 ½", price per dozen sheets $0.20. "Kodak VELOX paper was a very slow printing paper, producing a blue-black image, suitable for contact printing only, where the negative is placed in contact with the paper to produce a print of the same size. Kodak discontinued the manufacture of Velox paper in 1968."[55] "Velox Paper was first manufactured by Dr. L.H. Baekeland in 1894. It was a slow, silver chloride paper which could be handled before exposure even under weak electric light or yellow gaslight. In a photographic darkroom it could be handled under a bright yellow safelight. It later became known as 'Gaslight' or 'Contact' paper. In 1899 George Eastman bought the Velox process from Dr. Baekeland‡ for $1 million, and started to manufacture Velox paper in the U.S.A."[56] Velox paper was one of the earliest forms of "Development" paper. Prior to its advent, "Albumen" or "Printing Out Paper" or "P.O.P." was in use.[57]

‡ Dr. Leo Hendrick Baekeland was an industrial chemist who went on to develop an early plastic material that became know as "Bakelite" which was used in the manufacture of early telephones, auto steering wheels and other products. Encyclopedia Britannica, Inc., 2013, <http://www.britannica.com/EBchecked/topic/48620/Leo-Hendrick-Baekeland#ref22160>.

- AZO Postcard Paper, 3 ¼" x 5 ½". AZO was "one of the popular photographic papers used for printing"[58] real photo postcards and was also another popular form of silver chloride paper manufactured by the Eastman Kodak Company. Ansel Adams used silver chloride paper to make his contact prints.[59] AZO paper had several advantages over other papers.[60]
  1) Silver chloride paper seemingly lasts forever with a shelf-life of over 40 years without having to be refrigerated or frozen.
  2) Contrast control is easy to master using Amidol and a water bath.
  3) A long tonal scale allows AZO to do a better job of delivering grays than most other black and white papers.
  4) It is easier to use than other papers, especially enlarging papers. It takes less time to "arrive at the final print" because it needs less "dodging/burning than enlarging papers."[61]

Another insight that can be gleaned by examining Disfarmer's "real photo postcards" is that we can easily date the photos by examining the stamp boxes on the back of the postcards which varied over time. The stamp box is rectangle in shape with "AZO" centered on each side of the box with different corner symbols that indicate manufacturing dates for the paper as follows:

- Four triangles pointing up in corners – manufactured 1904 to 1918.
- Two triangles pointing up and two pointing down in corners – 1918 to 1930.
- Squares in the corners – 1927 to 1940.[62]

**5. Address side of Disfarmer Real Photo Postcard (RPPC) stamped "Penrose & Meyer Photographers Heber Springs, ARK." Postcard stock is Kodak AZO paper as noted in Stamp Block.**

Disfarmer's photographs were always "contact printed" which reproduced photographic prints in the same size and dimension as the negative image. The largest negative image produced by Disfarmer being 3 ¼ by 5 ½ inches but he also utilized a camera that produced photographs that were 2 ¼ by 3 ¼ inches in size. Contact printing is a simple process in which the dry plate negative is placed in a frame next to the photographic paper and then exposed briefly to a light source – daylight or an artificial source. The photographic paper is then processed through a series of chemical baths (developer, fixative, stop or wash) to allow the image to be permanently affixed to the paper.

This simple three step process for developing monochromatic or black and white photos was the same process used in the early 1900's as it was almost 100 years later until the advent of digital photography. Disfarmer apparently never invested in an enlarger for his dark room and relied on contact printing throughout his lifetime.

**Darkroom**

## Supposition 4c: Possible Dark-Room Equipment

- Kodak Dark-Room Lamp: No. 2, 5/8 inch wick, price $1.00.

Although electrical service began in Heber Springs in 1909 with the formation of the Heber Power and Light Company, it was not until 1920 that 24-hour electrical service was provided to the rural community.[63] It is unknown how Disfarmer's darkrooms were precisely equipped at his three studio locations in Heber Springs.

The Eastman Kodak Company did provide a number of lamp accessories that would work in a darkroom that was not supplied with electricity. Kodak Velox and AZO paper, preferred by Disfarmer, had a feature and benefit marketed by the company that these could be exposed rather quickly by a number of artificial light sources such as gaslights. Although Heber Springs likely never had gaslight, it surely had residents that relied upon kerosene lamps, in addition to electrical lights.

It is curious that Disfarmer never invested in a photo enlarger to provide his customers with pictures scaled beyond the native format of his cameras. Its possible that Disfarmer was simply reacting to a lack of demand for larger prints because his customers, being of modest means, were unwilling to pay for larger prints. Its also possible that Disfarmer was unwilling to invest the extra time required to process enlarged prints of his subjects (enlarging papers require two and three minutes to develop whereas AZO stock takes less than a minute).[64] Lastly, its possible that his darkrooms were not equipped with electricity even though the utility was available in the town as early 1909.

At least two photographs made by Disfarmer were enlarged to a larger format (approximately 8 by 10 inches) about 1934. These enlargements owned by a Disfarmer relative, were made from Disfarmer negatives by Geppert Studios of Des Moines, Iowa (one of the two enlargements I examined had the Geppert Studios stamp on the back side). An article from Radio Star Magazine dated October, 1934, titled *"KMOX – Their Studios Are Crowded at Sun-up"* explains how the Disfarmer negatives of his sister, Margaret Meyer-Minor and her husband, Theodore H. Minor, came to be enlarged by a studio in Des Moines, Iowa, in 1934. In the 1920's and 1930's, a very powerful radio transmitter located in St. Louis, KMOX, a Columbia Broadcasting System (CBS) affiliate, aired a broadcast each morning except Sunday at 5:30 a.m. targeting farmers in the middle of the country. The show was a "wholesome variety" show called the "Home Folks Hour." In March, 1934, Geppert Studios ran a series of short ads during the "Home Folks Hour" offering to make picture enlargements at twenty-five cents each. Geppert Studios had to work overtime to process the 1,080 orders it received. Its likely that Disfarmer may have sent the negatives of his sister and brother-in-law to Des Moines for enlarging to be given as a gift to his sister since she was taking care of their aging mother in 1934 just before her death.

## Backdrops and Props

Penrose & Meyer Studio:

- Backdrops: 1) a Greco-roman themed backdrop and 2) a darker, mottled backdrop.
- Props: Traditional period props - chairs, stools, benches and tables.

Meyer Studio:

- Backdrops: 1) a Greco-roman themed backdrop and 2) a darker, mottled backdrop.
- Props: Unclear.
- Meyer (Disfarmer) appears to have spent considerable time outside the studio taking photos of subjects in outdoor settings.

Disfarmer Studio:

- Backdrops: 1) a light colored or white backdrop with distinctive black tape, vertical and horizontal stripes clearly visible that was on a movable partition and 2) a darker, mottled, pull-down backdrop. The light backdrop with the distinctive black tape vertical and horizontal stripes has been the subject of much speculation about why Disfarmer chose to use such an non-conventional backdrop in his studio.

  Toba Tucker, in the documentary film on Disfarmer[65] provides a very plausible explanation on why Disfarmer chose to use the distinctive white backdrop with the black stripes. Ms. Tucker believes that on cloudy days when lighting was low, that Disfarmer would use the lighter background to enhance the natural lighting provided by the skylight. This backdrop appears similar to an E.K. Blush backdrop mentioned in Chapter 3.
- Props: very limited use of props – occasional use of a bench or stool.
- Disfarmer appears to have worked primarily inside the studio during this phase.

## Vignette: Rochester Camera and Lens Companies

"The photo-optical industry in Rochester was born in 1880. In that year Bausch and Lomb began to make photographic lenses; the Rochester Optical Company began to make cameras; and George Eastman began to make [dry silver gelatin] plates."[66] Mr. Rudolf Kingslake aided by Don Lyon published a research paper in 1974 for the Rochester Photographic Historical Society titled *"The Rochester Camera and Lens Companies"* which documents the "complicated story spanning almost 100 years" of history of the myriad companies that occupied the photo-optical industry in Rochester. A version of this fascinating and insightful research publication is available on the Internet.[67] Mr. Kingslake's engrossing, historical piece suggests the magnitude of the research undertaking required to follow the veritable maze of start-ups, mergers, acquisitions and failures of these enterprises some 100 years after-the-fact.

As stated earlier, Rochester, New York, was the "Silicon Valley" in the late 19th and early 20th Century. The city was a hot-bed of inventors, entrepreneurs, engineers, technicians, marketers and risk-takers all vying to capitalize on the exploding consumer demand for photography equipment and associated supplies that occurred in the early 20th Century in the United States and Europe. Certainly George Eastman's company, the Eastman Kodak Company, is the most successful and best-known company that grew up in Rochester however, in the infancy period of the industry, the business landscape in Rochester was littered with start-up enterprises attempting to cash in on the photography "gold rush".

Just like modern day Silicon Valley, the intellectual capital – the inventors and scientists – was very mobile at the end of the 19th Century. Key personnel left one enterprise and went to a competing enterprise or started up a new enterprise. Some of these start-up enterprises were under-capitalized and went out of business or were acquired by more successful enterprises. George Eastman was a deal-maker and had excess capital which allowed him to acquire the more desirable targets, often letting the acquisitions continue to operate under their old name for a number of years. This also allowed him to eliminate the competition thereby allowing him to create a virtual monopoly in the space.

Its beyond the scope of this publication to delve deeply into the history of the photo-optical industry in Rochester. According to Kingslake, the photo-optical industry began in Rochester in 1853 when a German immigrant, John Jacob Bausch opened a tiny spectacle business that had few customers. It mushroomed from there. Following are some of the companies addressed in Kingslake's publication:

Bausch and Lomb
The Rochester Optical Co.
The Ray Camera Co.
The Monroe Camera Co.
Photostat & Rectigraph
The Photo Materials Co.
Reichanbach, Morey & Will
Eastman Kodak Co.
Graflex (Folmer & Schwing)
Elgeet
Wollensak
Vogt Optical Co.
Gundlach
Century
Ilex
Sunart & Seneca
The Crown Optical Co.
Projection Optics
Gassner and Marx
Movette
Present

## Vignette: Eastman Kodak Company

George Eastman was an amateur photographer himself in the 1870's. But at that time, photography was a very cumbersome, costly and time-consuming hobby. One of the first big breakthroughs in photography was the development of the dry-plate process for creating the "film" or negative for use in cameras. In 1880, George Eastman developed a machine that could mass-produce the new glass plates coated with the dry, silver gelatin emulsion making them camera ready. In 1881, George formed the Eastman Dry Plate Company which became Eastman Kodak Company in 1889 and is more commonly referred to as Kodak.

The next big breakthrough for Eastman came in 1888 when he patented a box camera pre-loaded with a roll of photographic paper capable of capturing 100 exposures. This event also marked "[t]he beginning of the end for dry plates."[68] Eastman marketed the pre-loaded box camera to consumers at a price of $25. After "snapping" the 100 photos, the purchaser simply mailed the entire camera, paper roll and all, to the company in Rochester, NY. There, Eastman employees removed the paper and the camera was then reloaded and returned by mail to the owner for reuse. In the meantime, the 100 photo roll of paper was developed and cut into indi-

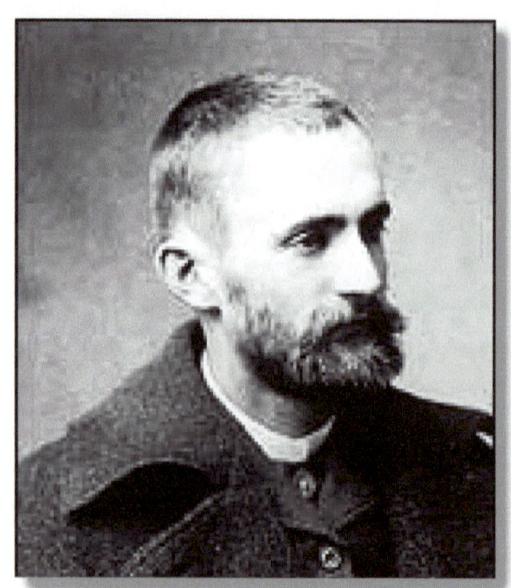

6. A young George Eastman.

vidual prints at the factory. The finished photos were then returned by mail to the amateur photographer.

The pre-loaded camera was relatively pricey and the quality of the final product was poor however, this represented a major break-through in photographic technology making it accessible to amateurs for the first time and setting off a technology revolution in the process. Eastman launched an advertising campaign featuring women and children operating the camera, and coined the memorable slogan: "You press the button, we do the rest."[69] These two events catapulted Eastman into entrepreneurial superstar status and provided the financial foundation on which his eventual conglomerate was built.

Building on the rolled paper concept, Eastman hired chemist Henry Reichenbach who eventually developed a rolled, translucent film which was patented by the company. The development of rolled film lead to the introduction of the “Brownie” box camera in 1900 which was one of the most successful consumer products of its day. In its early days, Kodak acquired a number of competitors and suppliers executing a monopolistic strategy similar to that employed by other “turn of the century” industrial titans such as Rockefeller, Carnegie and Vanderbilt. Kodak is still in existence today having survived a Chapter 11 bankruptcy proceeding which was filed in January 2012. Kodak dominated its industry throughout the 20th Century but lost its market advantage due to its failure to capitalize on new digital photography technology even though Kodak is credited with inventing the core technology now used in digital cameras.

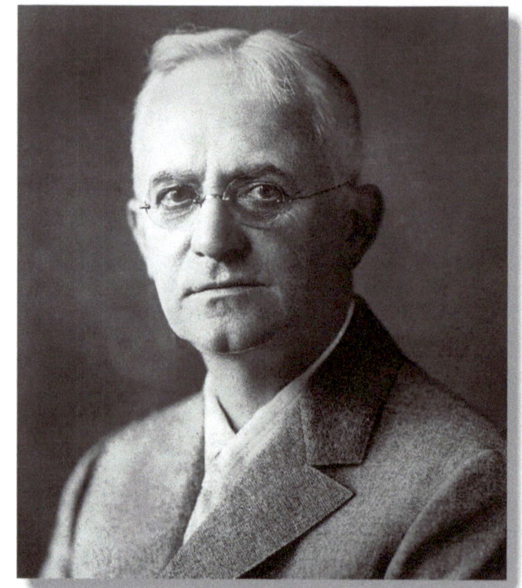

7. An older George Eastman.

George Eastman is a memorable inventor from the turn of the 19th to the 20th century but, more importantly he was a tough businessman and marketing genius. Like Henry Ford, he created a market for his new, consumer oriented photography equipment and products. “He set out to form a monopoly on photography and very nearly suc-

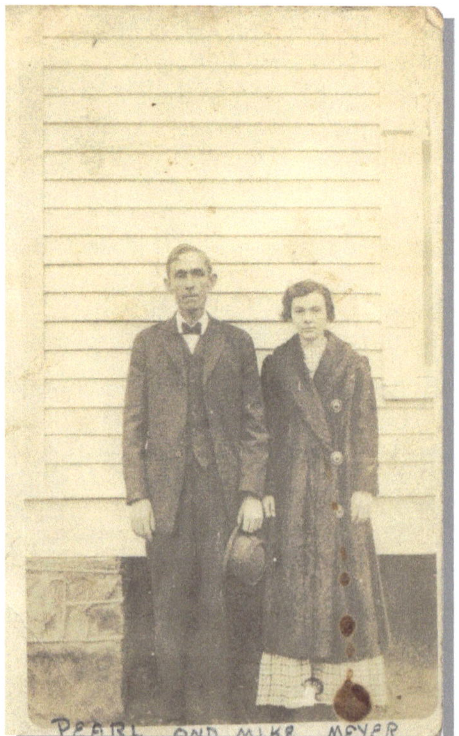


**8. Left: Real Photo Postcard (RPPC) of Mike Meyer / Disfarmer and his niece, Pearl Fricker, made behind Disfarmer’s Heber Springs home on Sugar Loaf Street, circa 1918.**

**9. Below: Address side of RPPC. Printed on Kodak AZO postcard paper stock as evidenced by stamp block in upper right-hand corner. Four triangles pointing up in corners date paper between 1904 and 1918.**

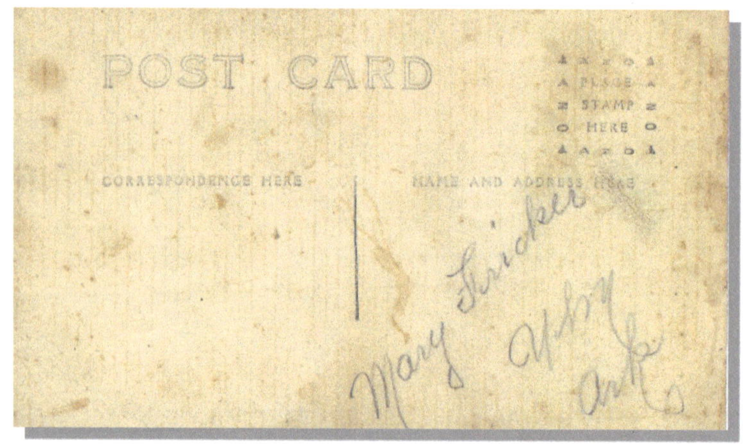

ceeded. Beyond his undeniably innovative discoveries in photographic science and engineering, his greatest achievement was in changing the psychology of photography."[70]

## Vignette: Real Photo Postcards

The term "Real Photo Postcard" ("RPPC") refers to real photographs printed directly to a postcard as opposed to commercially printed, mass produced postcards. RPPC's can be easily detected by viewing the photo side of the postcard under a magnifying glass. If the image is made up of tiny dot patterns, it was commercially printed whereas if the image is solid -- no dots – its a real photo postcard. Oftentimes, an RPPC was one-of-a-kind meaning that only one print was made from a negative.

Prior to May 19, 1898, the United States Postal Service held a monopoly on being the only entity allowed to print postcards. On that date, Congress passed the Private Mailing Card Act allowing private entities to print and produce postcards. On March 1, 1907, a second significant event occurred in the history of "penny postcards." On that date, federal legislation was passed allowing for the first time, the writing of a personal message on the address side of a postcard. Prior to that date, messages could only be written on the non-address side of the postcard. From that date forward, postcards had a line down the center of the postcard allowing a personal message to be written on the left side of the line and the intended recipients address to be written on the right side of the line. This new form of communication became the first pop culture form of text messaging and set off a postcard mailing craze that swept the nation with more than 677 million postcards being mailed in 1908.[71] [72]

**NOTES**

---

[41] Mia Fineman, "Kodak and the Rise of Amateur Photography," Heilbrunn Timeline of Art History, New York: The Metropolitan Museum of Art, 2000–, <http://www.metmuseum.org/toah/hd/kodk/hd_kodk.htm> (October 2004).

[42] "History of Kodak Cameras," Customer Service Pamphlet, Eastman Kodak Company, 1999.

[43] Scott's Photographica Collection, Eastman Kodak Company 3A Folding Pocket Camera, updated on March 12, 2002, <http://www.vintagephoto.tv/3afpk.shtml>.

[44] Louise Fricker, "Disfarmer Biographical Sketch," Appendix 1, page 81.

[45] Rudolf Kingslake, A History of the Rochester, NY Camera and Lens Companies, <http://www.graflex.org/articles/kingslake/>.

[46] "Historic Camera," Historic Camera History Librarium, 2002 – 2012, <http://www.historiccamera.com/cgi-bin/librarium2/pm.cgi?action=app_display&app=datasheet&app_id=1144>.

[47] "Historic Camera."

[48] "Historic Camera."

[49] Sandy Barrie, Old Negatives and Records / Photographers 1840 – 1940 Great Britain & Ireland, 2001, published by Ron Cosens, <http://www.cartedeviste.co.uk/faq/negatives/>.

[50] Sandy Barrie.

[51] Sandy Barrie.

[52] Sandy Barrie.

[53] Sandy Barrie.

[54] Sandy Barrie.

[55] Michael Talbert, Kodak Black & White Printing Paper pre- & post-1947, p. 1, last modified 4th June 2013, <http://www.photomemorabilia.co.uk/Kodak_Black%26White_Printing_Paper.html>.

[56] Michael Talbert. p. 3.

[57] Michael Talbert, p. 3.

[58] Martin Reed, Yesterdays Papers, 1998, revised 2004, <http://www.silverprint.co.uk/info/yespap.html>.

[59] John Bowen, "Advantages of AZO Silver Chloride Paper," Analog Photographers User Group, <http://www.apug.org/forums/forum37/67987-advantages-history-azo-silver-chloride-paper.html>.

[60] John Bowen.

[61] John Bowen.

[62] "Real Photo Postcards Stamp Boxes," <http://www.edinphoto.org.uk/0_pc_0/0_post_card_history_-_stamp_boxes.htm>.

[63] "HEBER SPRINGS COMMERCIAL HISTORIC DISTRICT, HEBER SPRINGS, CLEBURNE COUNTY," Arkansas Historic Preservation Program, <http://www.arkansaspreservation.com/historic-properties/_search_nomination_popup.aspx?id=2459>.

[64] Michael A. Smith, How to Print on 100-Year Old Paper / The AZO and Amidol Story, 1996, <http://www.michaelandpaula.com/mp/azoamidol.html>.

[65] Disfarmer: A Portrait of America, a documentary film written and produced by Public Pictures, 2010.

[66] Rudolf Kingslake.

[67] Rudolf Kingslake.

[68] Denise Ross, Gelatin Dry Plate Photography, <http://www.thelightfarm.com/Map/Books/cim/MapTopic.htm>.

[69] Mia Fineman.

[70] Denise Ross.

[71] "Postcard," Wikipedia, the free encyclopedia, last modified November 24, 2013, <http://en.wikipedia.org/wiki/Postcard>.

[72] "Real Photo Postcard," Wikipedia, the free encyclopedia, last modified September 17, 2013, <http://en.wikipedia.org/wiki/Real_photo_postcard>.

# Chapter XI. The Disfarmer Family Album

*"No matter how dreary and gray our homes are, we people of flesh and blood would rather live there than in any other country, be it ever so beautiful. There is no place like home."*

— L. Frank Baum, The Wonderful Wizard of Oz

*"I shall take the heart. For brains do not make one happy, and happiness is the best thing in the world."*

— L. Frank Baum, The Wonderful Wizard of Oz

One of the more significant questions surrounding the myth about Disfarmer's life that has remained unanswered until the publication of this biography has been whether he was largely a misunderstood character. Despite the Heber Springs townspeople's observations about his hermit-like existence and despite the well-documented "fact is stranger than fiction" story behind his petition to the court for a name change, many of his fans have clung to a belief that Disfarmer, deep down, was a people person. This group of people held the belief that in order for Disfarmer to take such soul-searching photos, surely he was just a recluse that really empathized with common people.

Some members of Disfarmer's own family believed that the crazy story about Disfarmer's name change had been made-up. Adding to the "out of focus" image that his own family possessed of Disfarmer were heirloom family photos, postcards and first-hand accounts that demonstrate that Disfarmer was in frequent contact with many of his sisters, brothers, in-laws, nieces and nephews until he reached age 51 in 1935, the year his mother died. After the matriarch of the family died, Disfarmer began to distance himself from his family, eventually ceasing virtually all contact with them. This chapter contains photographs of many of Mike Meyer / Disfarmer's family – mother, brothers, sisters, their wives and husbands, some of his nieces and nephews and great-nieces and nephews. Many of these photographs were made by Disfarmer in one of his studios, at scenic venues near Heber Springs or on one of his numerous trips to visit his family who lived in Prairie or Arkansas County.

For the first half of his life, Disfarmer appears to have been very close with his older sister, Anna, his youngest brother, Charley, and his first cousin, Pearl Fricker. This supposition is based on the fact that they were very close in age and the multiple photographs that are known to exist containing Disfarmer in combination with these relatives. It is not clear what year Anna married Dave Goodrich but their daughter, Ione, was borne on March 30, 1916. Since Anna was not living with Disfarmer and his mother in Stuttgart in 1910, she was probably married before 1910. According to a 1918 draft record, Dave and Anna, 36, were still living in Almyra, Arkansas where Disfarmer's family had first moved in Arkansas, which is about 20 miles south of Stuttgart. According to the 1920 U.S. Census, Anna, her husband, Dave, and young daughter, Ione, were living across the street from Disfarmer and their mother and must have moved there between 1918 and 1920. The 1930 Census show Anna and her husband, Dave Goodrich, living in Ajo, Pima County, Arizona. Sometime around 1933, Anna and Dave move to Santa Clara, California where she eventually dies and was buried in 1972. According to the Louise Fricker Biographical Sketch (Appendix 1), the Cleburne County Probate Court sent a share of the Disfarmer estate to Anna (Meyer) Goodrich, age 78, at 117 Gilman Street, Campbell, California.

### *Charley Meyer*

Details about Disfarmer's younger brother, Charles Heinrich Wolfgang Meyer, get a bit more sketchy following the 1900 Census when Charley was clearly living with Disfarmer, his mother and the rest of the clan. A June 5th, 1917 World War I draft registration record shows a "Charles Wilfert Meyer" who was single and living at a YMCA in San Diego, California. The draft card shows that Charles Wilfert Meyer was born on September 26, 1889, at Kellerville, Indiana. This date and place of birth are identical matches to those of Charles H. Wolfgang Meyer. The physical description matches that of Charles Wolfgang Meyer as well -- medium build, brown eyes and light brown hair. The draft card goes onto note that Charles Wilfert Meyer had reached the rank of "Sergeant" having served in the infantry for one year from the State of Arkansas. The record also notes that Charles was working as a telegrapher at the main office of Western Union in San Diego, California. These details confirm beyond a reasonable doubt that Charles Wilfert Meyer and Charles Wolfgang Meyer were, in fact, the same individual and was living in San Diego, California in 1917.

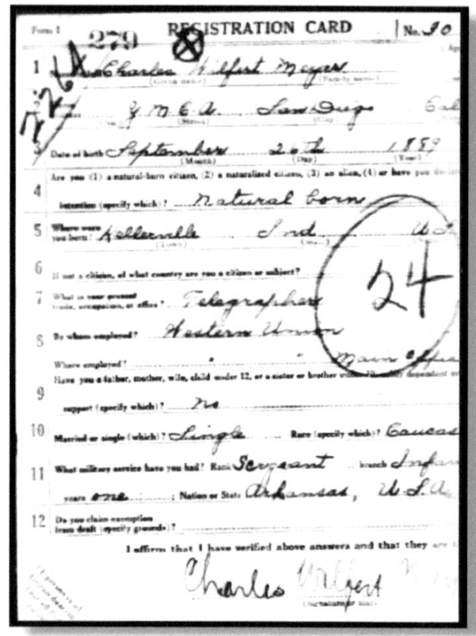

REGISTRATION CARD No. 90

279

1 Charles Wilfert Meyer (Given name) (Family name)

Y.M.C.A. San Diego (Street) (City)

Date of birth September 26th 1889 (Month) (Day) (Year)

4 Are you (1) a natural-born citizen, (2) a naturalized citizen, (3) an alien, (4) or have you declared your intention (specify which)? natural born

5 Where were you born? Kellerville Ind. U.S.A. (Town) (State)

6 If not a citizen, of what country are you a citizen or subject?

7 What is your present trade, occupation, or office? Telegrapher

8 By whom employed? Western Union

Where employed? Main office

9 Have you a father, mother, wife, child under 12, or a sister or brother under 12, solely dependent on you for support (specify which)? no

10 Married or single (which)? Single Race (specify which)? Caucasian

11 What military service have you had? Rank Sergeant branch Infantry years one; Nation or State Arkansas, U.S.A.

12 Do you claim exemption from draft (specify grounds)?

I affirm that I have verified above answers and that they are true.

Charles Wilfert Meyer (Signature or mark)

24

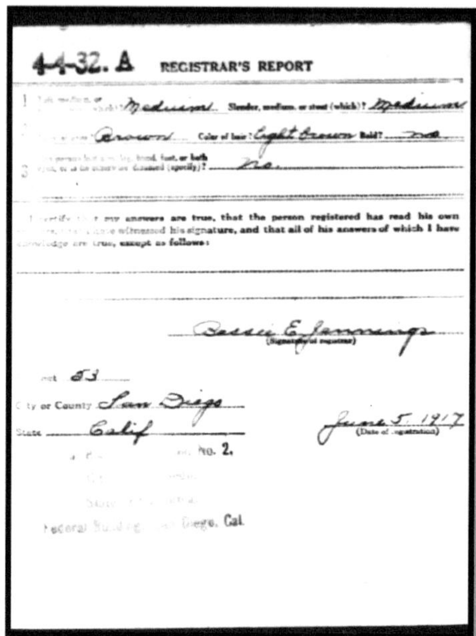

4-4-32. A REGISTRAR'S REPORT

1 Tall, medium, or short (which)? Medium Slender, medium, or stout (which)? Medium

2 Color of eyes? Brown Color of hair? Light Brown Bald? no

3 Has person lost arm, leg, hand, foot, or both eyes, or is he otherwise disabled (specify)? no

I certify that my answers are true, that the person registered has read his own answers, that I have witnessed his signature, and that all of his answers of which I have knowledge are true, except as follows:

Bessie E. Jennings (Signature of registrar)

Precinct 53

City or County San Diego

State Calif

June 5, 1917 (Date of registration)

No. 2.

Federal Building, San Diego, Cal.

**1. Charles W. Meyer's 1917 Draft Registration Card. Charles Meyer was Disfarmer's youngest brother.**

Why would Charles change his middle name? My supposition on the name change is that when Charles completed the draft card, he thought he might eventually have to fight the Germans along side other Americans and did not want the name "Wolfgang" to be a dead giveaway that he was of German descent and possibly sympathetic towards the enemy. Hence, the name change. As for why he moved to California, according to family accounts, Charley liked to hang around railroad depots where he learned telegraphy. He landed a job working for the railroad as a telegrapher and was eventually transferred to San Diego taking a job with Western Union.

Anecdotally, the Army Signal Corps for which the telephone and telegraph were the major technologies during World War I, established Rockwell Field at San Diego as an aviation school on Thanksgiving Day, 1912. Rockwell Field was originally known as Signal Corps Aviation School. Perhaps Charley ended up in San Diego as a result of his affiliation with the Army. According to the 1910 Census, Charley was not living in the Stuttgart home with brother Mike and his mother, Margaretha. Its possible, Charley was in the Army at time and may have been deployed with his Arkansas regiment to help quell the Mexican uprising led by Pancho Villa along the U.S. - Mexico border. Border skirmishes between Mexican Revolutionaries and U.S. Militia lasted from about 1911 until the entry of the U.S. into WWI in 1917.

Charley appears to have married and raised a family based on a real photo postcard showing Charley, his wife and two young children. It is not clear where the photo was taken. Extensive research does not clearly shed light on the name of Charley's wife or children. It appears that Charley may have lived out his life in California. Family accounting and a death record show that Charley died near Santa Clara, California, where his sister, Anna also live and died. According to the Louise Fricker Biographical Sketch (Appendix 1), the Cleburne County Probate Court sent a share of the Disfarmer estate to Charley Meyer, age 70, at 230 S. 13 Street, San Jose, California.

# Disfarmer's Mother: Margaretha (Weidenhammer) Meyer

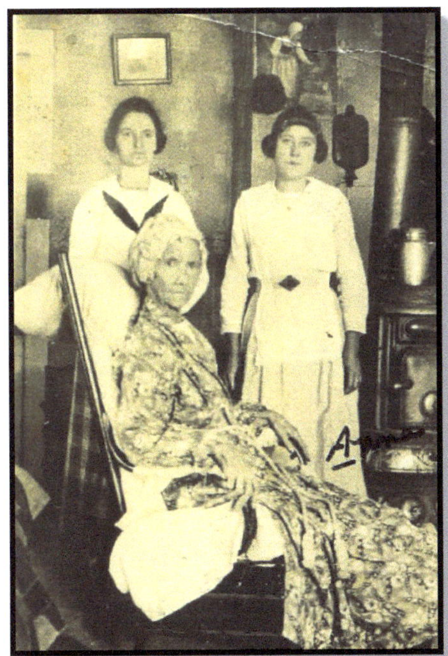

2. Margaretha (Weidenhammer) Meyer (seated), circa 1926, in Heber Springs home after her fall. She is being tended to by her daughter, Anna (right) and unidentified housekeeper (left).

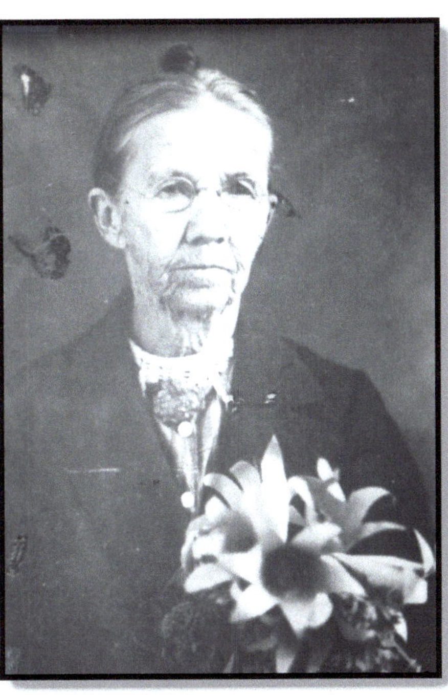

3. Margaretha (Weidenhammer) Meyer , circa 1919. Photo taken in Penrose & Meyer studio in Jackson Theater.

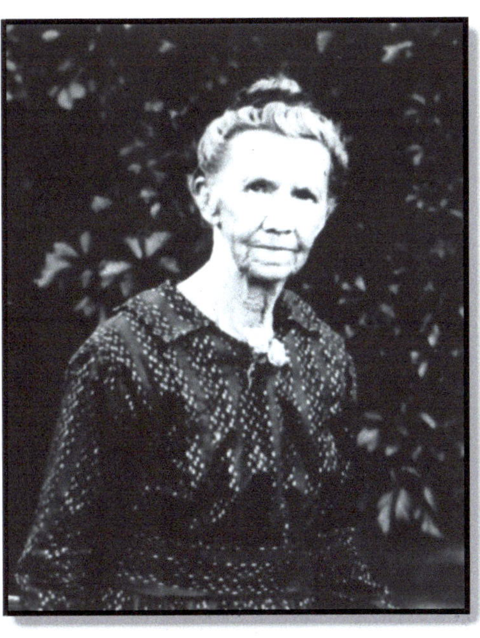

4. Margaretha (Weidenhammer) Meyer, circa 1932.

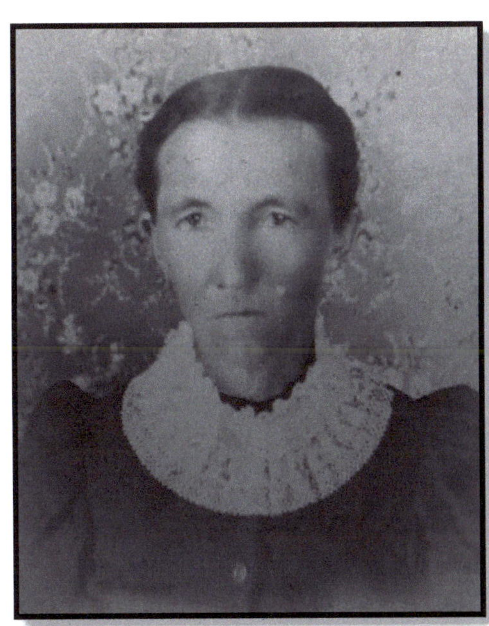

5. Margaretha (Weidenhammer) Meyer, May 5, 1915. Photo is believed to be made inside the Heber Springs, Arkansas, home of Mike and Margaretha Meyer. This is from a real photo postcard (RPPC) made by Mike Meyer / Disfarmer.

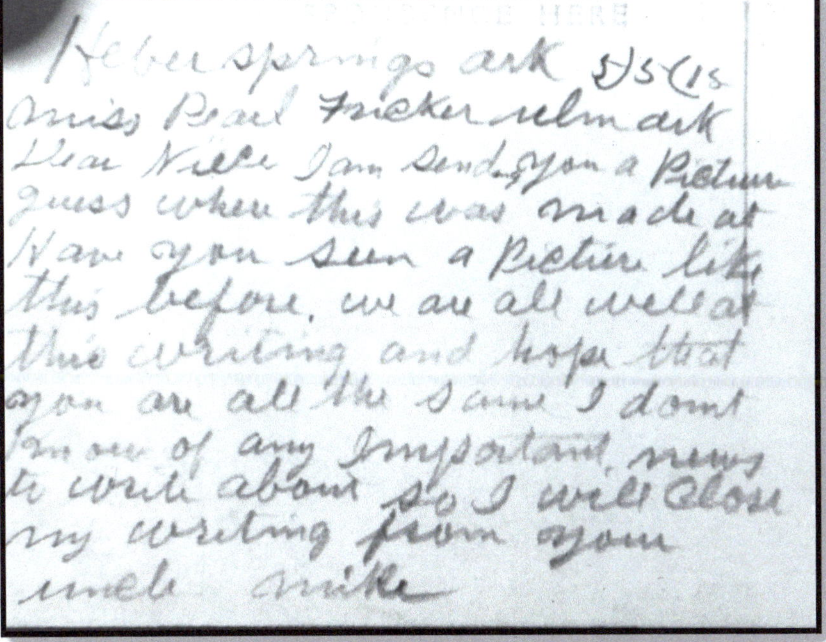

Heber springs ark 5)5(15
Miss Pearl Fricker ulm ark
Dear Niece I am sending you a Picture
guess where this was made at
Have you seen a Picture like
this before, we are all well at
this writing and hope that
you are all the same I dont
know of any Important news
to write about so I will Close
my writing from you
uncle mike

6. This is the "correspondence" side of the RPPC photo (left) of Disfarmer's mother. The inscription reads: "Heber Springs Ark 5) 5 (15 / Miss Pearl Fricker Ulm Ark / Dear Niece I am sending you a picture / guess where this was made at / Have you seen a Picture like / this before, we are all well at / this writing and hope that / you are all the same. I dont / know of any important news / to write about so I will close / my writing from you / Uncle Mike."

# Disfarmer's Oldest Brother: Andrew Meyer

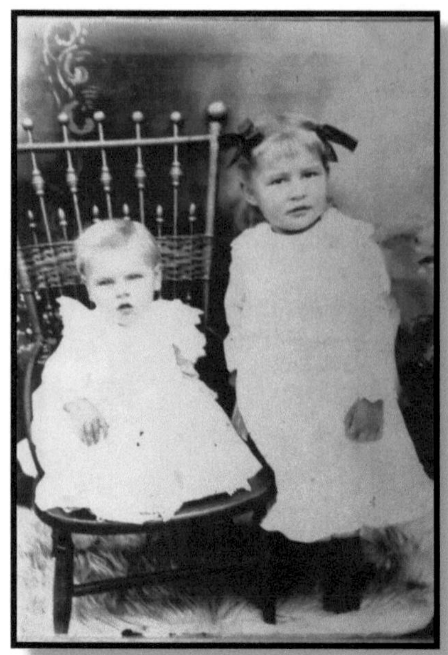

7. Children of Andrew and Lillian Meyer: Martin (left) and Tilly (right) circa 1901.

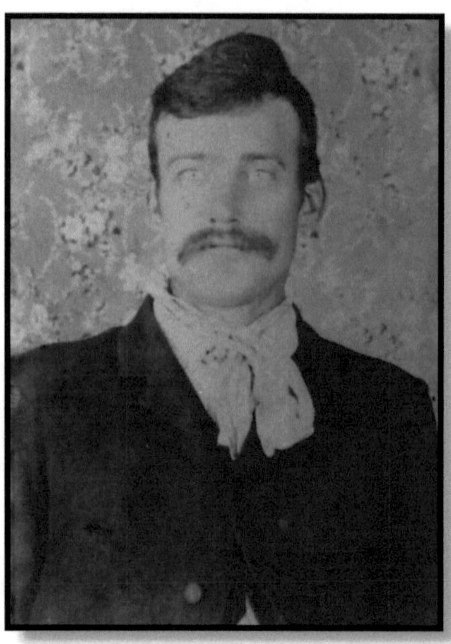

8. Andrew Meyer, Disfarmer's oldest brother.

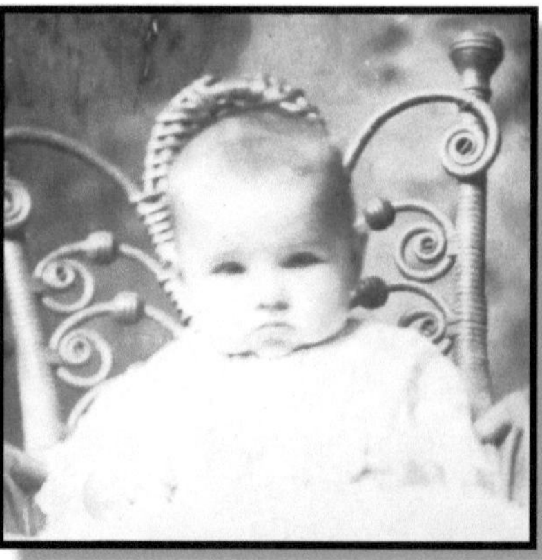

9. Evelyn Meyer, daughter of Andrew and Lillian Meyer. Photo taken in Charles Buerkle Studio in Stuttgart, Arkansas, circa 1908.

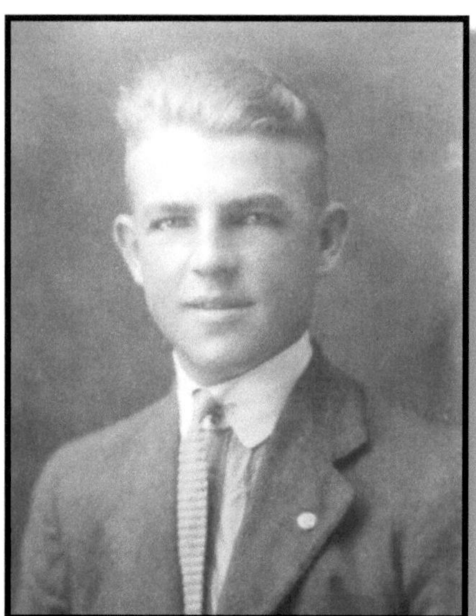

10. George Meyer, son of Andrew and Lillian Meyer, circa 1922.

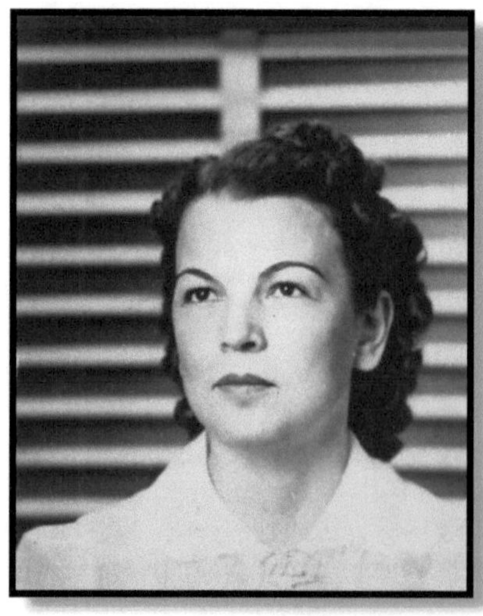

11. Evelyn (Meyer) Doyle, daughter of Andrew and Lillian Meyer.

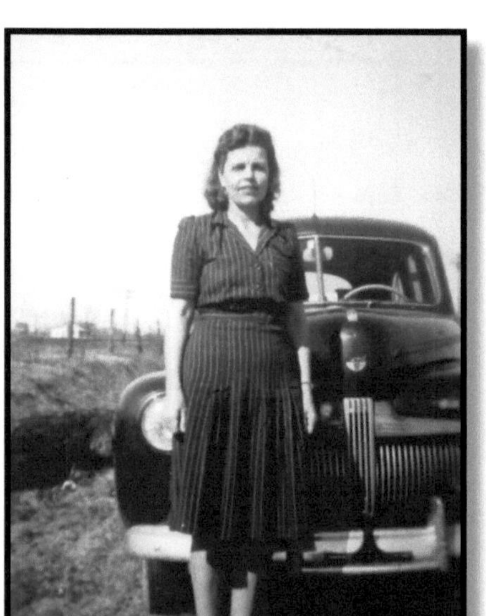

12. Pearl Marie (Meyer) McRae, daughter of Andrew and Lillian Meyer, circa 1935. Photo is believed to have been taken at funeral of Margaretha (Weidenhammer) Meyer.

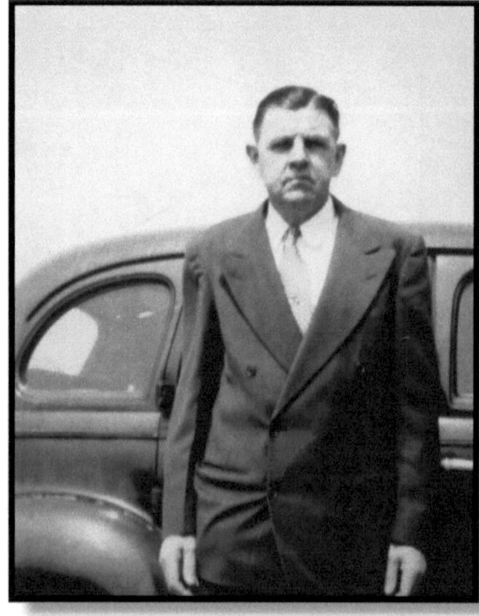

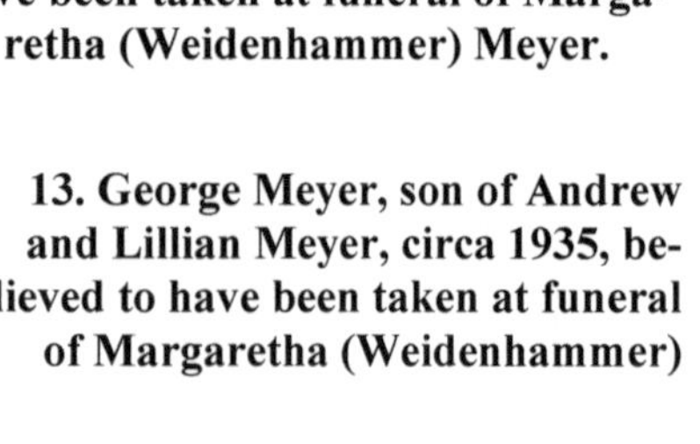

13. George Meyer, son of Andrew and Lillian Meyer, circa 1935, believed to have been taken at funeral of Margaretha (Weidenhammer)

14. Grace Wilma Meyer, daughter of Andrew and Lillian Meyer.

# Disfarmer's Sisters: Barbara (Meyer) Neukam and Anna Katherine "Katy" Meyer

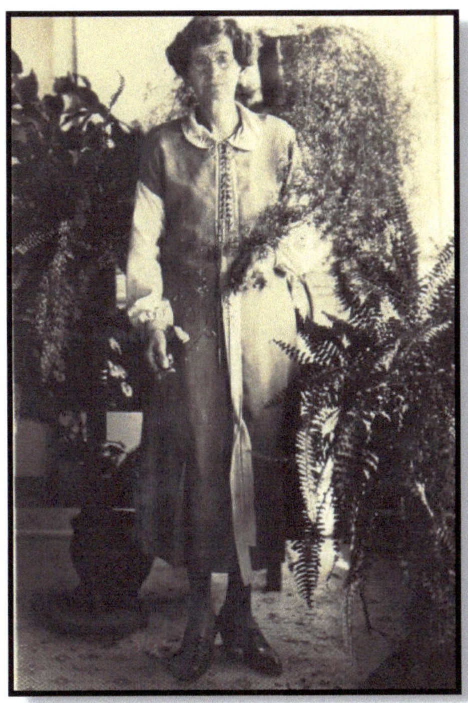

**15. Barbara (Meyer) Neukam, sister of Mike Meyer / Disfarmer.**

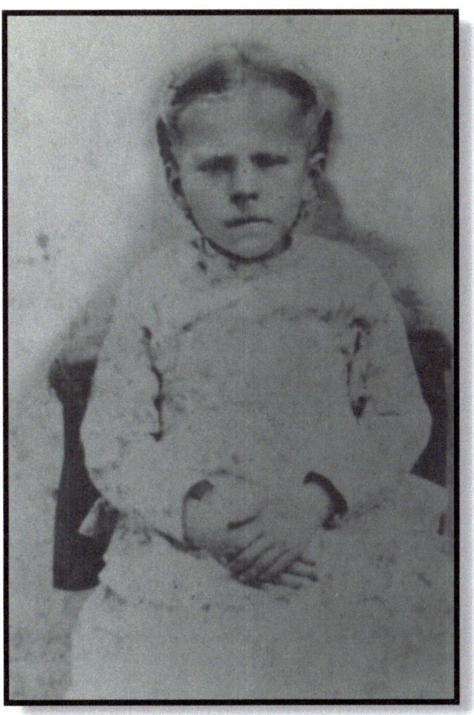

**16. Katy Meyer, sister of Mike Meyer / Disfarmer who died at age 6.**

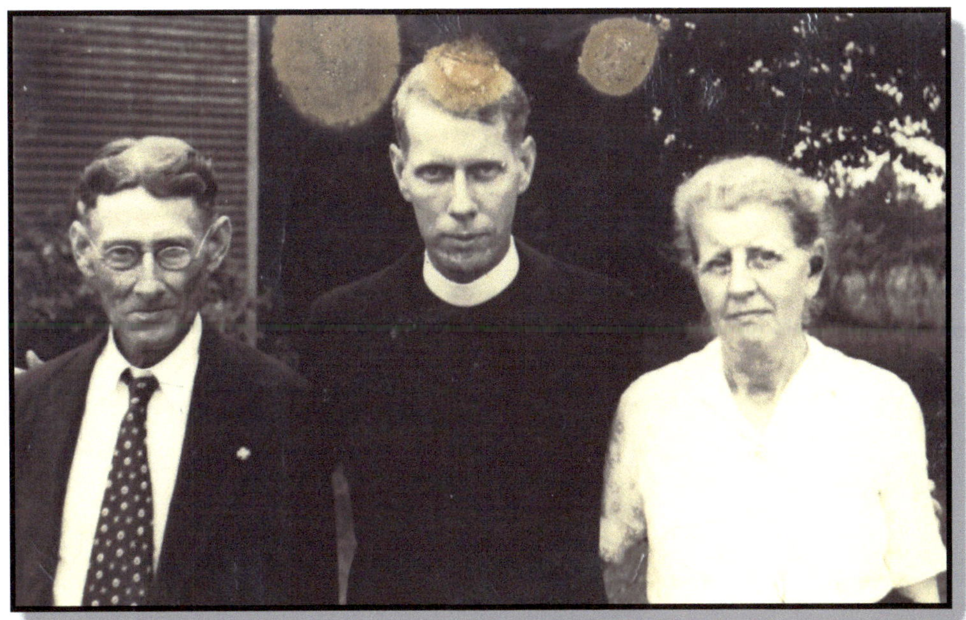

**17. Mike Meyer / Disfarmer (left), unidentified minister (center) and Disfarmer's sister, Barbara (Meyer) Neukam (right). Photo made circa 1935 possibly at the funeral of Disfarmer's mother, Margaretha (Weidenhammer) Meyer.**

# Disfarmer's Sister: Mary Ursula (Meyer) Fricker

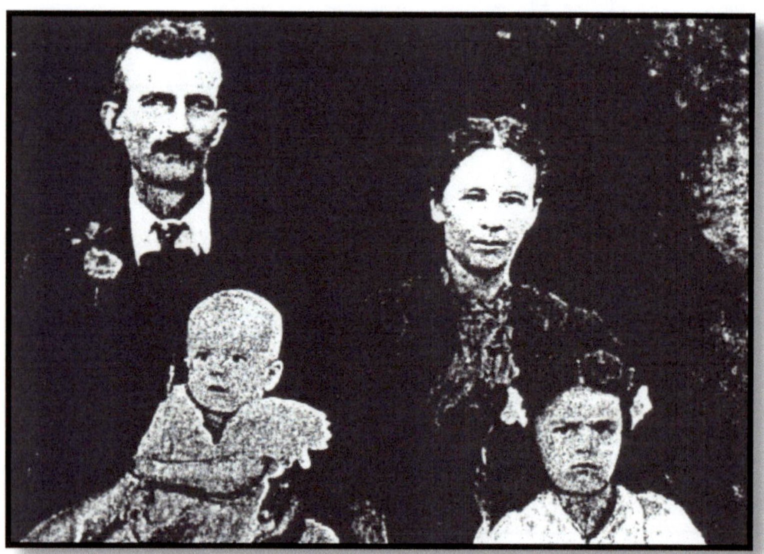

**18. John Joseph Fricker, Sr., his wife, Mary Ursula (Meyer) Fricker, and daughter, Pearl (left front) and son William (right front), circa 1901.**

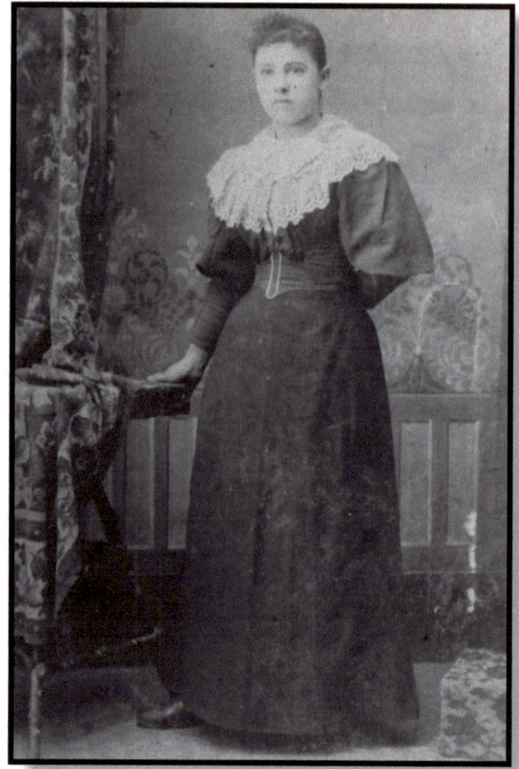

**19. Mary Ursula (Meyer) Fricker, sister of Mike Meyer / Disfarmer.**

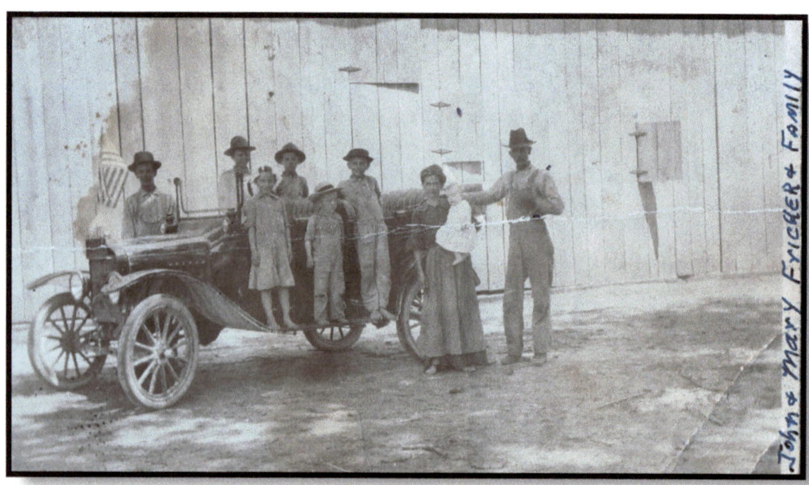


**20. Above: John Joseph Fricker and Mary Ursula (Meyer) Fricker and family in RPPC taken near Ulm, Arkansas, circa 1914. Below: Address side of RPPC stamped "Penrose & Meyer Photographers Heber Springs, Arkansas."**

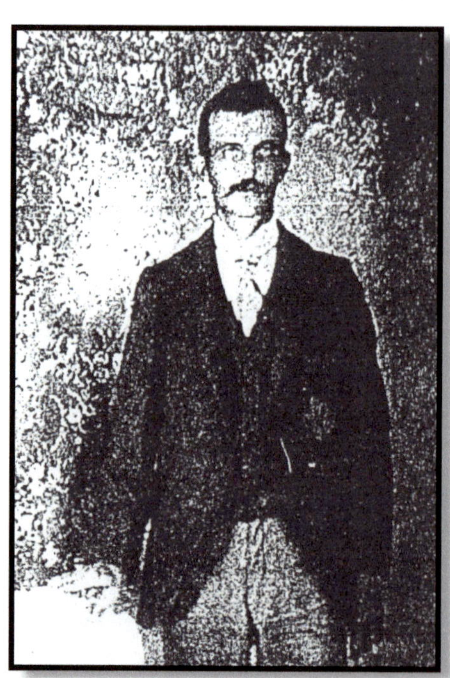

**21. John Joseph Fricker, Sr., son of Simon and Marie (Ackerman) Fricker.**

# Disfarmer's Sister: Anna (Meyer) Goodrich

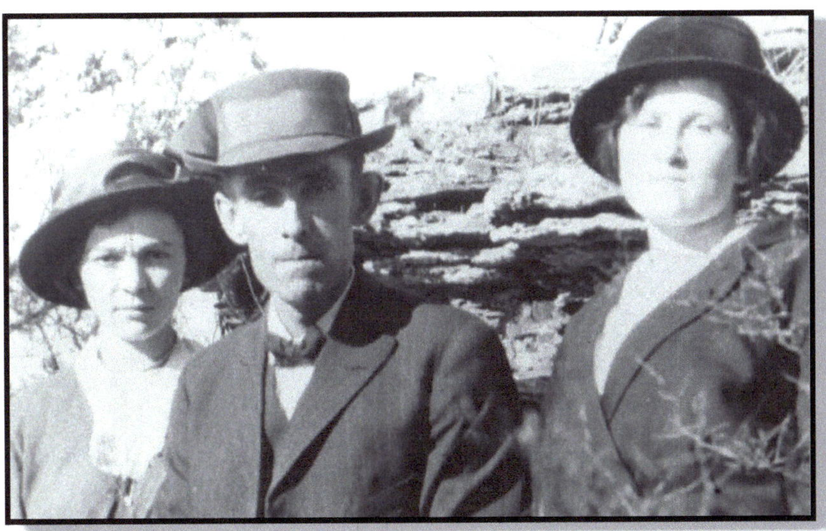

22. Pearl Fricker (left), Disfarmer's niece and daughter of his oldest brother, Andrew; Mike Meyer / Disfarmer (center) and his sister, Anna (Meyer) Goodrich (right). Photo taken on Sugar Loaf Mountain, Heber Springs, Arkansas, circa 1914.

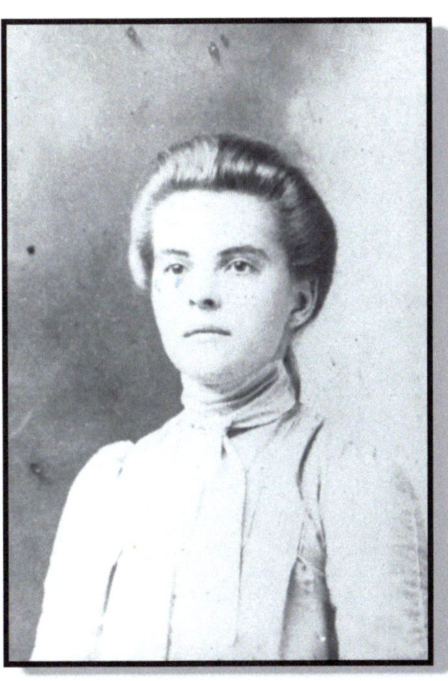

23. Anna (Meyer) Goodrich, sister of Mike Meyer / Disfarmer circa 1898.

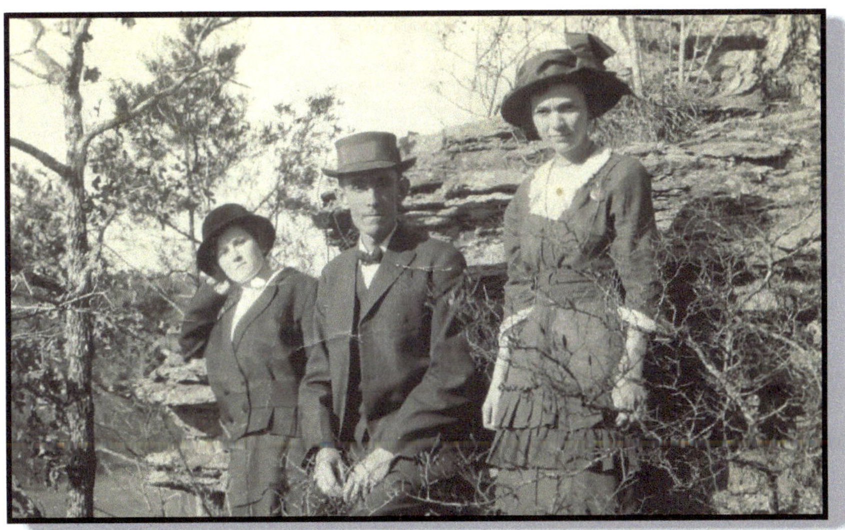

24. Anna (Meyer) Goodrich (left), sister of Mike Meyer / Disfarmer, Mike Meyer / Disfarmer (center) and Pearl Fricker (right), Disfarmer's niece and oldest daughter of his oldest brother, Andrew. Photo was taken on top of Sugar Loaf Mountain, Heber Springs, Arkansas, circa 1914.

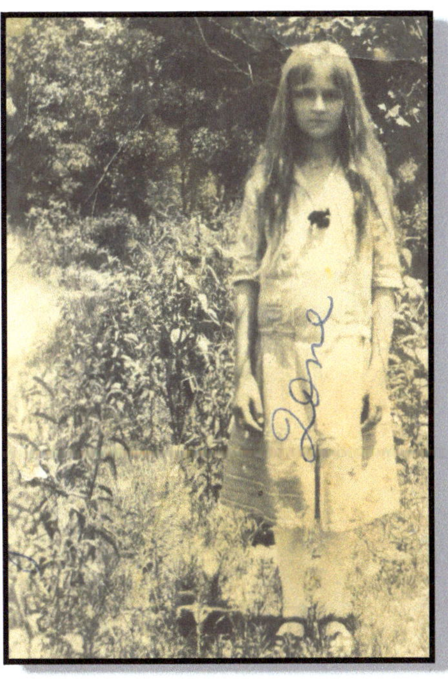

25. Ione Goodrich, only daughter of Anna (Meyer) Goodrich, and niece of Mike Meyer / Disfarmer circa 1924.

# Disfarmer's Sister: Margaretha "Maggie" (Meyer) Minor / Klinger

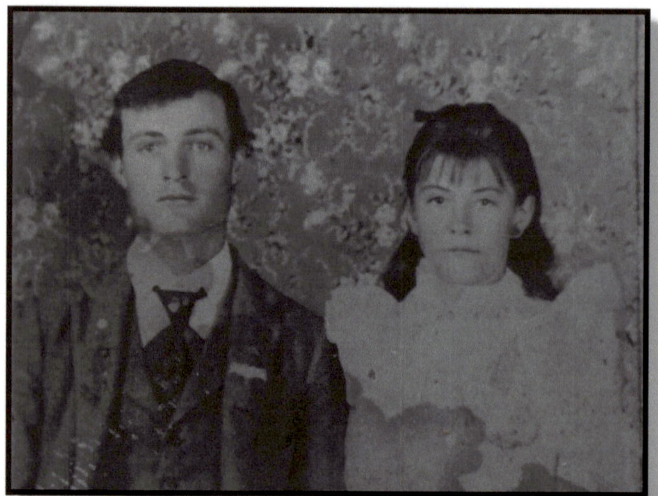

26. Maggie Meyer (right) and friend Bill Billings. Maggie played the piano and Mike Disfarmer played the violin.

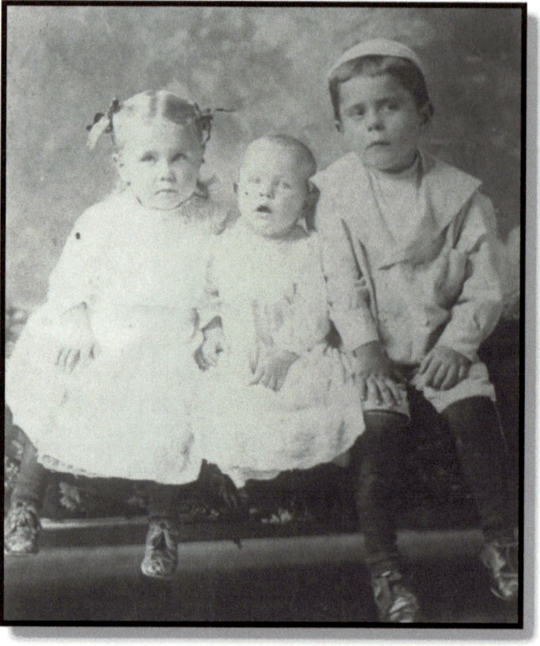

27. Children of Maggie and Hursley Minor: Anna (left), Mike, William (right).

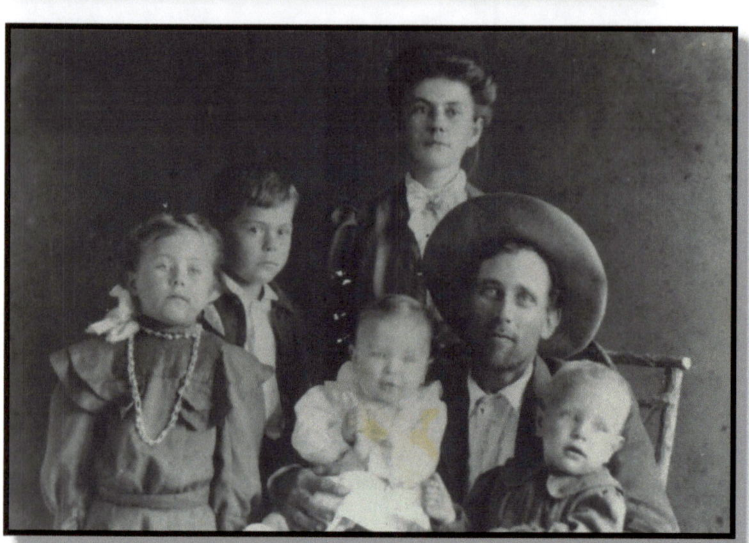

28. Maggie (Meyer) Minor, husband Hursley Minor and children (left to right) Anna, William, Marion and Mike.

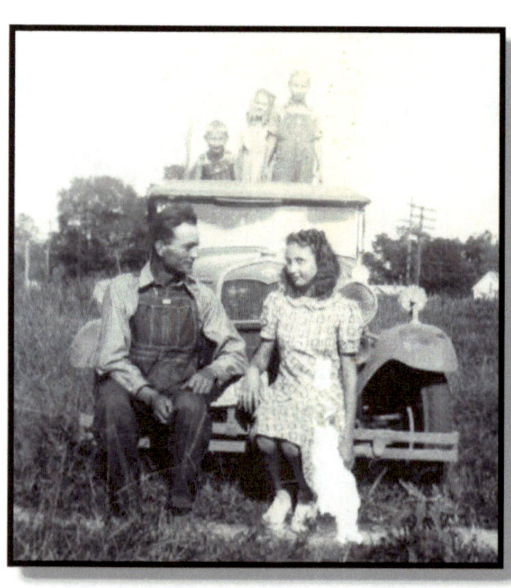

30. Mike Minor, his wife Velma and unidentified foster children.

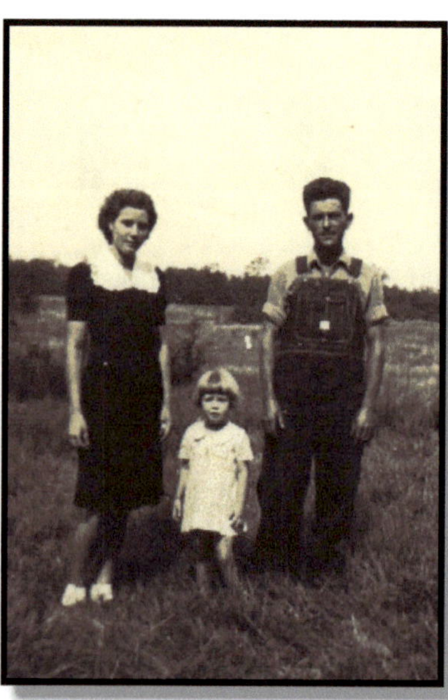

29. William Minor, son of Maggie and Hursley Minor and Disfarmer's nephew.

31. Marion Minor, his wife Clara and daughter, Mildred.

# Disfarmer's Sister: Maggie (Meyer) Minor / Klinger (continued)

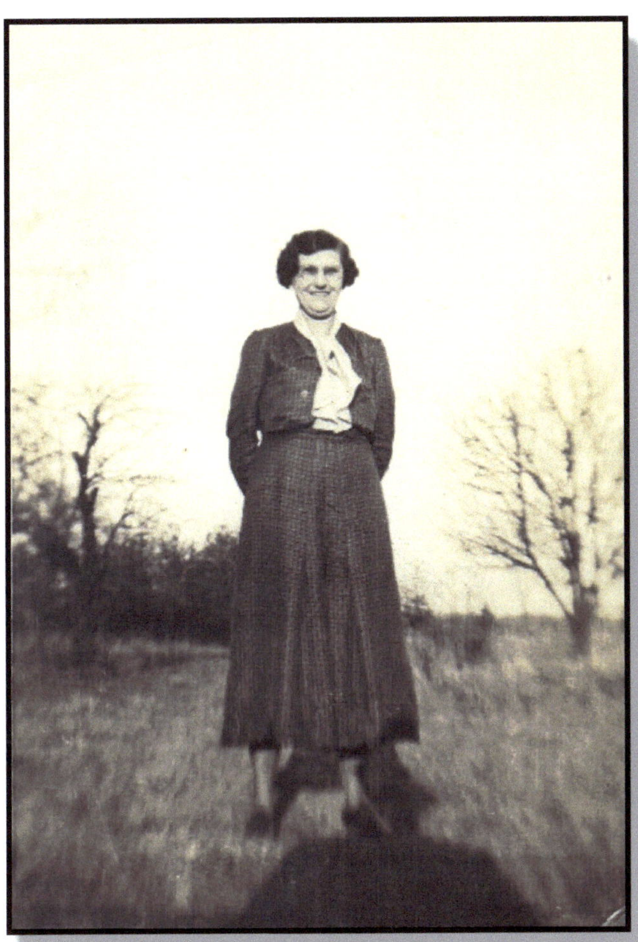

32. Photo made by Mike Meyer / Disfarmer of his sister, Maggie, on the Minor farm in De Valls Bluff, Arkansas. Disfarmer's unique shadow is clearly visible in the foreground of the photo. This photo and the one below of her husband, Hursley Minor with a cow, were both mailed to Geppert Studio in Des Moines, Iowa where they were enlarged to 8 X 10 prints.

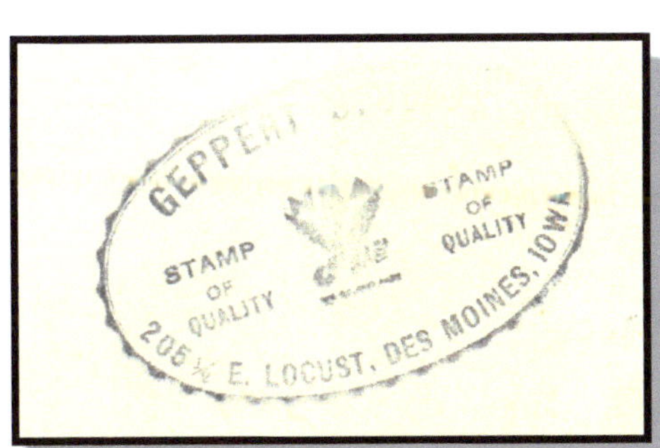


33. This stamp was clearly visible on the back of the 8 X 10 print of a 3½ X 5½ print that was made by Mike Meyer / Disfarmer. The stamp is from Geppert Studio in Des Moines, Iowa which made enlargements of Disfarmer negatives.

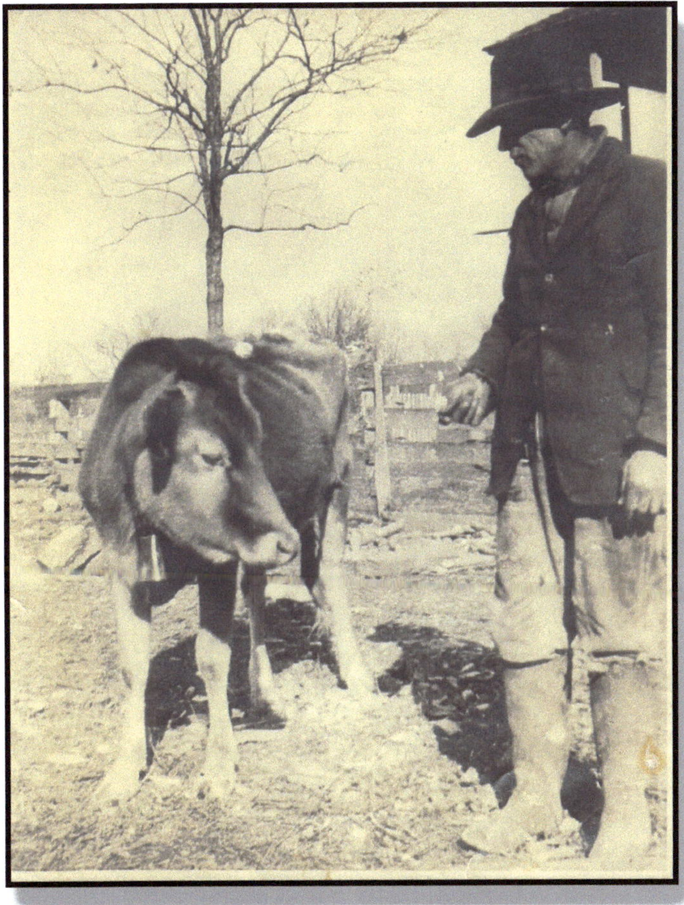

34. Photo made by Mike Meyer / Disfarmer of his brother-in-law, Theodore Hursley Minor, on the Minor farm in De Valls Bluff, Arkansas. This photo and the one above of his wife, Maggie, were both mailed to Geppert Studio in Des Moines, Iowa, where they were enlarged to 8 X 10 prints.

# Disfarmer's Sister: Maggie (Meyer) Minor / Klinger (continued)

**35. Maggie (Meyer) Minor, sister of Mike Meyer / Disfarmer, holding her dog with her husband, Theodore Hursley Minor on their De Valls Bluff, Arkansas farm. Photo made by Disfarmer circa 1934.**

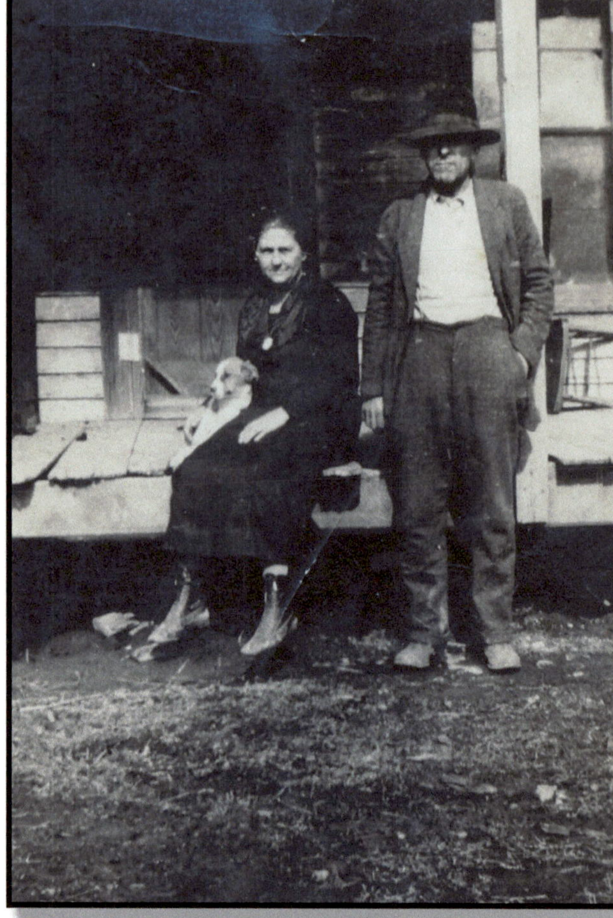

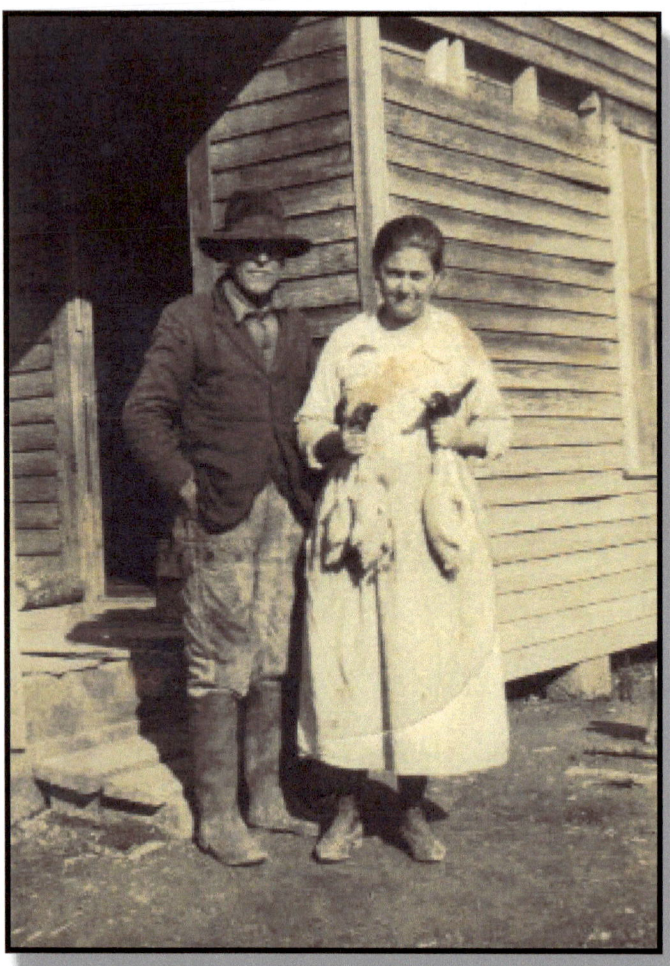

**36. Maggie (Meyer) Minor holding ducks with her husband, Theodore Hursley Minor, circa 1934. This photo was made by Disfarmer on a visit to the De Valls Bluff farm where Disfarmer traveled to visit his mother who lived with her daughter for the last few years of her life.**

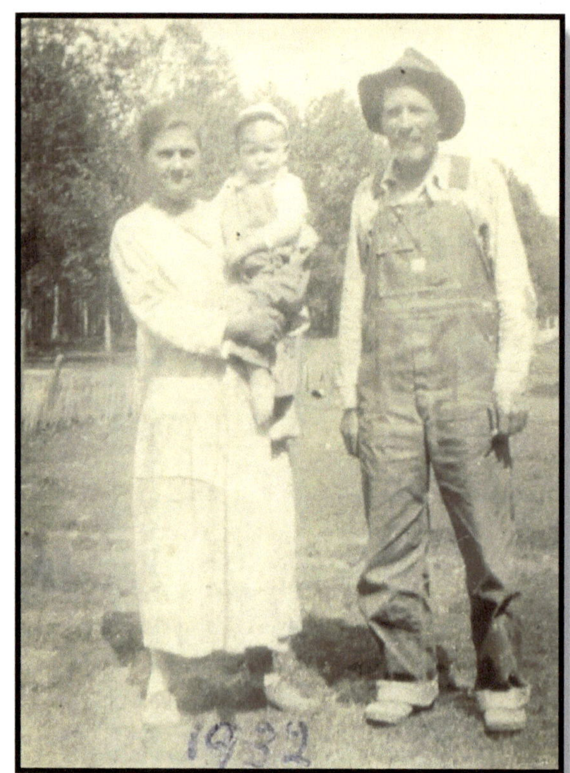


**37. Maggie (Meyer) Minor, youngest sister of Disfarmer and her first husband, Theodore Hursley Minor in 1932. Maggie is holding her first grandchild, James Calvin Minor.**

# Disfarmer and His Youngest Brother: Charles "Charley" Heinrich Wolfgang Meyer

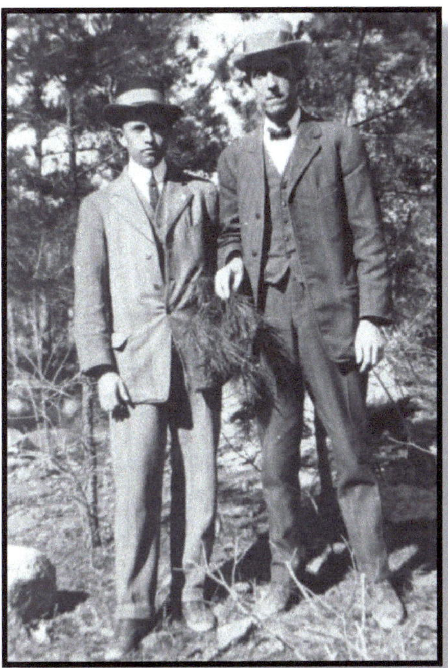

38. Charlie Meyer (left) and Mike Meyer / Disfarmer (right), circa 1914.

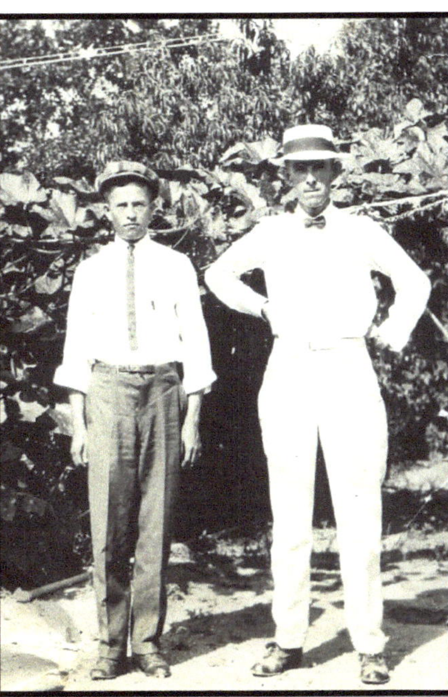

39. Charlie Meyer (left) and Mike Meyer / Disfarmer (right), circa 1915.

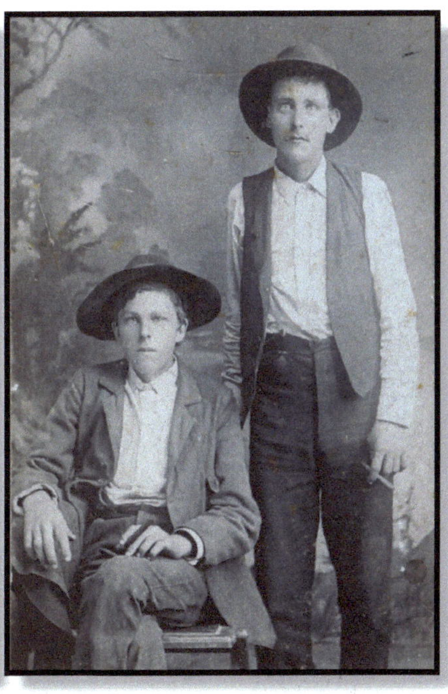

40. Charlie Meyer (left) and Mike Meyer / Disfarmer (right), circa 1900, in photo made by Dayton Bowers in his DeWitt, Arkansas studio.

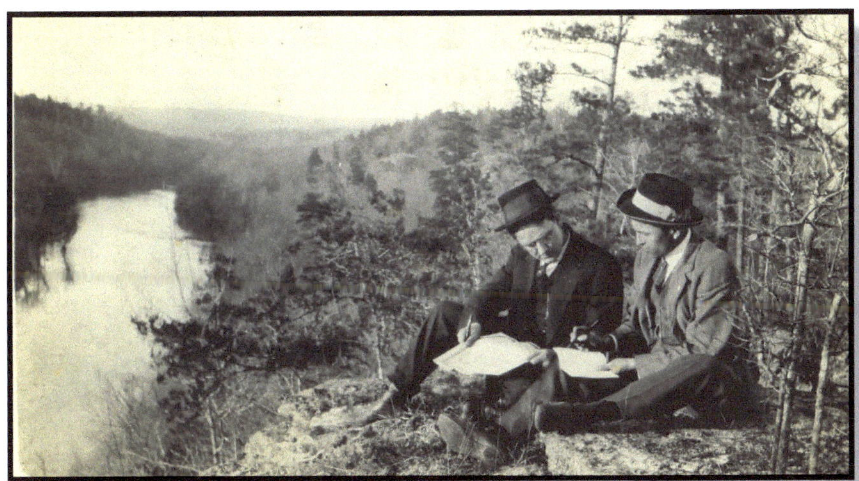

41. Charlie Meyer (right) and unidentified man on top of Sugar Loaf Mountain, Heber Springs, Arkansas, circa 1914. Notice similarity of Charlie's hat in this photo and the photo above on top left. The unidentified man is believed to be George A. Penrose, Disfarmer's early partner in the photography studio housed in the Jackson Theater in Heber Springs. This photo suggests that Charley may have played a small roll in the early partnership.

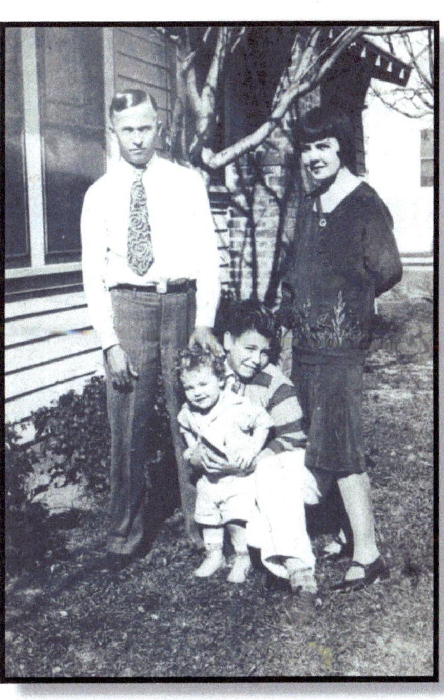

42. Charley Meyer and his wife and two children, circa 1930. This photo is believed to have been taken near Santa Clara, California.

# Disfarmer's Nieces and Nephews

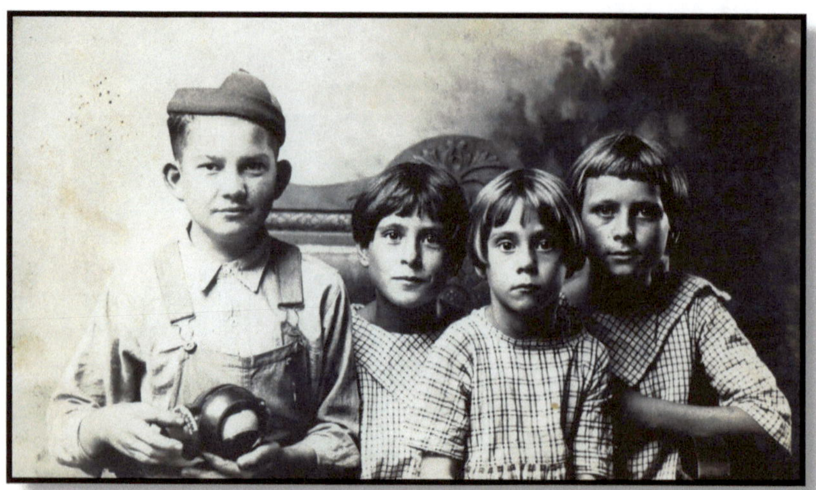

43. Real Photo Postcard (RPPC) made by Mike Meyer / Disfarmer, circa 1920. Inscription reads: "Margaret, Lucy, Martha Minor" "this is your good looking cousin Joe Neukam on this picture with the girls Mike made the picture while we was up here & wanted to sent them before now but forgot all the time"

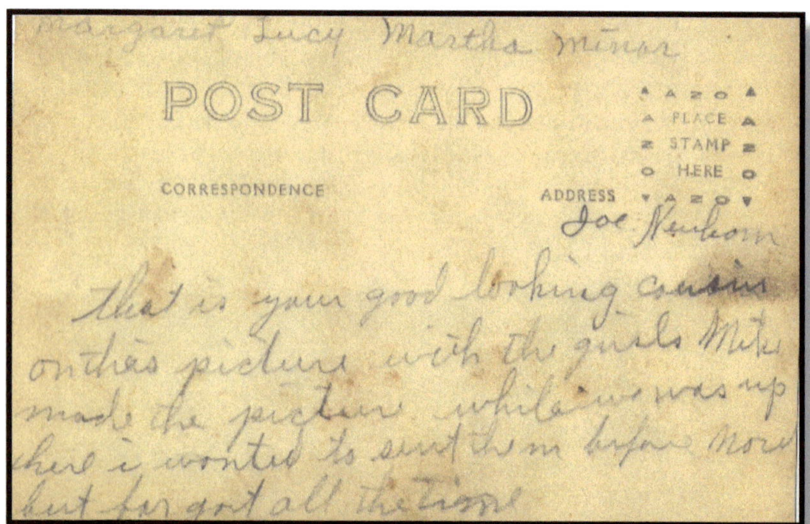

Margaret Lucy Martha Minor

POST CARD

PLACE STAMP HERE

CORRESPONDENCE

ADDRESS

Joe Neukam

this is your good looking cousin on this picture with the girls Mike made the picture while we was up here i wanted to sent them before now but forgot all the time

44. Joseph "Joe" Michael Neukam, nephew of Disfarmer in photo taken in Disfarmer studio circa 1922. Joe died in a swimming accident at the age of 22.

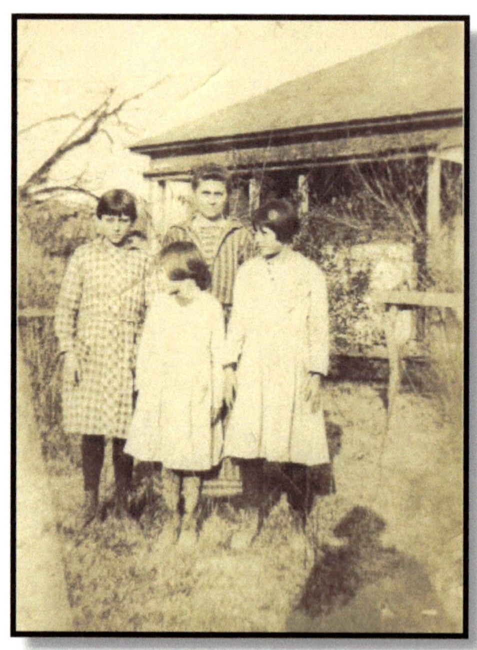

45. Left to right: Margaret, Martha, Maggie (mother) and Lucy Minor circa 1924. Photo was made by Disfarmer – his unique shadow is clearly visible in the foreground.

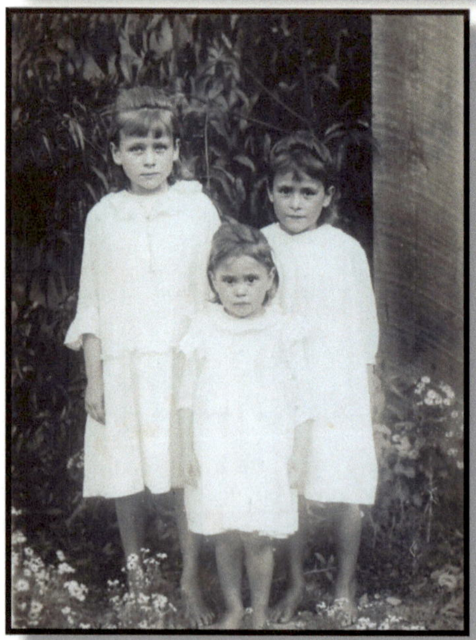

46. Left to right: Margaret, Martha and Lucy Minor circa 1919. Photo was likely made by Disfarmer.

# Disfarmer's Nieces and their Children

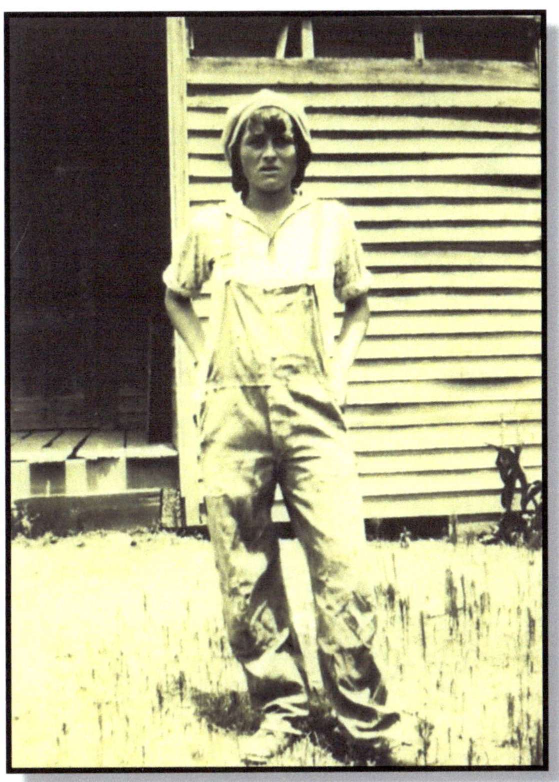

47. Margaret Minor, daughter of Maggie (Meyer) Minor and niece of Disfarmer on the Minor farm in De Valls Bluff, Arkansas, circa 1929.

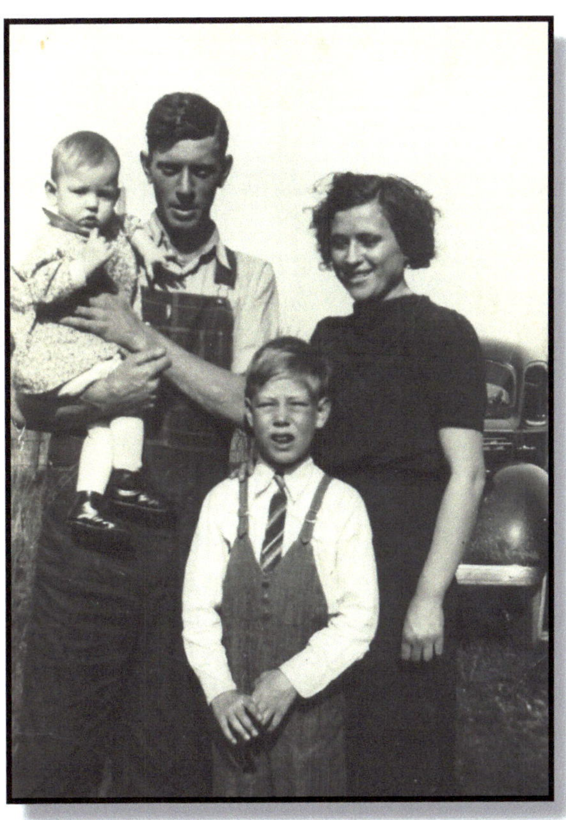

48. Margaret (Minor) Kirkemier with her husband Frank F. Kirkemier, Sr., her son, James Calvin Minor (front) and daughter, Ruth Kirkemier, circa 1938.

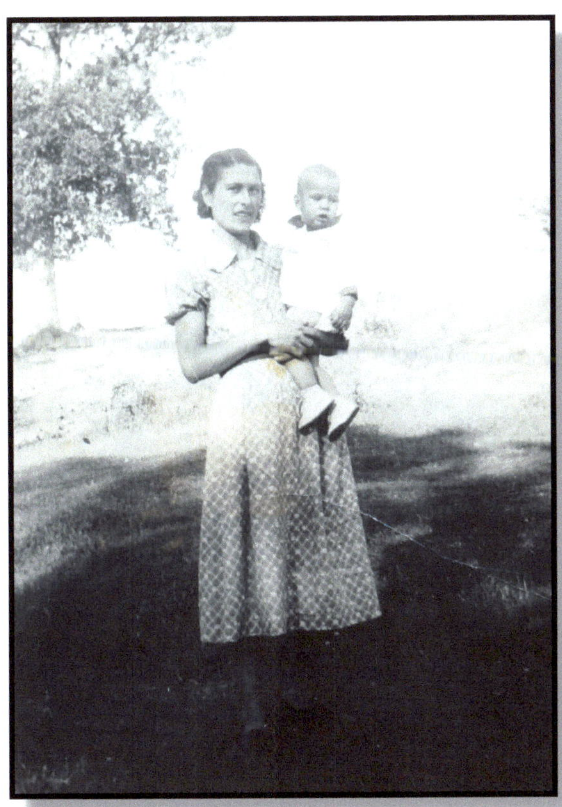

49. Lucy (Meyer) Kirkemier and her son, Lester Kirkemier, circa 1938. Lucy was Disfarmer's niece.

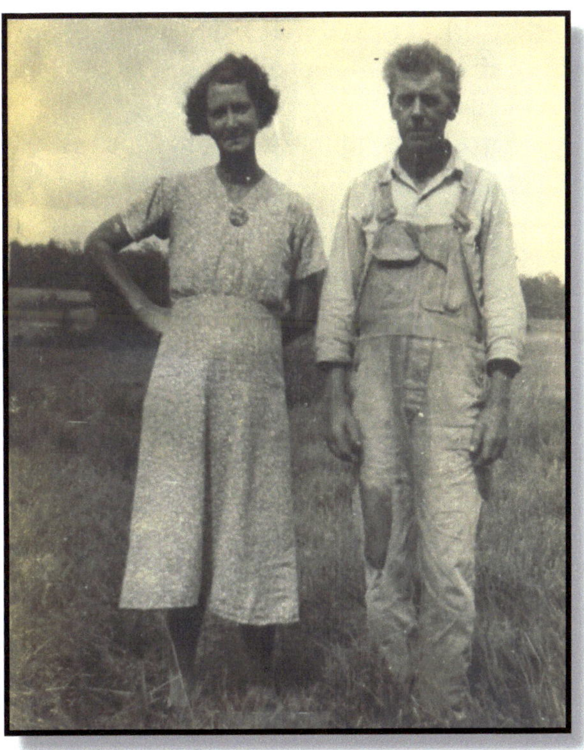

50. Stephen Henry Kirkemier and his wife, Ida Alvina (Deutsch) Kirkemier, grandparents of Ruth Kirkemier and cousin, Lester Kirkemier, circa 1932.

# Appendix 1: Disfarmer Family History as Told by Relatives to Louise Fricker

Louise Fricker, the wife of Disfarmer's nephew Roy Fricker, became the self-appointed family genealogist and historian during the 1980's and 1990's. She reached out to the various members of the large, extended Meyer and Fricker clans seeking personal remembrances and photographs she could use in documenting a comprehensive family genealogy. Anyone that has ever entered such an undertaking understands the significant commitment of time that is required to see the effort through to the finish line. Louise Fricker's task was made even more difficult and challenging because she tackled this task before the arrival of such tools as the Internet, Ancestry.com and by the large size of the Meyer and Fricker families. Ms. Fricker reached out to relatives via mail, phone calls and at family gatherings and reunions where she requested documentation to help her in her efforts.

Roy Fricker, Louise's husband was a nephew of Mike Meyer / Disfarmer and appears to have had a special and long-lasting relationship with Disfarmer. After Peter Miller and Julia Scully discovered the photographic genius of Disfarmer and brought his work to the international stage, Louise and Roy became particularly interested in preserving some of the details of Disfarmer's life. This involvement in documenting some of the details of Disfarmer's life led them to become intimately involved in the efforts of Toba Tucker in producing her book, *HEBER SPRINGS PORTRAITS Continuity and Change in the World Disfarmer Photographed*, copyright 1996. Ms. Tucker undertook a multi-year sabbatical to Heber Springs, Arkansas to re shoot some of Disfarmer's early photographic subjects some 40 to 50 years hence, and attempted to replicate Disfarmer's technique. The timeframe of Toba Tucker's effort coincided with the work of Louise Fricker to document the Meyer family genealogy. The Frickers shared information with Tucker about Disfarmer and vice-versa. The writings of Louise Fricker during this timeframe strongly suggest that she contemplated publishing her own biographical work on the most famous member of the family – Mike Meyer / Disfarmer. Unfortunately, Ms. Fricker's work did not result in an insightful, first-hand accounting on the life of Disfarmer. However, thanks to the generosity of David Fricker, son of Roy and Louise Fricker, and David's wife, Verma, who granted me permission to copy and use the fruit of her labor, I am able to build on the foundation that she laid. Her work was both inspirational and instrumental in my efforts to produce a factual biography of Mike Disfarmer's life.

In this appendix, I have attempted to reproduce some of the more significant documents contained in the Louise Fricker genealogical record. The following pages are an accurate reproduction of the material contained in the Fricker materials. Some of the following material was written by a relative of Mike Meyer / Disfarmer and provided to Louise Fricker. A significant portion of the material itself was written by Louise Fricker in what appears to be her early efforts to produce a narrative on Disfarmer's life. I have attempted to reproduce accurately the original documents preserving spelling, syntax and punctuation of the original authors. A close reading of this material will help substantiate the dichotomy of views about the true persona of Mike Disfarmer. Some of Disfarmer's own family members have conflicting views of the man behind the camera. At least one relative did not believe the story behind his name change and thought that the newspaper reporter that originally covered the story in 1939 should have been fired for making up such a story. In this biography, I have attempted to provide clear and compelling facts on which the reader can form his or her own opinion about the real Disfarmer and to lay to rest some of the myth and legend about the man behind the camera.

# The Meyer Family History as Told by Harry Neukam

*[This Meyer Family History was sent to Louise Fricker by Harry Neukam on April 15, 1991. Certain minor aspects of this Family History are inconsistent with research findings made by the author of this biography relying primarily on Ancestry.com.]*

Christopher Meyer, paternal great great grandfather to Harry Neukam, was born April 21, 1809 in Germany. He married Ursula [Maier?] in Germany and came to the United States in 1841. They landed at Baltimore, Maryland then moved to Dubois County [Indiana] and sometime later to Crawford County, Indiana. They had one son, Martin. It is not known when Christopher died or, where he is buried.

Harry's great-great-grandmother Ursula Meyer was born in Germany in 1814. On December 27, 1881, Christopher and Ursula Meyer sold 40 acres of land to John C. Harder, Martin Meyer and John Licht, Trustees of the Emmanuel Lutheran Hill Church, Dubois, Indiana for $5.00. In the 1890's, she came to Almyra [Arkansas] and made her home with her son Martin, where she lived until her death in 1898 at the age of 84. She is buried beside her son, Martin, in Almyra Cemetery at Almyra, Arkansas.

Harry Neukam's maternal great-great-grandfather, Johann Weidenhammer was born October 3, 1812, at Mistelback, District Bayreuth, Bavaria, Germany. On November 25, 1839 and May 25, 1841, the U.S. Government deeded 40 acres to Johann Weidenhammer. February 5, 1841 he married Barbara Krodel in St. Paul's Lutheran Church, Jasper, Indiana.

Children of Johann Weidenhammer and Barbara Krodel were:

1. Eva - born Jan. 27, 1842
2. Anna - born Jan. 30, 1845
3. Margaretha - born Mar. 24, 1849 (Harry's Great-Grandmother)
4. John - born Feb. 23, 1853

There is no record of Johann Weidenhammer's death or, where he is buried. Johann Krodel was appointed Guardian of the family in 1862 or 1863.

Harry Neukam's maternal great-great grandmother, Barbara Krodel Weidenhammer was born August 21, 1821 in Germany. She was the daughter of Johann Krodel 1st. After Johann Weidenhammer's death, she married Michael Greener [Griiner] on June 18, 1860. She died Sept. 16, 1906 at the age of 85. Michael Greener was born Feb. 15, 1828 and died April 5, 1904 at age 76. Both are buried in Emmanuel Lutheran Hill Cemetery, Dubois, Indiana.

Harry Neukam's great-grandfather, Martin Meyer, was born June 2, 1846 in Indiana. On Aug. 25, 1864, he was mustered as a regular soldier in Company A 49th Indiana Veteran Voluntary Infantry and served over a year, receiving his discharge Sept. 18, 1865. Margaretha Weidenhammer became his wife on May 26, 1868. He was a carpenter, harness-maker, musician and farmer. He moved with his family to Arkansas in 1892. He died August 30, 1898 at age 52 and is buried in Almyra Cemetery at Almyra, Arkansas.

Harry Neukam's great-grandmother, Margaretha Weidenhammer was born near Haysville, Indiana, March 25, 1849. She was baptized in infantry [sic] and confirmed at age 13 in the Lutheran Church at Haysville, Indiana. She moved with her family to Arkansas in 1892 and settled on a farm south of Almyra, later moving to Stuttgart. In 1927, she fell and injured her hip which left her and invalid. For some years she lived at Heber Springs with her son, Michael who was a photographer there. She spent her remaining years with her daughter, Maggie, at De Valls Bluff, where she died Feb. 18, 1935 at the age of 85. She is buried beside her husband, Martin Meyer, in Almyra Cemetery at Almyra, Arkansas.

Children of Martin Meyer and Margaretha Weidenhammer were:

1. Andrew
2. Barbara
3. Mary Ursula
4. Anna Kathrina
5. Anna
6. Michael "Mike"
7. Anna Margaretha "Maggie"
8. Charley Wolfgang

## What I Can Remember About Uncle Mike
## Written to Me [Louise Fricker] by Marie Fricker Fillman July 1, 1986

It has been a long time and one sure can forget a lot, but I will try. I do not remember when he visited our home, but I do remember some of the times we were there [Heber Springs]. First of all I do know that Uncle Mike always had his right mind he was as sane as any other sane man. I remember he had a studio uptown in Heber springs

I would go down almost every day. He always let me be there and look at everything. He talked to me about his picture taking but I don't recall him ever taking my picture, there, but I have a picture of me standing by a tree when I was 8 or 10 years old. Pearl had one taken then, too. He must have been to see us then also, when we were in Heber Springs. If a storm came up he was always, watching them. I remember one night he was out in the street looking up at the clouds and I went out there (I think I always followed him as I was Probably 10 or 11 years old) and he talked to me about the clouds, etc. and I thought that was great. He was always checking on the storms, as they had a storm cellar in the yard, and if it looked bad enough everybody went to the cellar, sometimes the neighbors, too.

I loved to go to "Grandma's and Uncle Mike's." I do not believe that story about the tornado blowing him away as a baby and someone else raising him. That I think is a lot of B.S. Pardon the expression. I think if it were so, It would have bee mentioned years ago. Ione [Goodrich] might know something. They lived across the street from Uncle Mike before they moved to California.

Joe and I went up one time. I know Mom and I went up and I would guess that Roy went too. We went by train to see them and I remember that we had to change trains, somewhere and while we were in the depot a man came up to me and said if you will go with me to town I will buy you some candy, and I went to Mom and she told me, don't go with him because he may take you away and I'll never see you again. That is still so vivid in my mind, I can still see us.

I remember Grandma always kept the bread and sugar, etc. on the table between meals and when she was not around I would sneak one or two slices of bread and eat them raw. We never had store bought bread at home. It was so good. I always felt Grandma knew I swiped it.
Grandma sold garden produce that she raised. One morning I answered the knock on the door and a young girl was at the door. She said to me "My Mom wants one dozen "un-jons" (onions) I have never forgotten that.

I am sorry I don't know more about Uncle Mike, he also looked like Uncle Andrew, Aunt Barbara, Maggie and Mom. I wonder who could ever have started that story. Someone must have made a pile of money out of it. That man who put it in the Paper, should not have done so. Can he prove it? If he can't and I don't believe it, It should not have been printed. He should lose his job.

## Ione Goodrich Riedell-neice [sic] of Mike Meyer Who Lived in Santa Cruz, California Wrote:

"It was wonderful to hear from you and very exciting to hear that there may be a book about Uncle Mikes photography I used to have so much fun when I was a kid in Heber Springs. Uncle Mike used to let me help spread Pictures to dry after he printed them and he would let me watch him make prints in the dark room and would explain everything as he went along."

## Roy's [Fricker] Memories of his Uncle Mike:

Roy remembers Uncle Mike coming to visit them when he was a young boy and they lived north of Ulm. Before Roy's Mother died in 1926, he visited them and his brother Andrew in Stuttgart. He drove a Model T Ford. He enjoyed talking about the route he had taken from Heber Springs to Ulm with Roys Father. He talked of the towns he came through and what he had seen. He talked a lot about incidents around Rosebud, and Quitman. Evidently he had friends that lived there. One of his favorite gripes was "Why should I, who makes two or three trips a year, have to pay the same for licenses as a man that drives his car every day?"

He sent off for radio parts and built a radio inside his home, but he put the speakers on the porch. He said the reason for this was it was too loud but Roy thought maybe the reason he did this was his way of sharing the radio with his neighbors. Not all had radios. He had a studio south of the court house in those days. Roy, his sisters Elsie and Marie and their Mother rode the train from Brinkley to Heber Springs to visit his Grandmother and Uncle Mike when Roy was a small boy. Uncle Mike was always very nice to Roy's family when they visited him and his Mother. He took them on tours to the top of Sugar Loaf Mountain, the water works, to Candlestick Rock, and Sulphur Springs. Roy remembers once when they were on top of Sugar Loaf Mountain, his brother Joe had a box camera. Uncle Mike showed Joe how to keep low and as the buzzard soared low, snap a photo of the buzzard when it was a short distance away.

When Uncle Mike and his Mother lived in Heber Springs they had a lovely flower and vegetable garden. They also raised rabbits. One day his grandmother went outside and stepped into a hole a rabbit had made. She fell and broke her hip. IN time it healed but she fell and broke it again. She became bedfast. For a time they had a housekeeper. After the tornado destroyed their home she went to live with her daughter Maggie and family at De Valls Bluff near Peppers Lake. Uncle Mike stayed on at Heber Springs and built his studio-home on Main Street. His Mother died in the home of Maggie 25, March, 1935. She is buried at Almyra, Ar. beside her husband Martin Meyer, who died 30 Aug. 1898.

When Roy and his Mother visited his Grandmother at his Aunt Maggie's, his Grandmother lay and looked out the window, she told them she saw a picture show, but of course it was caused by the pain killer she took to keep her from hurting so much.

IN 1931 or 32 Mike moved his studio into the building near the park. Roy and I visited him a couple of times a year in later years. Uncle Mike was always glad to see Roy and they enjoyed visiting. He didn't talk to me very much, so while they visited I entertained myself by looking at his photo covered walls. Roy Knew Uncle Mike enjoyed beer and since Cleburne County was dry he always gave Uncle Mike a couple of cans of beer before we left. The last time we visited Uncle Mike was in the fall of 1958. When we were ready to leave Uncle Mike walked to the car with us and shook hands with both of us which was very unusual. He usually said goodbye and stayed in his studio. Roy gave him the two cans of beer, he thanked Roy and Roy asked if he could take a picture of Uncle Mike. He seemed pleased and said Roy could and holding a can of beer in each hand behind his back, he posed for Roy. He asked us to come and see him again, but that's the last time we saw him. We wish he could have known how famous he was to become.

None of Uncle Mikes neices [sic] or nephews that knew and loved Uncle Mike were contacted or questioned, before the book was published. Roy was very hurt by some of the things said about Uncle Mike in the book. Uncle Mike was a very intelligent person bordering on genius, and people of that type of intelligence are often misunderstood and looked on as strange. Had we known about the book before it was published perhaps something could have been done, but after a book has been published and time has elapsed, nothing can be done.

## Mike Meyer / Disfarmer Biographical Sketch by Louise Fricker

Michael Meyer B. 12 April 1884 Portersville Ind. D. 26 Oct., 1959 Heber Springs Arkansas. In 1884 he and his family moved to Arkansas. In the late 1800's, he farmed with his father Martin Meyer, for a time, then lived in Stuttgart. He worked as a night watchman for the ricemill [sic]. His brother Charlie enjoyed being around the railroad depot where he learned to be a telegraph operator and was later sent to California to work for the railroad.

After the death of his father, in 1898, he and his mother, Margaretha Weidenhammer, moved to Heber Springs, Arkansas January 8, 1914. He operated a portrait Studio for the next 40 years. He was a Mason and he enjoyed his beer. His first love was photography and his second was music. He played three instruments - Violin, accordian [sic], and piano.

A tornado in the 1930's destroyed the Meyer home and his Mother, who had broken her hip when she had fallen, went to live with her daughter "Maggie" at De Valls Bluff, Arkansas. Mike built a studio-home on Main street near the park in Heber Springs, Arkansas. It had a big 20 foot x 30 foot glass skylight that faced the north, a large camera he had made, was mounted in the partition between the studio and the darkroom where he developed his own negatives. His living Quarters were in the back. He used glass 5"x7" negatives and later he used 3"x5 1/2" postcard sized glass plates. His studio props consisted of a couple of crude wooden benches and a table. For background, a black roll down curtain and a white wall explicably [sic] striped with black tape. He developed his own negatives. His photographs included items other photographers would have omitted such as a paper fan in an old woman's hand, a snapshot tucked in a youths hatband, or a suitcase by a soldiers feet. The fervent patriotism of the time of war is there in the buttons worn by the women, in the sailor posing with his girl, the uniforms, the simple gestures of the subjects touching-hands on shoulders, arms around each other and without understanding or articulating it how the people he photographed were interesting, because of the strength of charachter [sic] they projected.

He was termed, a good citizen and a decent man who minded his own business. He always knew he was a good photographer and it showed in his work. "A slender, ichabod type fellow with a long face" as described by Judge Reed. George Olmstead recollects he was a very colorful character, who wore a beard, a [P]rince [A]lbert coat and always wore a black hat. The people would line up to have their picture made on Saturdays. The country people loved to have their picture made. It was a fad. At the end of World War 11 [sic] his business declined.

The character of the people in the Heber Springs portraits portrayed a peculiar American Character shaped to a great degree by the rugged farm life and small town culture of America. The country people he photographed were largely cotton farmers scratching bare [sic] exhistances [sic] from the thin soil of Cleburne County in which Heber Springs is located. They supplemented cotton crops with corn, peanuts and sorghum. One man said "The people never knew there was a depression, because the times weren't any harder than they used to be."

Mikes [sic] life was deeply affected by the tornado that destroyed the Heber Springs home he shared with his Mother, the injury of her broken hip and her move to the home of her daughter in De Valls Bluff. In 1939 Mike had his name legally changed to Mike Disfarmer. He had forgotten the place of birth and his parents names were unknown to him and about three years after his birth he was blown in a tornado to the home of Martin and Margaretha Meyer who lived near Kellerville, Indiana.

The power of the Heber Springs Portraits lies in the character of the people portrayed in the moment of time in witch that character was revealed. Mike Disfarmer developed a strong personal style for his Portrait Studio. North light gave an overall illumination by which he recorded every detail of his subjects appearance as they stood for a relative long exposure required by the slow glass plates. He did a minimum of arranging, and posing his subjects. The rough stools and benches were his only props. He pressed the shutter when his presence was the least intrusive. With directness and simplicity he achieved a revelation of character of these plain country people that haven't been duplicated by more sophisticated photographers. His portraits present a clear and honest record of what people looked like in that part of rural America at an emotional and historic turning point in history. Visual documentation of the period between 1941 and 1946 is scanty. The broad picture of depression in America was Magnificently recorded. Photographers of this era went with their cameras where

American troops were fighting, with little photography to fill the gap between the 30's and 50's. These seem to fill the void and from what we know and can surmise, a self-contained and remote society was severely shaken by the war and that gives the Heber Springs Portraits their historical character by Disfarmer's Genius in allowing his subjects soul to show.

Before he died he had appointed his brother Charlie as administrator of his estate. When he died Charlie lived in California and was unable to come to Arkansas and asked that another Administrator be appointed by the court. U.S. Hensley, President of the Arkansas National Bank of Heber Springs was appointed.

Before his death he had gotten, weak and all he would eat was chocolate ice cream, recalls Cartel Haywood a grocer. He and Lesby Davis hadn't seen Mike in a day or two. They went over and forced the door open- Mike was laying behind the counter on newspapers, on the floor dead. He had been dead for a day or two.

At the estate sale, Joe Albright, past mayor of Heber Springs, local realtor and a photography buff paid $5.00 for the complete collection of more than 3,000 glass negatives made by Mike and the entire contents of Mikes Photographic Studio-home. Hoping to find some interesting photographic equipment to add to his collection. Albright saved the box of glass negatives thinking they might have some historic value. They lay in storage 15 years until Peter Miller editor of the Arkansas Sun, a weekly newspaper ran some old photographs titled "Do you Know who this is!". When Joe Albright saw them he thought of the Mike Meyer collection of glass negatives stored in his garage. He took them to the newspaper office for Peter Miller to see. His photographers eye recognized that the portraits were much more than quaint pictures. He made a few enlargements and sent them to Modern Photography Magazine. He said, "these pictures are very moving to me, there is a kind of straightforwardness about the way they posed...they left a wad of tobacco in their mouth, came in for a picture, paid Their $2.00 and left with a family heirloom. The subjects didn't pose. They just looked at the camera, baring their souls in an honest and straight forward way typical of the people of Arkansas. It might also be interesting to note the way that the people in the photographs related to each other. The way they placed their children in relationship to themselves, how they put their arms around each other. I hope that you will see the beauty of these pictures as I do, and hope you will use them."

Peter Miller and Julia Scully, editor of Modern Photography Magazine received a grant of $6,500.00 from Arkansas State American Revolution Bicentennial Commission to produce the book Disfarmer: The Heber Springs Portraits l939-1946. It was published in December 1976 by Addison House, and for the collection of 42 photographs, Peter Miller and the Group donated to the Art Center Exhibition, which became a permanent collection of the [Arkansas] Art Center.

I understand the 5000 copies of the book, Disfarmer: The Heber Springs Portraits, 1939-1946 that we paid $22.50 for in 1975 and the book Aperture no. 78 that has a chapter on Mike Disfarmer, Heber Springs, Arkansas, that we paid $9.50 in 1977 were a complete sell-out and are now collectors items and worth considerable more.

We went to the Disfarmer Art Exhibit at its first showing in Little Rock. It consisted of 42 enlarged black and white portraits about 2 feet by 5 feet. They were amazing to see. We were very impressed. A large room was devoted to the portraits of Uncle Mike. The large black and white portraits were as sharp - no blurs or flaws - as the original glass negatives. Roy stood and looked at these enlargements arranged around the four walls of this large room and said "I am amazed, I knew Uncle Mike was good at his work but I am impressed with this."

Photocopies of clippings of articles about his work, sent to me by Peter Miller were from Publications like New York Times, Art News, Publishers Weekly, Penthouse, Photoworld, Country Journal, Blackwater Gazette, Australian Publications, Creative Camera and others, were appreciated.

The exhibition of the portraits were shown in cities like Cologne, Germany, New York, Copenhagen, Paris, Zurich and many cities in the United States. Today his works are known nationwide and featured in Photography Encyclopedias, Time [L]ife books and libraries. Julia Scully writes, "Mike probably wasn't trying to produce a historical, socialogical [sic] document. He probably had little expectation that his photographs would be valued after his death, but because he recorded the faces of a small town during the difficult years of World War 11 [sic]." She calls the portraits, a microcism [sic] of small town America at that point when it's endurance was severly [sic] tested.

The sad part of it is ,Uncle Mike always knew he was good at what he did, Too bad he couldn't have known, how the people nationwide now knows how good he was.

At his death his estate was valued at $18,146.80 and after payment to U.S. Hensley, the administrator of his estate, the funeral home, home bills, income taxes, Attorneys fees, court costs leaving $14,850.00 in his estate to be disbursed to the living heirs.

| | | | |
|---|---|---|---|
| Charles W. Meyer | 70 | brother | San Jose California 230 S. 13 St. |
| Anna M. Klinger | 73 | sister | R.F.D.l DeValls Bluff, Ar. |
| Anna Goodrich | 78 | sister | 117 Gilman St., Campbell, Calif. |
| Heirs of Andrew Meyer | deceased brother | | Stuttgart, Ark. |
| Heirs of Barbara Neukam | deceased sister | | Almyra, Ark. |
| Heirs of Mary Fricker | deceased sister | | Ulm, Ark. |

In 1989 a unique bit of Cleburne County history seemed to be repeating itself now, as a professional documentary portrait photographer studies Heber Springs own Mike Disfarmer.

New York portratist [sic] Toba Tucker recently moved to Heber Springs to work on a project inspired by Disfarmer's work. She said "Disfarmer's portraits were an inspiration to me because they are very strong and compelling." His work helped her decide on a career in portrait photography. A grant from the Arkansas Endowment for the Humanities, as well as a grant from First Electric Cooperative in Heber Springs helped finance her two to three year project.

Toba uses no mechanical strobes - needed a studio with good light. She usually photographs Native American Indians in color but she prefers black and white. Her works are in a permanent collection of the Metropolitan Museum of Art and the Museum of the American Indian and the New York Museum of Modern Art.

She came to Heber Springs to locate as many people as she can who were photographed by Disfarmer and photograph them and their families for a new book she will call "The Heber Springs Portraits: Continuity & Change." She visited us in our home, took portraits of Roy and me, Joe Fricker and wife Dorethy [sic]. She ate supper with us, spent the night and left early the next morning after breakfast for little Rock to see if her application for a grant to help continue with her work had come through but it was unavailable and she would have to return to New York and work on another project. It was a pleasure having her in our home. We visited her in her home in Heber Springs before she left. She said she planned to return someday and finish her book on Uncle Mike's work and portraits. She had borrowed things from our Meyer Family History Book and in return had given us photographs, newspaper clippings and legal documents that we did not have. March 24, 1991 we received an invitation to an exhibition and reception for her sponsored by the Cleburne County Arts Council. It was very interesting and enjoyable. Her portraits are sharp, clear black and white, very like Uncle Mikes. Her portraits of her Heber Springs subjects lined two walls of a very long hallway in Heber Springs Middle School. Uncle Mikes portrait was centrally located and next to him on the right was the portrait she had taken of Roy and me and on the left was a portrait of Roys cousin Harry Neukam and one of Roy and his brother Joe. The reception was crowded with people she had photographed. Harry Neukam and his wife Norma, Joe and his wife Dorethy [sic], Roy, David and I were the only members of Uncle Mike's that attended the exhibition and reception.

Toba later returned to New York and was busy photographing Indians on Long Island the last letter we had from her. Maybe Someday she will get to return and finish her work and we will have yet another book about Uncle Mikes portrait Photography.

# Appendix 2: Meyer Family Timelines

## Timeline Report for Martin Meyer

| Yr/Age | Event | Date/Place |
|---|---|---|
| > 1846 | Birth | 02 Jun 1846<br>Haysville, Indiana, United States |
| > 1849<br>2 | Birth (Spouse)<br>Margaretha Weidenhammer | 25 Mar 1849<br>Haysville, Indiana, USA |
| > 1868<br>21 | Marriage<br>Margaretha Weidenhammer | 26 May 1868<br>Dubois, Dubois, Indiana, USA |
| > 1869<br>22 | Birth (Son)<br>M. Andrew Meyer | 04 Feb 1869<br>Burbison County, IN, USA |
| > 1871<br>25 | Birth (Daughter)<br>Barbara Meyer | 16 Aug 1871<br>Wickcliff, Indiana, USA |
| > 1874<br>28 | Birth (Daughter)<br>Anna Katherine Meyer | 16 Aug 1874<br>Indiana, USA |
| > 1877<br>31 | Birth (Daughter)<br>Mary Ursula Meyer (Fricker) | 29 Sep 1877<br>Crawfordsville, Montgomery, Indiana, USA |
| > 1880<br>33 | Residence<br>Marital Status: Married;<br>Head of Household | 1880<br>Patoka, Crawford, Indiana, USA |
| > 1881<br>34 | Death (Daughter)<br>Anna Katherine Meyer | 1881 |
| > 1881<br>34 | Birth (Daughter)<br>Anna M. Meyer | 23 May 1881<br>Indiana, USA |
| > 1884<br>37 | Birth (Son)<br>Michael Meyer | 12 Apr 1884<br>Portersville, Indiana, USA |
| > 1887<br>40 | Birth (Daughter)<br>Margaretha "Maggie" A. Meyer | 04 May 1887<br>Kellerville, Indiana, USA |
| > 1889<br>43 | Birth (Son)<br>Charles H Wolfgang Meyer | 26 Sep 1889<br>Kellerville, Indiana, USA |
| > 1890<br>43 | Marriage (Daughter)<br>Barbara Meyer (Neukam) | 1890 |
| > 1892<br>45 | Residence<br>Marital Status: Married; | 1892<br>Almyra, Arkansas, Arkansas, USA |
| > 1895<br>48 | Death (Father)<br>Christopher Ulrich Meyer | 13 Jan 1895<br>Patoka, Crawford, Indiana, USA |
| > 1895<br>49 | Marriage (Daughter)<br>Mary Ursula Meyer (Fricker) | 24 Dec 1895<br>Almyra, Arkansas, Arkansas, USA |
| > 1896<br>49 | Marriage (Son)<br>M. Andrew Meyer | 1896 |
| > 1898<br>51 | Death (Mother)<br>Ursula Meyer (Maier) | 1898<br>Almyra, Arkansas, Arkansas, USA |
| > 1898<br>52 | Death | 30 Aug 1898<br>Almyra, Arkansas, Arkansas, USA |

# Timeline Report for Margaretha Weidenhammer

| Yr/Age | Event | Date/Place |
|---|---|---|
| > 1849 | Birth | 25 Mar 1849<br>Haysville, Indiana, USA |
| > 1850<br>9 mos | Residence | 1850<br>Harbison, Dubois, Indiana |
| > 1860<br>10 | Death (Father)<br>Johann Weidenhammer | Bef. 1860<br>Indiana, USA |
| > 1862<br>12 | Confirmation (LDS)<br>Lutheran Church | Abt. 1862<br>Haysville, Indiana, USA |
| > 1868<br>19 | Marriage<br>Martin Meyer | 26 May 1868<br>Dubois, Dubois, Indiana, USA |
| > 1869<br>19 | Birth (Son)<br>M. Andrew Meyer | 04 Feb 1869<br>Burbison County, IN, USA |
| > 1871<br>22 | Birth (Daughter)<br>Barbara Meyer | 16 Aug 1871<br>Wickcliff, Indiana, USA |
| > 1874<br>25 | Birth (Daughter)<br>Anna Katherine Meyer | 16 Aug 1874<br>Indiana, USA |
| > 1877<br>28 | Birth (Daughter)<br>Mary Ursula Meyer | 29 Sep 1877<br>Crawfordsville, Montgomery, Indiana, USA |
| > 1880<br>30 | Residence<br>Marital Status: Married;<br>Relation to Head of House: Wife | 1880<br>Patoka, Crawford, Indiana, USA |
| > 1881<br>31 | Death (Daughter)<br>Anna Katherine Meyer | 1881 |
| > 1881<br>32 | Birth (Daughter)<br>Anna M. Meyer | 23 May 1881<br>Indiana, USA |
| > 1884<br>35 | Birth (Son)<br>Michael Meyer | 12 Apr 1884<br>Portersville, Indiana, USA |
| > 1887<br>38 | Birth (Daughter)<br>Margaretha "Maggie" A Meyer | 04 May 1887<br>Kellerville, Indiana, USA |
| > 1889<br>40 | Birth (Son)<br>Charles H Wolfgang Meyer | 26 Sep 1889<br>Kellerville, Indiana, USA |
| > 1890<br>40 | Marriage (Daughter)<br>Barbara Meyer (Neukam) | 1890 |
| > 1892<br>45 | Residence<br>Marital Status: Married; | 1892<br>Almyra, Arkansas, Arkansas, USA |
| > 1895<br>46 | Marriage (Daughter)<br>Mary Ursula Meyer (Fricker) | 24 Dec 1895<br>Almyra, Arkansas, Arkansas, USA |
| > 1896<br>46 | Marriage (Son)<br>M. Andrew Meyer | 1896 |
| > 1898<br>49 | Death (Spouse)<br>Martin Meyer | 30 Aug 1898<br>Almyra, Arkansas, Arkansas, USA |

# Timeline Report for Margaretha Weidenhammer (continued)

| Yr/Age | Event | Date/Place |
|---|---|---|
| > 1900 | Residence | 1900 |
| 50 | | Crockett & Keaton Townships, Arkansas, Arkansas, USA |
| > 1902 | Marriage (Daughter) | 1 Nov 1902 |
| 53 | Margaretha "Maggie" A Meyer (Minor) | Almyra, Arkansas County, AR, USA |
| > 1906 | Death (Mother) | 16 Sep 1906 |
| 57 | Barbara Krodel | Dubois, Dubois, Indiana, USA |
| > 1910 | Residence | 1910 |
| 60 | | Stuttgart Ward 1, Arkansas, Arkansas, USA |
| > 1920 | Residence | 1920 |
| 70 | | Heber Springs, Cleburne, Arkansas, USA |
| > 1926 | Death (Daughter) | 13 Mar 1926 |
| 76 | Mary Ursula Meyer (Fricker) | Ulm, Prairie, Arkansas, USA |
| > 1930 | Residence | 1930 |
| 80 | Age: 81; Marital Status: Widowed; Relation to Head of House: Mother-in-law | Watensaw, Prairie, Arkansas, USA |
| > 1935 | Death | 18 Feb 1935 |
| 85 | | De Valls Bluff, Prairie, Arkansas, USA |

# Timeline Report for Anna M. Meyer

| Yr/Age | Event | Date/Place |
|---|---|---|
| > 1881 | Birth | 23 May 1881<br>Indiana, USA |
| > 1892<br>45 | Residence<br>Marital Status: Married; | 1892<br>Almyra, Arkansas, Arkansas, USA |
| > 1898<br>17 | Death (Father)<br>Martin Meyer | 30 Aug 1898<br>Almyra, Arkansas, Arkansas, USA |
| > 1900<br>18 | Residence<br>Age: 19; Marital Status: Single;<br>Relation to Head of House: Daughter | 1900<br>Keaton, Arkansas, Arkansas, USA |
| > 1916<br>34 | Birth (Daughter)<br>Ione M Goodrich | 30 Mar 1916<br>Arkansas, USA |
| > 1918<br>36 | Residence<br>Source: Dave H. Goodrich WWI Draft Card | 1918<br>Almyra, Arkansas, Arkansas, USA |
| > 1920<br>38 | Residence | 1920<br>Heber Springs, Cleburne, Arkansas, USA |
| > 1930<br>48 | Residence<br>Age: 48; Age: 42; Marital Status:<br>Married; Relation to Head of House: Wife | 1930<br>Ajo, Pima, Arizona, USA |
| > 1934<br>52 | Residence | 1934<br>San Jose, California, USA |
| > 1935<br>53 | Death (Mother)<br>Margaretha (Margaret) Weidenhammer | 18 Feb 1935<br>De Valls Bluff, Prairie, Arkansas, USA |
| > 1956<br>74 | Death (Spouse)<br>David Henry Goodrich | 22 Jan 1956<br>Santa Clara, California, USA |
| > 1972<br>90 | Death | 24 Feb 1972<br>Mountain View, Santa Clara, California, USA |

## Timeline Report for Michael (Meyer) Disfarmer

| Yr/Age | Event | Date/Place |
|---|---|---|
| > 1884 | Birth | 12 Apr 1884<br>Portersville, Indiana, USA |
| > 1892<br>45 | Residence<br>Marital Status: Married; | 1892<br>Almyra, Arkansas, Arkansas, USA |
| > 1898<br>14 | Death (Father)<br>Martin Meyer | 30 Aug 1898<br>Almyra, Arkansas, Arkansas, USA |
| > 1900<br>15 | Residence | 1900<br>Crockett & Keaton Townships, Arkansas, Arkansas, USA |
| > 1910<br>25 | Residence | 1910<br>Stuttgart Ward 1, Arkansas, Arkansas, USA |
| > 1914<br>29 | Residence<br>Moves to Heber Springs, Arkansas | 8 Jan 1914<br>Heber Springs, Cleburne, Arkansas, USA |
| > 1918<br>33 | Address<br>Source: WWI Draft Registration Card | 1918<br>Heber Springs, Cleburne, Arkansas, USA |
| > 1920<br>35 | Residence | 1920<br>Heber Springs, Cleburne, Arkansas, USA |
| > 1930<br>45 | Residence<br>Age: 45; Marital Status: Single;<br>Relation to Head of House: Head | 1930<br>Heber Springs, Cleburne, Arkansas, USA |
| > 1935<br>50 | Death (Mother)<br>Margaretha Weidenhammer | 18 Feb 1935<br>De Valls Bluff, Prairie, Arkansas, USA |
| > 1939<br>54 | Changes Name<br>to Mike Disfarmer | 29 Mar 1939<br>Heber Springs, Cleburne, Arkansas, USA |
| > 1942<br>57 | Residence | 1942<br>Heber Springs, Cleburne, Arkansas, USA |
| > 1959<br>75 | Death<br>Age at Death: 75 | 26 Oct 1959<br>Heber Springs, Cleburne, Arkansas, USA |
| > 1959 | Burial | Heber Springs, Cleburne, Arkansas, USA |

# Appendix 3: Heber Springs Times and the Headlight Article on Name Change

*[The following is a transcription of an article that appeared in the April 13, 1939 edition of the front-page article that appeared in the Heber Springs Times and Headlight newspaper regarding Disfarmer's name change.]*

## Photographer Changes Name After Residing Here Twenty-Five Years

Truth's stranger than fiction.

This much-used phrase becomes truer as time passes.

And there is no fiction stranger and more interesting than the life story of Mike Disfarmer, local photographer who up until the recent special term of circuit court here was Mike Meyer, manager of the Meyer Studio here.

Circuit Judge Garner Fraser and attorneys here agreed that the case "in the matter of the change of name of Mike Meyer to Mike Disfarmer" was most unusual. In the petition, presented by Mr. Meyer (beg pardon, Mr. Disfarmer) through his attorney, Gean P. Houston, he stated that he was a citizen of and resident of Cleburne county and had been since January 8, 1914; that he was 56 years of age, and had never at any time been charged with, indicted for or convicted of any crime or misdemeanor and was not at the present time being charged with any violation of the laws of the United States or the of the State of Arkansas.

Mr. Disfarmer stated that he was supposedly born near Portersville, Ind. August 16, 1882; that neither his father's name or his mother's name had ever been know to him.

About three years after his birth, Mr. Disfarmer stated, he was blown in a tornado to the home of Martin Meyer and his wife, Margaretha Meyer, who lived near Kellerville, Ind. and that he lived with this family until each died. Martin Meyer died in August 1898, not knowing the name of the young fellow he befriended. Mrs. Meyer died and was buried at Almyra [Arkansas] in 1935.

Mr. Disfarmer also asserted in his petition that because of his parentage and line of decent being unknown the Meyer family by whom he was reared and their many relatives and kinsmen had on many occasions been embarrassed and humiliated, and that because of the petitioner's status, the Meyer family often expressed themselves as being desirous to disown him.

So, he has planned for some time to change his name.

Since "meyer" means "farmer" in German, and since the petitioner was not a farmer, he chanced upon the name "Disfarmer," "Dis" is said to mean "not" in German.

And so, the Heber Springs photographer is now Mr. Mike Disfarmer.

# Appendix 4: James Calvin Minor, Sr., Country Music Star and Great Nephew of Mike Disfarmer

*[Story by Todd Minor of De Valls Bluff, Arkansas – photographic images provided courtesy of the James Calvin Minor, Sr. Family.]*

James Calvin "Jim" or "Jimmy" Minor was an American Country Music guitarist, singer-songwriter, producer, publisher and record label owner. He was born in De Valls Bluff, Arkansas on January 20th, 1931, the son of Margaret Minor, Disfarmer's niece (see Chapter 11, photos #47 and #48). Jim learned to play and sing at a very early age. He won the Arkansas Livestock Show talent contest when he was just a young teenager and his prize was an opportunity to play with Wilma Lee and Stoney Cooper at radio station KCLU in Blytheville, Arkansas.

Jim served in the United States Army from 1947 to 1950. He was stationed at Church Hill, Canada and in Washington, D.C. where, in 1949, he got to perform. He was living in Evansville, Indiana in 1953 and playing in a local country band called "The Ranch Hands". In November, 1953, Evansville, Indiana got its first TV station WFIE, channel 62. The station owners hired the band to do a live, 30-minute TV show titled "Jimmy Minor and the Diamond K Ranch Hands." The band made 26 episodes of the show. It was the first country music TV show in the state of Indiana. The show was sponsored by Kay Jewelers which is still around today.

At the same time, Jim also had two TV shows running in Princeton, Indiana, on station WRAY, channel 52. One of those shows was called "The Big E Jamboree." On February, 1954, he opened a show at the Evansville Coliseum for Little Jimmy Dickens, Johnny and Jack, Kitty Wells and Del Wood. In 1954, he moved to Flint, Michigan where one of his first jobs was as a DJ at country radio station WBBC. He had his own show and was Michigan DJ of the year in 1955.

While working for General Motors, Jim met Bob Cloud who was a song-writer. Jim and Bob ran a talent and promotional agency, a recording company and a publishing company. They published music on Mayflower Music and Mercury Records for Narvel Felts, Jimmy Edwards, Connie Dycus, Vada Belle and Alice Berry -- all rockabilly artists. Jim recorded his first record in 1955 for the Western Chuck Wagon record label of Flint. Jim opened shows for Pee Wee King, Tex

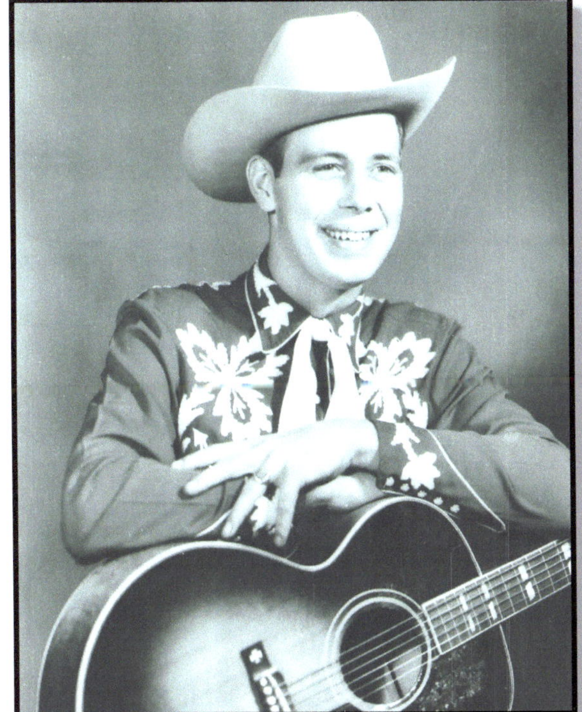

**1. Promotional photo of Jim Minor, with Radio Station WBBC, Flint, Michigan and Chuck Wagon Recording Artist.**

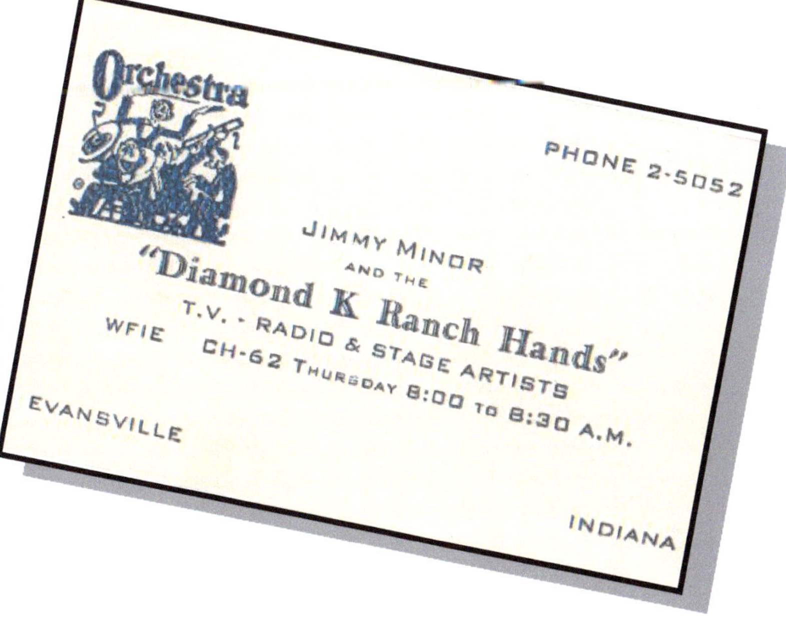

Ritter, George Morgan, Wilma Lee and Stoney Cooper, The Wilburn Brothers, Ernest Tubb, Lonnie Barron, Casey Clark and many, many others.

In 1957, Jim and Bob Cloud heard a song on a little label in Flint called "The Love Bug Crawl." It was recorded by some local boys and Jim and Bob knew that this song had Nashville potential. So they took James Bullington to Nashville where Art Talmadge of Mercury Records changed his name to Jimmy Edwards. They went into the RCA Studio in Nashville and remade the song. It became an instant, hot top 100 hit.

Minor was Edwards manager and the two were whisked out on tour in January of 1958 on Irving Feld's *Greatest Teenage Recording Stars Tour* which starred Buddy Holly and the Crickets, The Everly Brothers, Eddie Cochran and many others. Jim and Bob were owners of Colt "45" Records of Flint, Michigan in 1959 which was a Country and Western label featuring such artists as Connie Dycus, Donna Chrysler/Donah Hyland, Paul and Larry and Eddie and Don.

Jim Minor recorded Country Music from 1955 to 1965 for four different labels with two labels being major labels Mercury Records and United Artists. He was the first country artist to appear on the United Artists label in 1960. He made a guest appearance on the Saturday night "Grand Ole Opry Show" on Sept. 30th, 1961 and then played at the Midnight Jamboree at the Ernest Tubb Record Shop.

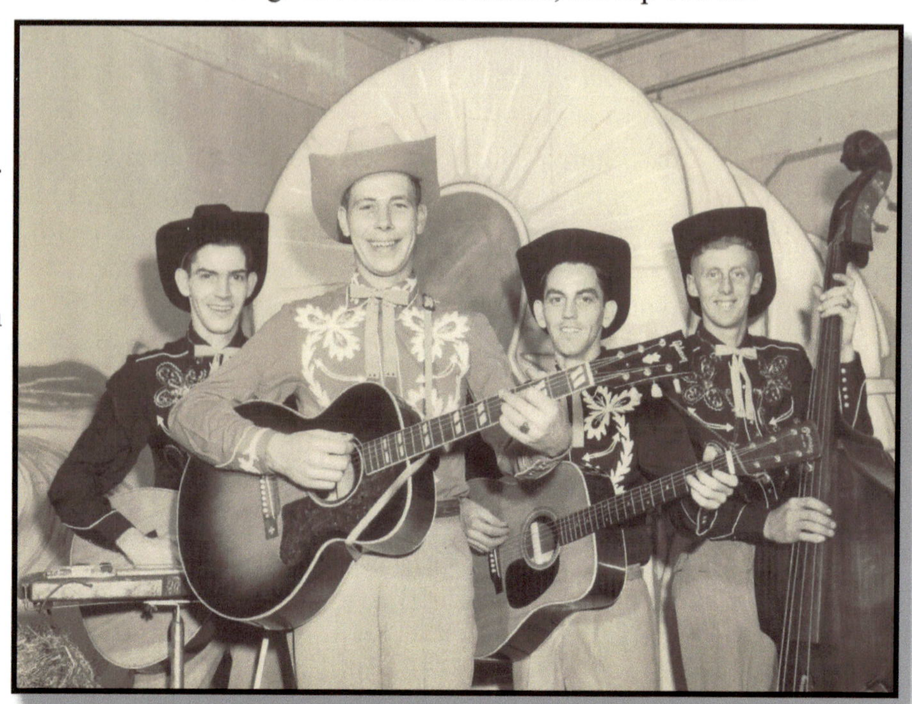

**2. Jimmy Minor and the "Diamond K Ranch Hands" - TV, radio and stage artists for station WFIE in Evansville, Indiana.**

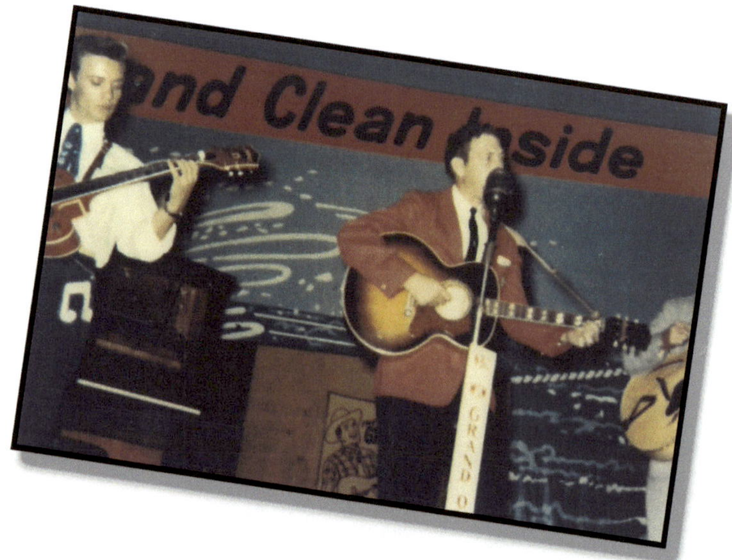


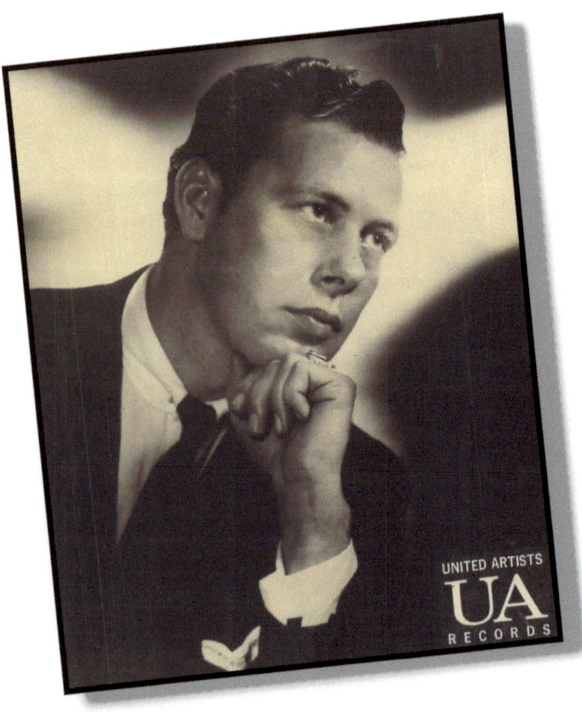


**3. Above: Jim Minor appearing on the "Grand Ole Opry."**

**4. Left: Jim Minor promotional photo released by United Artists.**

Jim recorded his last record in 1965 for the SOUND, INC. record label out of Michigan. He continued to do shows around the Flint, Michigan area through the mid-1970's. By all accounts, he was a well respected entertainer. He retired from General Motors Fisher Body Plant in Grand Blanc, Michigan in 1978 and moved his family back to his Arkansas hometown of De Valls Bluff where he died on November 7th, 2009. Jim was inducted into the Rockabilly Hall of Fame on March 10, 2011 and was inducted into the Michigan Country Music Hall of Fame on September 2nd, 2011. Jim's music and original recordings can be heard on the following website: http://www.reverbnation.com/jimminor

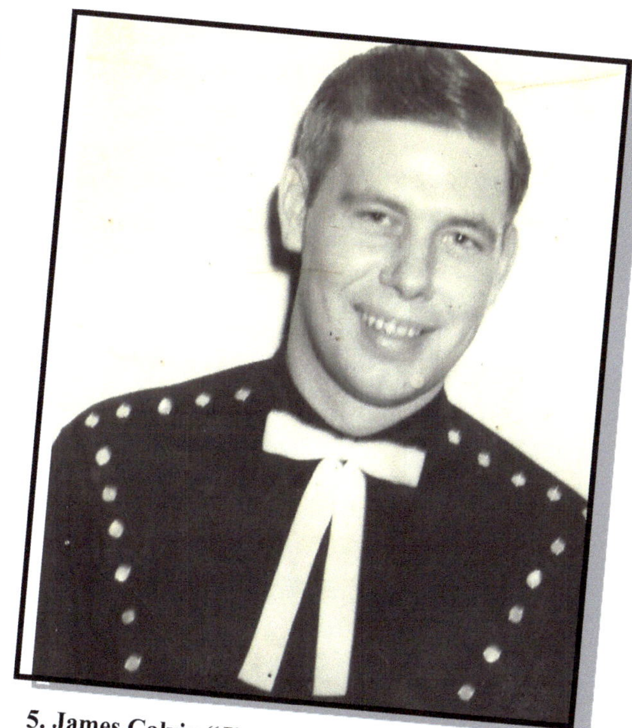

**5. James Calvin "Jim" or "Jimmy" Minor circa 1950.**

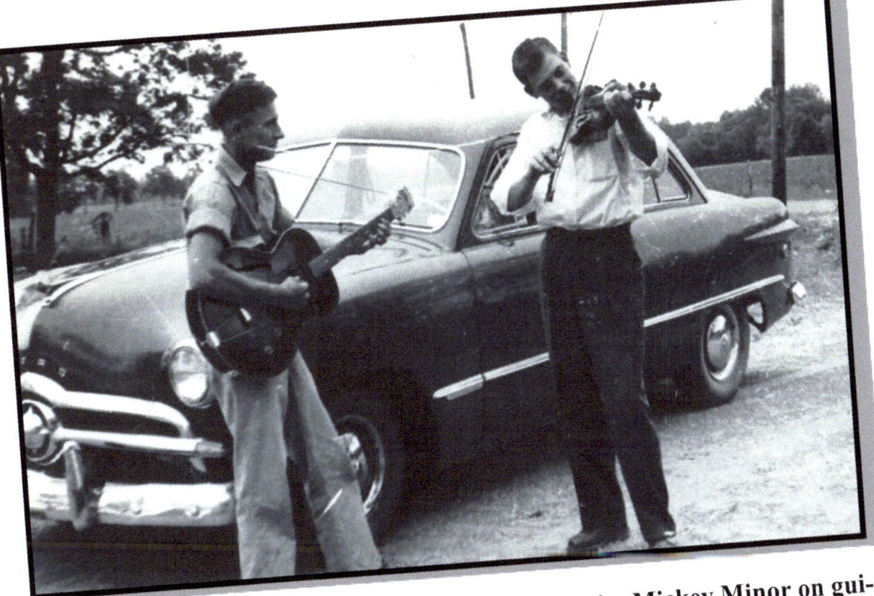

**6. Jimmy Minor playing the "fiddle" and his cousin, Mickey Minor on guitar, circa 1949.**

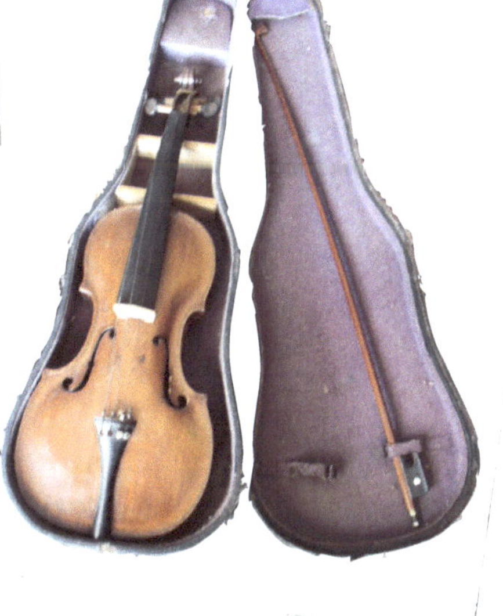

**7. Disfarmer's violin and carrying case owned by the James Calvin Minor, Sr. Family.**

## Appendix 5: Disfarmer Exhibit - Cleburne County Historical Society, Heber Springs, Arkansas

*[These photos were taken by the Author of the Disfarmer Exhibit at the Cleburne County Historical Society Building located in Heber Springs, Arkansas.]*

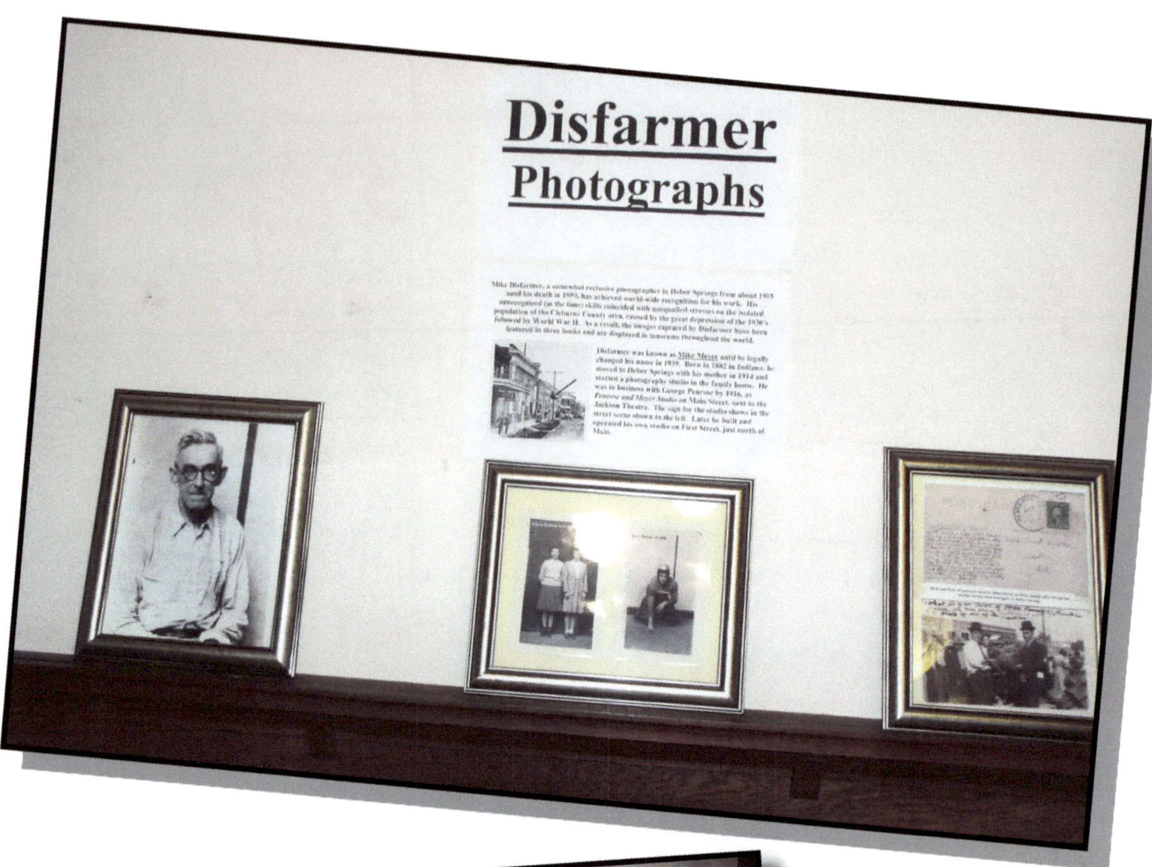


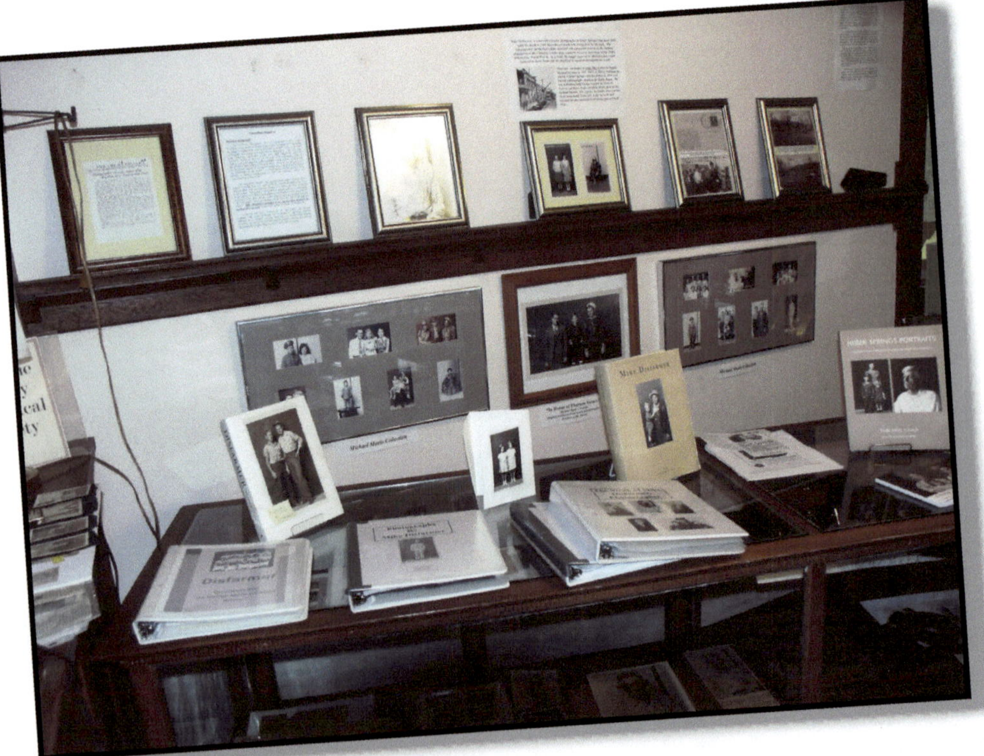

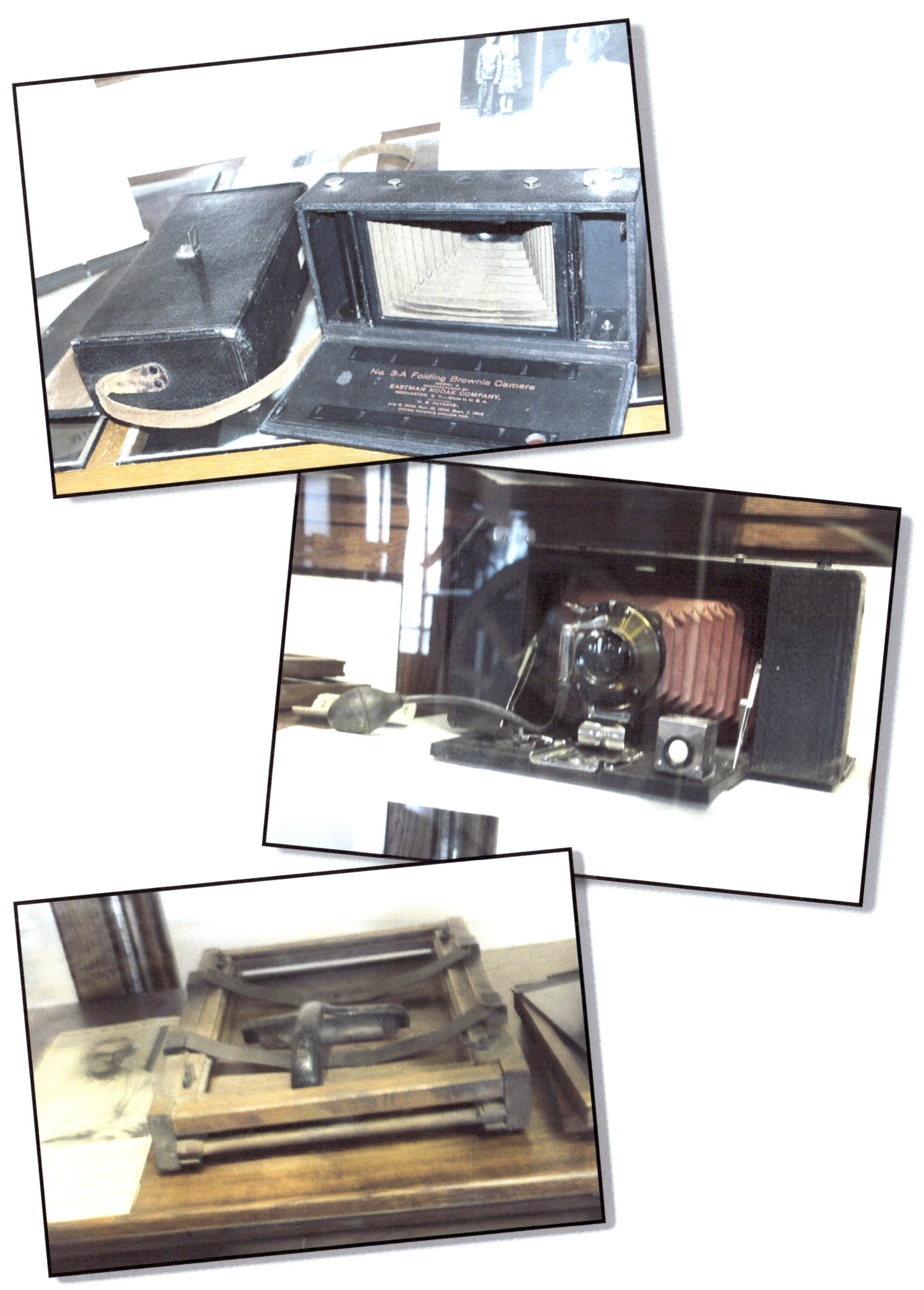
No. 3-A Folding Brownie Camera
EASTMAN KODAK COMPANY,
U. S. PATENTS:

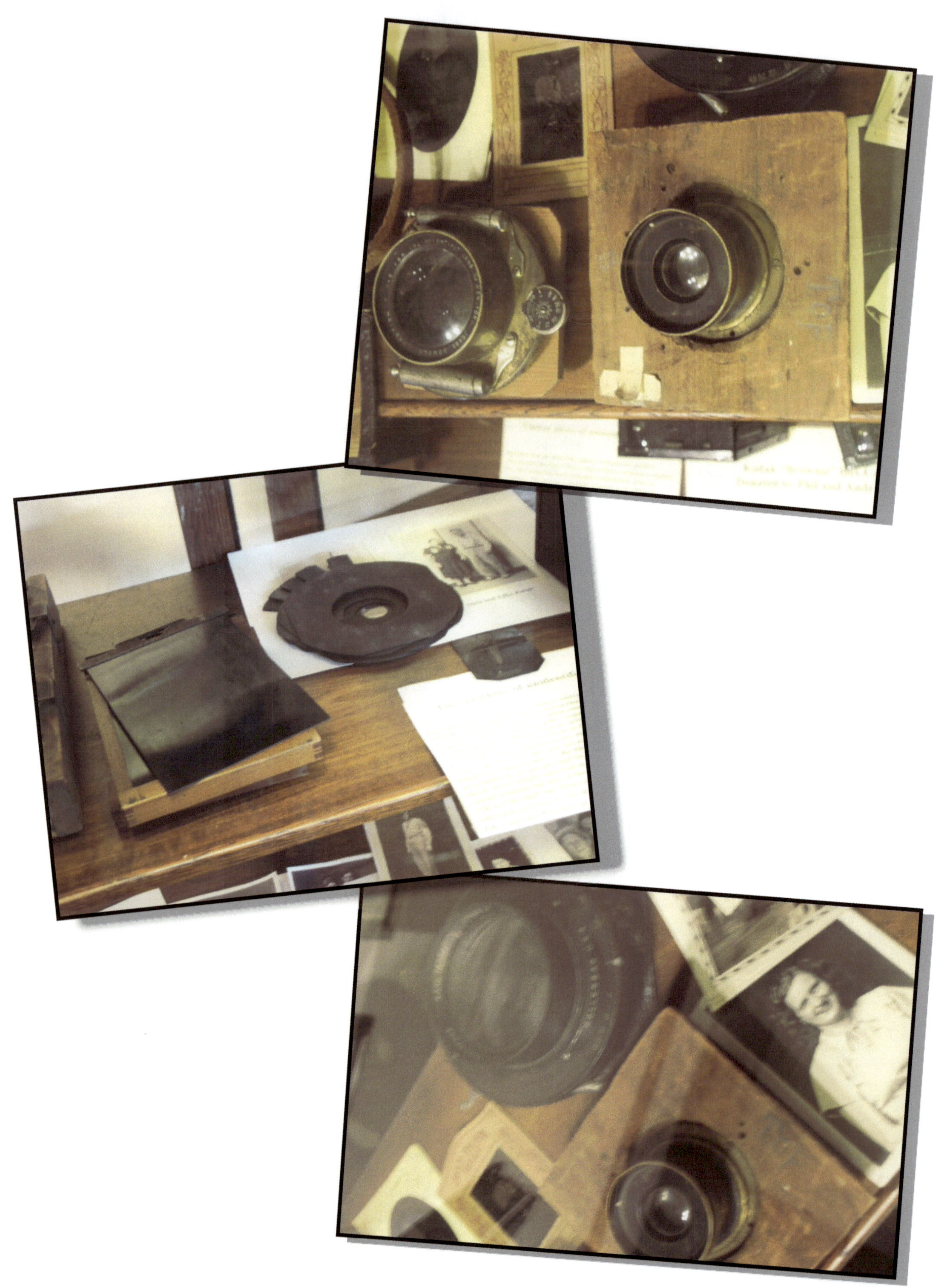

# Links to Disfarmer Photos

To see more of Disfarmer's unique photographs, please refer to the following websites:

http://disfarmer.org/

http://www.disfarmer.com/

http://www.disfarmer.com/gallery/

http://www.amazon.com/Disfarmer-Vintage-Prints-Edwynn-Houk/dp/1576873048

http://www.americansuburbx.com/2012/01/mike-disfarmer-disfarmer-rediscovered.html

https://www.google.com/search?q=disfarmer+photos&tbm=isch&tbo=u&source=univ&sa=X&ei=zO_3UoE7x6nIAZXKgbgB&ved=0CCcQsAQ&biw=1600&bih=799

http://www.stevenkasher.com/exhibition/69/#!2007

In addition to these websites, several high-quality books have been published of Disfarmer's photos. Many of these books are no longer in publication but, used and like-new copies can be purchased through popular auction and book market websites.

# About the Author

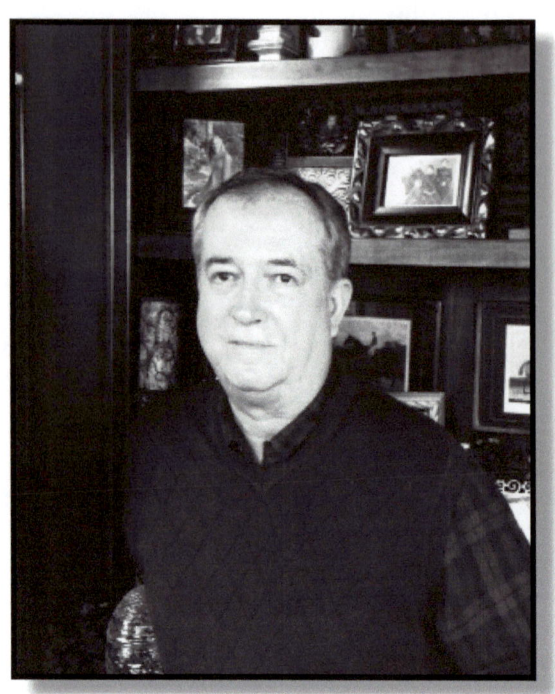

Kim O. Davis currently resides in Sherwood, Arkansas, a suburb of Little Rock. He was raised in Ashdown, Arkansas, a small town in southwest Arkansas lying about 30 miles from Hope, the birthplace of President Bill Clinton. He was the Valedictorian of his high school class. Mr. Davis is a graduate of Baylor University where he received a B.S. in Biology and an M.B.A. He is a charter member of the Texas Lambda Chapter of Phi Delta Theta, a national fraternity. He has been married to his wife, Judy, for 27 years and has one daughter, Sydney, a college freshman.

This non-fiction work is his first publishing endeavor but he has plans for another non-fiction work and may venture into fiction in the future. He considers himself a history buff and became interested in Mike Disfarmer after attending an exhibit of Disfarmer's work at the Greg Thompson Gallery in North Little Rock, Arkansas. After attending the Disfarmer exhibit, Mr. Davis began to conduct some research into Mike Disfarmer's photographs and life. Through extensive research, he became acquainted with several descendants of Mike Disfarmer and learned that the family had first-hand accounts and family photographs that could form the basis for a much needed biography on the life of Mike Disfarmer. Mr. Davis' email address is AuthorKimODavis@gmail.com.

www.ingramcontent.com/pod-product-compliance
Lightning Source LLC
LaVergne TN
LVHW070129110826
845147LV00002B/214

* 9 7 8 0 9 9 1 3 9 4 3 2 6 *